LUCID

LUCID

A MEMOIR OF AN EXTREME DECADE
IN AN EXTREME GENERATION

LUCY HOLDEN

GALLERY BOOKS UK

First published in Great Britain by Gallery Books,
an imprint of Simon & Schuster UK Ltd, 2022

1 3 5 7 9 10 8 6 4 2

Simon & Schuster UK Ltd
1st Floor
222 Gray's Inn Road
London WC1X 8HB

www.simonandschuster.co.uk
www.simonandschuster.com.au
www.simonandschuster.co.in

Simon & Schuster Australia, Sydney
Simon & Schuster India, New Delhi

Some names have been changed to protect the guilty –
and the innocent.

A CIP catalogue record for this book
is available from the British Library

Hardback ISBN: 978-1- 3985-0037-2
Trade Paperback ISBN: 978-1- 3985-0038-9
eBook ISBN: 978-1- 3985-0039-6

Typeset in Bembo by M Rules
Printed and bound by CPI Group (UK) Ltd, Croydon, CR0 4YY

For my parents, for everything.

And to anyone who has ever been made to feel they're losing it completely.

At times, late on those nights when
the dancing, the slight intoxication,
my wild enthusiasm, everyone's violent
unrestraint would fill me with a tired
and overwhelmed rapture, it would seem
to me – at the breaking point of fatigue
and for a second's flash – that at last I
understood the secret of creatures and of
the world. But my fatigue would disappear
the next day, and with it the secret; I
would rush forth anew.

The Fall,
ALBERT CAMUS

Contents

Prologue

I walked on tiptoes until I was ten years old.

My Achilles tendons are roughly a quarter of the length of other people's, so I had to train my heels to touch the ground after I learnt to walk. My dad took me to the hospital appointments, and I remember sitting on a bed with a paper towel topping and a doctor stretching my legs to see what they would and wouldn't do.

More than the hospital I remember walking around the streets of Falmouth with him afterwards, following his verbal instructions with my own. Tiny and with a blonde tangle of ringlets, saying, 'Heel, toe, heel, toe, heel, toe,' as he did, like it was a thrilling new game, which is how I learnt to walk like other people in the end.

I still walk on tiptoes sometimes, if I'm thinking about something else entirely, or trying to be quiet or invisible, like I got used to doing when my dad worked nights, later on, and was sleeping when my brother and I came home from school and we had to be as silent as possible until he woke up. In my twenties, I used tiptoes to sneak in or out of the flats I'd tried to make a home while different men slept or raged, quickly learning the creaks of the floorboards and avoiding them, but feeling like my heart beat louder than any step would groan if I trod on one.

The words still run through my head sometimes, silently, as

though repeating *heel, toe, heel, toe, heel, toe* will get me through anything. Thinking that if that mantra taught me to walk on level ground when I was a child, that it might walk me through whatever uneven time I find myself in again. I wondered whether there was a metaphor in there for a while. Like being born with less of an Achilles tendon than other people might mean I had no Achilles heel, but I knew I did and I knew it came largely down to one man.

When I saw his name on my phone after almost ten years and felt my breath catch in shock and the ground shift beneath my feet, I knew I had two options. I could tiptoe unconsciously or fearfully through what was about to happen, or I could dig my heels in and repeat my *heel, toe* lines to myself again, knowing it was the harder, more painful way to walk, but understanding that silence wouldn't achieve anything. If I'd learnt to walk once before when my body didn't want to, I hoped that this time I could walk my mind to a place it didn't want to go but needed to be.

I sat on my bed and breathed in, to stop myself tiptoeing to the kitchen to get a bottle of wine, which is what I felt like doing. I knew I needed to be completely sober when I sent this message, and I knew I'd only get one chance. I stayed where I was and felt the breath sink to my stomach and my jaw clench as I asked the man I hated more than anyone in the entire world for his email address, the muscles in my throat tightening and something like heat creeping into the corner of my eyes. I didn't ask why he'd taken nine months to respond, I just waited, and when he gave me what I needed, I opened my email and asked if he had any idea what this was about.

An hour later, he told me it sounded serious, and I wondered whether he really could have *no idea*; whether that was even a possibility. But I knew he had to say that. I knew he was smart. And this could be evidence, if I ever wanted it to be. I wondered, as I had several times in the past nine months, whether he had read the message when I'd first sent it and had been deciding whether he should ever reply. I wondered about the power of the mind to block out memories completely for those who wanted to forget the past. I knew how powerful my own mind had been, most of the time, in building a wall and not looking over it to a house on the coast on New Year's Eve, but I knew that I'd always known what was the other side, even if I never looked.

I took a deep breath and I started typing, not feverishly, but lucidly; more conscious than I've ever been. It took less than ten minutes, because I'd known for a long time what I should say. Then I read the message three times and pressed send, knowing I'd gone over every possibility of a reply and that I had a high chance of not getting what I wanted, or needed.

Even clearer than that was the knowledge that in the old days I would have sent it and gone straight out into the world and sought chaos. Drank and shouted conversation and chain-smoked and followed the night into the morning or the morning after so that I didn't think about anything at all.

But I didn't. Instead, I went downstairs with my heels as close to the ground as they'd go, thinking *heel, toe, heel, toe, heel, toe*. I put my trainers on and I walked the country lanes that wove around the blankets of fields near my parents' house and I started sprinting.

I'd been running away from things for a long time, but it didn't feel like I was running to escape anything this time. It felt like freedom. Like learning to walk.

1

TESTAMENT OF YOUTH

Every generation seeks to define and understand itself, but I never thought mine would be given a war so fiercely personal and frighteningly public that forced us to sit with our identities in 2020, crystallising our own testament of youth as other generations had in post-war years.

A month after I turned thirty, a pandemic with many of the same conclusions of death, chaos, loss and revaluation either locked us into or threw us out of the lives we'd made and I felt my private life break down in the middle of a collective, public collapse. The main difference in this new war was that we weren't waiting for bombs to drop and men to disappear, younger and younger, to the trenches. The danger was less tangible and we watched the generals in charge of our fate on TV, ordering Deliveroo for dinner so we didn't have to risk our lives breathing an invisible virus that could kill us outside.

The slim reward of war, perhaps always, is perspective, and leaving the life I'd run towards since I left home at twenty gave me a distance that lit my last decade in clarity. I saw then that the society and culture in which my generation had lived was directly formed by, and was responsible for, the conditions we'd found ourselves in, which for me was a life of impermanence puffed to nothing in London. From my parents' house in Bath the future seemed unimaginable and uncertain and with life in the present suspended, there was nowhere to go but backwards. To work out how I'd come to be locked in a pretty rental flat with a man I thought I'd marry but now realised I had to escape.

When London and the parties closed to me in March 2020, and I left everyone I knew behind me to flee the city in the midst of this new war, it was hard not to feel the past was more present than ever. I'd run from it for a decade, but now there was nowhere else to go.

In life, regardless of what you choose to do with it, there comes, inevitably, a time when people ask *when* you decided to do with yours what you did, and quite often the person asking is ourselves. But the flaw in the question is the idea that you can pin with the thin gold steel of certainty *the moment* of axis, decision or change. Thinking like that suggests the path you walked didn't feel out of your control, or your consciousness entirely, most of the time.

I was twenty-three when I arrived in London in the autumn of 2013 to try to catch my life and pin it down. I was built then on fresh-faced naivety, ambition, adrenaline and a play of arrogance that disguised youthful insecurity and self-doubt. When I thought about who I wanted to be, it was in relation to who I *didn't*, and a process of trial and error had left some fear in my eye, but more often a look of daring, because I also had faith. We were a generation pot-planted in meritocracy and watered daily with the idea of delayed gratification, and I believed in the promise that if we worked hard enough we could have it all, regardless of who we were and where we came from.

My mother said I knew before I'd even reached my first birthday what I wanted, and what I wanted was to be in the front seat. That meant arching my back anytime they tried to put me in the baby seat in the back, and just *wailing* until one of my parents took pity on me and let me sit up front with them. Who knows how quickly we become who we become, but I was being dangled off death slides by my dad before I was even old enough to climb the steps to the drop myself and I wanted to go on the fastest ride at the fair before I was ten. I went on them alone because my parents' heads spun if they tried to accompany me and my younger brother seemed to have been born with the fear I didn't have, as well as his own.

After my wild-child beginnings, I wanted light, having already seen darkness one morning at the start of my final school year, when I'd woken up prematurely frail and stopped going in entirely. Up until then I'd been a model, box-ticking student, 'gifted and talented' the letters that came through the door said, but the pressure, after fourteen years in an education system leathered by hard, academic drive, hit me like a train. Psychosomatically, I was immobilised and my attendance after that morning was zero.

My mum tried everything she could think of to work out what I needed using the same process of elimination that parents use to stop crying babies. I could talk, but I didn't have the language to explain what was going on, so she bought vitamins that smelt like cat litter in case my plummeting mood was diet-related; boots because it was winter and she thought the rain was soaking through my shoes. Everyone felt worse when they had wet feet, she said. She brought home the schoolwork I was missing, and I taught myself alone in my bedroom, sitting on my bed like a sickly Victorian child as family members and friends arrived out of the blue to ask what was going on. They nodded, urged, or took me out to lunch, where they asked me about my biggest fears and, on one occasion, imparted a metaphor about a sports car driving up tight lanes that scratched the sides, which might or might not have been about mental health. It was hard to tell.

I was taken to two doctors, and I cried as much in front of a GP who said I was burnt out (not depressed, as others had wondered) as I did in front of the homeopathic one who asked me about my dreams. I cried at the kindness of friends who brought me a cake they'd made after school to try to make me feel better, seeing tragedy in the way the Smarties had run their colours all over the sponge. I cried from guilt when my mum had to take time off work, for second-hand stress. At a loss, my dad settled on a guilt trip that said I was hurting her by not going in, which only made it worse. My brain had become a bomb and being asked to do anything, or even get out of bed some days, made me melt into something close to hysteria.

In the mornings I would leave the house and wander around Bath alone, waiting for the pubs I looked old enough to drink in to open, then for my older boyfriend to finish work. Sid was a chef who worked doubles and had a break in the middle of the day, but there was always someone around, those that didn't follow conventional routines for their own reasons. I swapped book recommendations with the drug dealers Sid knew, but found they mainly just liked *The Alchemist*, which seemed to be always on the bookshelves at the care homes they'd often grown up in. I'd started to feel so much like an outsider that I preferred to be around people who'd experienced raw, difficult life, feeling an empathy and shared understanding with underdogs, and having a chameleon-like ability to slot in anywhere which felt powerful, clever, helpful. I didn't realise then how much of my sense of self was already being lost in this constantly morphing act. I was just whoever someone wanted me to be in the moment, like an actor in a dozen different parts, while underneath I felt hugely lost, and completely alone. When Sid went back for his evening shift, I went home and did my homework, and passed my exams fine in the end, but felt stared at in the exam hall I guess no one thought I'd return to.

When the head of sixth form told my mother that many students were already taking medication and having therapy to get them through their exams, I felt pure anger that we'd been pushed so hard in the first place. But I'd gone to a good, mixed, state comp and I didn't believe for a second that it was operating in a uniquely harsh way. The teachers cared, and many were brilliant. The pressure came from governmental reforms to the curriculum and the idea that we should be pushed for the sake of results. The real result was that children were being made to believe that *grades* were a matter of life or death, which filled them with such anxiety they had to be drugged to enter the exam hall.

Later, I credited that time with making me fear failure less, because at uni I saw others fall apart harder and far from home. Failure to me then was not getting into Oxford, and getting AAB instead of straight As, even though I'd taught myself during my toughest year at school and got 100 per cent in an exam I'd been told I wouldn't be allowed to take because of my poor attendance. Now I realise the fact I saw any of that as failure was absurd. It was the zeitgeist, and we were caught in a system in which we were expected to be everything, all of the time, and not break. When I'd fallen apart I was head girl, captain of a national-level sports team and persuaded to apply for one of the best universities in the world. The fact I fell apart then wasn't a coincidence; my life was a pressure cooker.

The stress was said to be even worse at private schools; and worse still at expensive all-girls' schools where perfect-girl syndrome raged and eating disorders were the plat-du-jour.

What the fuck's going on? I thought, anarchy charging through me. Every school had become a dystopian bear pit where we were made to compete against each other in every area of our lives, reflections cast online thanks to a new social media that measured popularity and success in friend counts and vanity. It was the start of the selfie era.

Real connection in the new online spaces got lost, not only because boys who were too shy to say hello in the playground could talk to you on MSN for two hours after school (sowing the idea that online flirtation was as good as real-life romance) but because the important stuff, like the anxiety we felt about the constant competition, was squashed under the veneer of false happiness. We learnt while we were still teenagers that you presented online a picture of who you were pretending to be, and left the doubt and the fear and the confusion in your mind.

At school I felt different from everyone else there, especially the girls, who argued about GHDs and turned their back on me when I got a boyfriend in lower sixth and 'left' them. Many of them had grown up in Bath and gone to primary school together, their mothers all cliquey friends, while I'd left my childhood behind in Cornwall when I was eight, and didn't feel tied to anyone or anything. By the time I was seventeen we'd moved seven times and I saw home and the people in the catchment areas around it as temporary. I couldn't stand being left at new schools by my parents, who were the only constant in a shifting world of people and places. As my education finally neared its end, I felt a desperate *need* to get out of there and ennui weighed heavy until that summer when it was finally over.

Anxiety wasn't even a word in our vocabularies back then, but my taste of the pressure made me try to avoid it in the years to come. I never stopped competing, just knew I'd duck out before I snapped again, because it wasn't worth it.

Refusing to jump through hoops of fire and glass, I turned my back on convention and took two years out to live as unacademically as possible. I got a job in a restaurant in Bath and on lunch breaks I sat on the floor of the travel section in Waterstones staring at the spines of the world and wondering where I'd find life. Sid and I went all round Europe soon after I left school on Interrail tickets part-funded by his second job as one of Bath's part-time coke dealers. He showed me how to mix narcotics with babies' teething powder from Boots, then wrap it in tiny origami envelopes made from band fliers; mindfulness in a very unmindful task. The numbed gums of Bath's middle-class addicts funded our entry to the Sistine Chapel and the Colosseum, the Louvre and Parc Güell as we covered fifteen cities in thirty days, staring up at the Brandenburg Gate and through the railings of the Spanish Riding School in Vienna as though we were looking through the doors of the world. I was an unlikely pseudo-gangster's moll, but my eyes were wide that winter after the trapped confines of the classroom. I felt free.

The world seemed so enticingly open after a relentless school routine and I said yes to it all, feeling like I was starting to like this life thing again. Back in Bath, at the restaurant, I served the owners of a ski company in Méribel who got drunk at the table, said I had nice teeth and offered me a job as a chalet maid, so off Sid and I went, he cooking for twenty in the chalet we were assigned. We skied for a month before we were fired by the awful boss whose racist, homophobic views we'd failed to be sycophantic enough towards. 'Hitler' Sid called him to his reddening face before we left, marching around our snowy balcony in his ski gear like a Monty Python Nazi before we were sped out of there to the plane. 'One month of skiing is more than enough anyway,' I told Sid after we'd found our seats. 'Repetitive *as*.'

Despite having nothing in common but a desire for excitement, Sid and I had been together more than two years before we finally broke up. I bought a ticket to Sydney from the money I'd made slogging in the restaurant we both worked at, not wanting to go back, and wondering what I should do in Australia when the transfer flight landed in Hong Kong. I had a panic attack and called my mum on a pay phone from the airport in the middle of the night to ask if she knew.

But in the hostels, I quickly found an international crowd of all ages, each of them looking for life, too, and settled into a motley crew of ever-changing people for three months, my chameleonising again helpful. By then I noticed it had become so extreme that people couldn't guess my nationality any more, often assuming I was Russian, German or Iranian if they weren't calling me Patsy (from *Ab Fab*). When the money ran out and I came home, I was ready to go to university, which now seemed safe after Melbourne's worst bush fires in a decade and the distance from home that had made me feel small and vulnerable had also proved to me I could survive a lot more than I'd felt I could at seventeen.

Arriving at the University of Leeds in 2010 felt like I was returning to a mental health ward after a period of recovery. Those who'd come straight from school hadn't yet learnt that failure didn't kill you and were letting it rock them savagely, pressure redoubled if anything, because this was our last chance to prove ourselves before the real world. Suddenly I was comforting crying friends who'd dropped single marks on (first-class, unassessed) essays or having cognitive behavioural therapy and retaking a whole year because they'd been so paralysed by the idea of handing in anything less than perfect. Perfectionism was destroying us, I thought as I skipped lectures again to watch *Jeremy Kyle* and drink Carlsberg with my flatmate in halls. Years later we were described as *generation medication* as well as *generation perfection* and I wasn't surprised at all – the latter being the reason behind the former.

A spate of suicides at Russell Group universities embodied the pressure. Bristol, a known second choice for those who'd failed to get into Oxbridge, was one of the worst and suffered several casualties, and in Birmingham, a friend of a friend jumped out of the fourth-storey window of the library, unable to deal with the weight of being the top of his year. The words 'student welfare' were bandied about, but little changed, and lower down the ladder, then education secretary Michael Gove's plans to make GCSEs 'more challenging, more ambitious and more rigorous' made me shudder, knowing about the antidepressant-swallowing kids who saw the goalposts move constantly; the increased pressure to achieve it all and make it look easy. The paralysing fear of hitting the bar.

Between 2010 and 2011, 43.3 million prescriptions for antidepressants were being signed, a 28 per cent increase from just three years earlier, according to a *Guardian* article. Amongst children and young people, prescriptions for the same drugs were also rising annually and were up by 15 per cent in England between 2016 and 2018. While the recession was being part-blamed for the rise in adult use, the increase in the number of children on medication was reasoned to be the fault partly of longer waits for mental health services.

Meanwhile, everyone around me seemed to be telling themselves that ruined mental health was a worthwhile by-product of success, knowing that when pretty much everyone went to university you had to do more before, during and after it to stand out. Combined with this need to achieve, and lurking behind the almost religious idea of meritocracy, there was a suspicion floating around like a conspiracy theory that the job market we'd be landing in was a ghost town.

Ahead of me, my friend Anna had graduated with a 2:1 in international relations but despite applying for many jobs for which she was more than qualified, she was now shelf-stacking in Boots. Her boyfriend Danny was working at Jamie's Italian in Gatwick airport where he served beers and burgers to on-the-piss holidaymakers at 6 a.m., knowing they'd get closer to the planes than he would, despite his engineering degree. Everyone that left university said you didn't feel like you had a minute to get one foot in the door before another batch of graduates were churned out into a depleted job market damaged by the recession. In 2008, when the economic crash was fuelling unemployment and austerity, I'd just left school, and by the time I left university in 2013, the downturn still wasn't over. That made people in their final year start MAs out of pure, procrastinating fear, and while I told myself that I didn't fear failure any more, the truth was that the world we were washing up into looked tough as hell. Watching those rush into the world ahead of me felt like watching soldiers running at barbed wire.

I didn't know until my final year at Leeds that I wanted to be a journalist, worrying I wasn't cut-throat enough, but again, I was working out what I wanted to do by what I *didn't* and I didn't want to write press releases about leggings made of tree sap that encouraged weight loss while you walked, or anything else I'd done during one of myriad work-experience weeks in PR offices during the holidays.

Instead I moved into the student newspaper office, which smelt of chicken chow mien, and began begging interviews from anyone I thought was interesting, hoping tapas with Howard Marks, coffee with Alastair Campbell, sushi with Mariella Frostrup, muffins with Caitlin Moran and a taxi to *The One Show* with Jay Rayner might help get me to Fleet Street more quickly than Icelandic fiction with Professor Bat. *Nothing comes of nothing*, I told myself, having memorised a single line of *King Lear* from the seven different versions I was studying in another module.

It was my unconventional friendship with one of my professors that helped most during that time. When I needed a steadying older influence in the face of such uncertainty, I found it in Everleigh, as I immediately and exclusively referred to him. Having barely known any of my grandparents, I found in Everleigh the kind of unconditional support other people had from blood relations two generations above. My last remaining grandparent died in Fresher's Week, and then there Everleigh was.

'What do you talk about?' friends my own age asked, unable to imagine how I could drink and chat for hours with a grumpy lecturer in his mid-sixties who berated us for not turning up to seminars (or if we did, for not having done the reading).

'Anything,' I said. 'Everything.'

We sat in the musty, crepuscular light of Whitelock's, a pub where seventeenth-century poets had drunk hideously warm ales before us, eaten fish and chips (maybe) and discussed love, death, relationships, London, culture, education and politics (almost definitely). I loved our lunches because during them I heard from him how things used to be, while he listened to how they were now. 'Egg freezing,' he'd say. 'Tell me what you think about it because for my generation it's almost Frankensteinian.'

Everleigh didn't go anywhere after I left Leeds, and we emailed regularly as the years flew on, or met in Lunnon (as he called it when deviating from 'the Great Wren') where he was often at the British Library for research, messaging me from amongst the bookshelves to say he was surrounded by excessively tedious scholars and craving a drink already, at 12.30 p.m. Later he'd stare at the jam jars our drinks had been served in at some hip venue I'd picked and say the too-loud music was at least antidote to Thomas Creede. 'Who?' I said. 'Don't ask,' he replied.

Our communications reflected, as time went by, his retirement, fears of old age, the birth of his first grandchild and the funerals of friends, while mine included negotiations with jobs, housing and relationships, and the first marriages and children of my contemporaries.

'Which one's this?' he asked of new men, trying to keep up with the four serious boyfriends and two casuals I'd had by twenty-three, as I tested the waters of what life could be like via the lives others had carved for themselves. The only thing my boyfriends had in common was that they were all older, evidence I was always chasing the future, perhaps, and wanted to see what was ahead.

At sixteen I'd learnt *Normal People*-love was escapist with a trainee fireman who carried me up the hills of Bath in exchange for doing his homework, and then at seventeen there was Sid who taught me to cut lines and onions. At twenty I realised how much people feared Monday mornings through a city lawyer in London who was so stressed on Sundays he drank a crate of strawberry cider and watched *Blue Planet* to calm down. A brown bottle of herbal anxiety pills stood on his dresser and as we slept he had nightmares, shouting and flailing and accidentally hitting me in the face. Jonnie showed me what being driven by money looked like, because we both knew he'd never leave his six-figure salary despite the furious tension constantly raging in his office: iPhones smashed at desks over lost deals and stories of people 'getting out' to start boar farms in Kent. I saw my first heartbreak with him, too, when he stopped running along train platforms every time I had to leave, his hand jammed through the window as though we were in a black-and-white film, and broke up with me instead, the day before my twenty-first birthday, which is also when I learnt to cry in the shower, to hide the sound. I bought a puppy called Alfie with my student loan to get over him, and Jonnie bought a Maserati, but pet therapy calmed me much more than 100 mph.

As did human affection, I found, via a boy called Sam who worked the bar of the restaurant I waitressed at in Leeds. He was a photography student who enveloped me in a 6ft 4in embrace, seeming to like me a lot just as I was, despite the fact I launched my door keys out of the fourth-storey window so he could let himself in; a show of not caring that hid the fact I expected to get hurt. It was him I messaged from Thailand that summer when I fell off a motorbike and had forty stitches up one side of my body. Three years later Sam and I would be in love, but I didn't know that yet.

In the meantime I turned twenty-one and allowed myself to be picked up in Bristol by an organic wine salesman who quickly took me home to meet someone called 'Granny' because he was about to inherit a family house so historically important it was half managed by the National Trust. For that – I learnt – he was expected to have a wife, and as we toured the house in our pyjamas, walking its three wings amongst paying visitors to closed-off rooms where Guy Fawkes' associates had once sat, I learnt it wouldn't be me. His life didn't feel like mine either, and he seemed to have the mildly amusing idea he was rescuing me from poverty, I realised, when he drove to Bath to give me a Christmas stocking, shocked I didn't get one at twenty-one, which made me feel like Oliver Twist until I opened it, and realised it was full of gin and G-strings more worthy of Moll Flanders. He taught me privilege didn't make you clever, and that men don't know what a size 8 looks like. The underwear, when I tried it on, cut me like a cheese wire through Brie.

By twenty-two, I was seeing a teaching assistant from Bath who had better conversation but walked around his mother's house, naked, writing me poetry about love that transcended the M1, which wasn't for me either.

Then, at twenty-three, just when I was wondering where love was, I met Liam, a musician who was everything. Maybe we don't forget the first summer after we graduate, whoever it's spent with and wherever that is; the freedom itself as alluring as anyone in it. The world seems so full of possibility, with everything ahead and yours to decide what to try to do with it, and I was addicted then to our world in his flat, his movements, black coffee, exploding laugh, hair smelling like tea tree, glinting eyes; sometimes pouty, often grinning. He shook off compliments, but I was head over heels as I watched the sea billow out from the beach from his front room, and the dogwalkers gather below in Regency Square, wondering if they knew a life – mine – was about to start above them.

After five years of circling each other with mutual interest in Bath, we'd finally fallen for and at each other over Christmas in my final year in a red, old-fashioned phone box that's windows steamed up as much as we did inside and made us quote a Larkin line about staggering skirmishes in telephone booths ever after – and by the summer we'd been together six months and I was spending most of my now purposeless time at his flat in Brighton watching his routine unfold as he carried his cafetière reluctantly to a desk to make the first cold calls of the day. I moved sleepily

to the sofa to lie cocooned in a duvet that smelt of sex, then listened to him babble before getting bored, picking up a guitar,
playing a few chords, then poking his head around the door and
screeching 'Squirrel Nutkin' at me as though we were Beatrix
Potter characters, with a huge smile on his face. He'd give me
a kiss, scuttle about the kitchen, then pluck something off the
bookcase and hand it to me before retreating back to the job that
depressed him.

This view of working life, the idea that you had to wait years for
a career that made you happy to take off, gratification always out of
reach, worried me, and Liam took antidepressants to handle it on
top of grief from other things. He was the second serious boyfriend
I'd had who relied on prescription medication to survive their
current, day-to-day life and when Liam ran out of pills, I walked
across Regency Square to the pharmacy with his passport in my
pocket to pick up the prescription, hoping I wouldn't one day need
one, too. On the other side of the square a man in Reebok trainers
soliloquised on a mattress as strewn with rubbish as Tracey Emin's
bed, and I felt the total, wonderful freedom of empty days that I
knew would be filled with routine as soon as I got a job, while the
idea that I might need a prescription to cope with it worried me
as much as Jonnie's nightmares.

The *Jurassic Park* sounds of bin lorries rattled around the houses
as I walked up Preston Street thinking that maybe you gravitated
towards people who'd touched darkness if you'd ever seen it yourself. I'd started to feel like I saw it easily in others now, like it left a
different look in your eye, and I wondered if I'd have been able to
see it in my grandmother's eyes if she hadn't decided she couldn't
go on any more when my mum was the age I was now.

'Can I have one?' I joked of the pills when I got back to the flat,
seeing he was embarrassed to be handed the white paper bag, and
he gave me a look of surprise that was almost hard and sceptical.
'You know you can lean on me, don't you?' I said, but he said he

didn't want to and I knew he felt it too much of a risk to rely on anyone who might leave.

Maybe if I hadn't said that, he wouldn't have broken up with me a few weeks later, on that street I'd walked to the chemist, saying it wasn't working and other things, probably, that I failed to hear in the shock, and there was nothing to do but pack my bag and make the meandering, three-hour journey back to Bath on the train, trying not to cry. At the other end I called, and he didn't answer, and I guess I learnt then how quickly you can be locked out of love, and I felt so stupid for trying to let someone in after Jonnie. For letting myself be hurt again, this much. *What did you expect?* I thought savagely, through the tears.

I looked desperately for clues about why I'd been cut out of Liam's life in Alain de Botton's *Essays in Love* which he had given me for Valentine's Day, and I read that people say 'I love you' when they want to hear it back, thinking he must have never loved me at all. Then I looked for insight into depression in William Styron's *Darkness Visible* and absorbed it feverishly, reading that being with someone when they're in the throes of blackness is like standing on a shore watching someone drowning, unreachable, and I felt the same. I read his tiny scrawled dedication in *Keep the Aspidistra Flying* a hundred times, not realising it was an analogy for the London I was about to enter, alone.

Six years later Liam told me it had been hard watching me about to make it, which I hadn't felt was happening at all, and I saw how we really did feel pitted against each other, always, even in love, when the zeitgeist of competition made others' success or ambition fuel our own jealousy and self-doubt.

If I'd known that at the time, it might have helped, because I only felt smashed into a thousand pieces, and I wondered what made our private world and language, what made me, so unworth fighting for. I wondered whether relationships were just about getting used to someone else being around all the time, and trying not to feel empty when they were gone. But when you know everything about someone: their movements, range of voices, worries, previous life, and were used to seeing their name on your phone screen all day long, a void is all there is. As I called him, despair was hearing the phone ringing and left unanswered in a world that now didn't exist.

Desperate not to feel like I did when I was seventeen again, I ran the country lanes around my parents' house until my legs shook, my head tripped with faintness and the air cut out of me in rasping breaths like blades. Relief was not being able to cry any more, and the pain injected in my side was a comfort, because it meant something was changing. I couldn't have been impressive enough, thin enough, nice enough, I thought, and my weight dropped as I took grief out on my body, wishing more than anything that I was tiny and cute and 5ft 2 or something else that was easier to look after.

Back home I fished a beer can from the fridge and felt the cold burn like static on my hot fingers, carrying it upstairs and drinking it in the bath until the water turned cold and my emotions quietened, blanketed by alcohol that overrode sadness until I could sleep. I couldn't stand feeling vulnerable, and didn't realise vulnerability is exactly what I hadn't shown Liam, or anyone else, when we were together, which might have saved us. When he'd told me what scared him, I said *nothing* scared me with a kind of dreadful irony that kept silent the fact that lots did and had already, I was just too scared to say what.

Instead, I resorted to well-worn, fuck-you post-break-up tactics and felt even more driven to make it. *He'll miss me when I'm famous*, I thought, *or at least successful*. Or maybe half-successful, and thinner, I negotiated, using ambition for distraction because I thought about him all the time and didn't want to anymore.

To earn money for a life I was desperate to hurry up and happen, I went back to the secondary school I'd left prematurely, enduring minor PTSD to paint the walls of the classrooms for another year of fresh-faced kids I hoped wouldn't break like I had.

Then in August, the interviews I'd done in Leeds began to attract some attention, and I was given a week at the *Guardian* to prove myself worthy of a job offer, sofa surfing the spare rooms of people my mum had known at uni and had to have a glass of wine before phoning to ask if I could stay. I commuted nervously to King's Cross where, at the *Guardian*'s offices, I sat at a desk covered in someone else's toppling papers, Googling: 'What's an MP?' while another young woman opposite me answered the phone with the words: 'Hello, Greggs. I MEAN THE *GUARDIAN*.'

'Greggs', as I thought of her from then on, had won a place on a scholarship scheme at City University, where everyone who could afford it did an MA in journalism before trying to worm their way onto the few remaining grad schemes at the nationals. But her MA had in turn only won her two casual shifts a week at the paper, so she had to offset the lowly pay by flogging sausage rolls at Greggs for minimum wage, too.

My job was to call as many MPs as it took to persuade eight to tell me whether they were worth a recent pay rise to £66,000, so I thought I'd better find out what they were supposed to be doing for it first. *Fucking politics*, I thought, like a placard-wielding punk.

'How's it going?' Greggs asked.

'Edwina Currie paused our conversation to pick up dog shit,' I told her. 'I assume it was her dog but – yeah.'

She laughed. In actual fact, I had quotes from six MPs (past, present and *I'm A Celebrity* MPs like Nadine Dorries included), which meant I needed two more if the feature was going to lead to a job. That hadn't been said, but I understood my week in the office wasn't dissimilar to the trial shifts I'd done in restaurants where you just had to smile and not drop anything.

Later that night I kicked my wheely suitcase back to King's Cross buoyed on the cheap red wine Greggs and I had raised to each other across other people's desks as the evening darkened, musing half-drunkenly that we'd probably live together if I got the job. She'd return home from work on the Greggs days with out-of-date pastries and we'd commute to London from a hovel near Shipley that still had an electricity metre, I considered. Our neighbours would probably be in a domestically violent relationship but we'd learn to shape sausage rolls into twenty-pence-shaped pieces and plug those into the metre so we could read game-changing law policy across the puff pastry light, I thought, as my bag jammed in a crack in the pavement and the reverie shattered.

I remembered Liam then and wished I was getting a train to Brighton instead of back to Bath, knowing he'd find it funny that I'd spent a week in *The Thick of It* and wishing I could still talk to him. Then I cursed Bath's MP Don Foster for the tenth time that week for refusing to help me with a comment. I'd met him at school and he'd been sycophantic enough for the photo ops. But what was the point of celebrating youth if you were then unwilling to help a single part of it get somewhere when they needed you, I wondered?

Sir Peter Bottomley woke me up the next morning, and I got my eight MPs and my first feature in a national paper (and therefore my first pay cheque: £400) despite Foster. Then I got a job offer, some weeks later: two days a week, the same as Greggs. But I couldn't afford to take it, knowing no estate agent would accept a casual contract paying £200 a week as assurance I could magic three to four times that in rent. Now the classrooms were painted, I sat on the reception of my old school, slyly reading Alan Bennett under the desk, and wondering with disdain what pushing myself to the point of breakdown had all been for if it was this?

In Leeds I'd imagined I only had to be stronger, better and more imaginative to make it in a harder world, seeing the route to Fleet Street as though on a satnav screen that automatically recalibrated when a road was closed. I'd failed my driving test twice, so that was as far as my road analogy went, but for those failures I blamed the phobia my rugby prop of a driving instructor had given me, his weight rolling the car downhill every time I tried to start it. That felt like a metaphor now I was trying to drive to the start of my life and felt the car stalling often; roads ahead closing every time I changed direction.

I needed to shift gear, I thought, thinking that a *second* job offer (preferably not at Greggs) might mean I could take the *Guardian* one and afford London, where all the national papers were based. I'd spent a week at another national newspaper earlier in the summer covering someone's holiday, and so I went back to the quick-talking Gillian Anderson lookalike who'd been in charge of me then, dreaming that she'd take my fate in her hands.

But she had a different idea, I realised. 'Pitch,' she emailed, and then a minute later my phone rang with her name.

'What can you write?' she asked, as I stood in the playground of my old school trying to think of anything I had to say. Anything that felt important. The answer, I realised, was staring right at me. So I gave her my story so far: the pressure and the competition and the exhaustion and . . .

'When can you write it?' she said.

A week later I was on the cover of the features section and Gillian Anderson called back to ask if I could now do a British version of a viral *New York Times* piece. Sex on Campus: the female perspective, and that, I thought, would be easy. Within a month, she'd told me to come up and start work. Now all I needed was a flat.

Dear Lucy,

I have incorporated a quotation from Lucy Holden in tomorrow's lecture on Sidney. 'University is a massively sexed-up school camp, and while it used to be widely considered that men were the chief authors of any liaisons dangereuses, it is girls who now hold all the cards.' Which does indeed fit with the argument that the sonnet lover is abject before the woman he celebrates.

The other feature made me think. Why didn't I, or most of my contemporaries in the dim and distant past, feel as pressured as your generation?

I wonder if the answer is that 'pressure' actually comes from everywhere except the 'good' internal pressure that leads one to want to do a task well. In the olden days the 11+ was a particular site of anxiety, but the fetishisation of marks and league tables have created that atmosphere of desperate competitiveness which has stifled teaching, making it ever more exam focused and children have internalised that sterile competitiveness perhaps.

The same triumph of league tables over actual, real value is also now firmly embedded in the staff world: get more grants/better student assessment/better scores/be in the top x of international league table etc. etc.

Does this opinion from a geriatric make sense?

Best wishes and good luck arriving in the Great Wren,

Everleigh

2

Girls of Slender Means

So there I was, *finally* in London, twenty-three years old and as extraordinary and ordinary as everyone else who'd just landed in the capital trying to find their future. My life so far was already drawn in my appearance: my tiptoe walk, bike crash scars and a broken nose from defending a friend in a fight at fifteen. 'The wild streets of Bath,' people said. 'The fucking Bronx,' I agreed, still having the dent of the girl's ring visible on the bridge of my nose to prove it and occasionally still wondering if I should have tried to hit her back.

I'm straightening my hair religiously because I think it makes my face look thinner and I'm told constantly (by men) that I'm tall for a girl, and that I'm *funny* in a tone that suggests it's surprising. I can chameleonise anywhere as long as it's not a place with rules. I'm quietly ruthless because people have been ruthless with me, and I do nothing by halves because my generation knows it can't afford to. I drink too much, want to work too hard, know rent's going to ruin me, but my parents are proud as hell that I've landed a job at one of the most famous newspapers in the world.

If we'd stayed in Cornwall maybe I'd have still been happy amongst the waves, but in London I was going to make it, I thought, considering myself halfway there because I knew what a pisco sour was and owned a pair of Chanel boots, even if they were an apology from the city lawyer who never answered his phone and which didn't suit me at all. They were still Chanel, I considered, regretting not accepting the other lavish presents he'd tried to buy me back with after messing me around, but still cringing about the hyperventilating, eight-minute voicemail I'd left him after we'd broken up and my cat got run over.

When I made it, things would be different, I told myself: I'd not have nightmares or need to drink crates of cider on Sundays. I'd not need to pop meds to get by and I'd not give a fuck when a cat died or a man dumped me. I'd not give a fuck *in Chanel.*

In our newly acquired flat, Welly – a friend from Bath who'd moved up with me – and I sat in the kitchen of our new world staring at a large section of wall that had been covered over with wrapping paper like a moving-in present.

'What do you think is behind that?' I asked him.

'Previous tenants?' he said, shaking floppy blond hair out of his face.

'Lovely,' I said, going to the fridge to open the only thing in it, a bottle of wine.

It was move-in day and this was the last place we'd seen during a boiling summer's day viewing London's expensive dumps. It was nice – bar the wrapping paper and the mice and the snails in my bedroom – but we would've signed anywhere at that point, just to end the search.

'You won't find better than this,' an estate agent with a 2-4-1-cocktails face told us when we'd looked around, and we didn't doubt it, having already viewed one flat in complete darkness, that estate agent prodding what looked like a festering sleeping bag, but might have been a corpse, with his clipboard. 'We'll get lightbulbs when you move in,' he'd said as we shook our heads.

So, at the *Hunger Games*-style viewing we'd walked into in Clapham we'd stared at a chapped patio the size of a Tokyo train station sushi bar, then at the faces of the other millennials broken from the hunt, and collared the Burton-suited boy agent to tell

him we'd take it. He leaned mock-conspiratorially on the neighbour's front hedge and slid through fake density.

'The landlord would favour a two-year contract ... ' he said,
brushing dirt off his shoulder like a nylon Jay-Z.

'Fine,' we said, as he shook Welly's hand and failed to extend
his to mine. I'd known he had a pseudo-feminist jug of Woo Woo
written all over him.

The only slight problem was that it was a three-bed flat, so I'd
persuaded Danny and Anna to join us from Brighton, where Anna
was growing ever more depressed shelf-stacking at Boots, and as
I clunked my wine glass against Welly's, I just hoped they'd like
each other. I already knew Welly and Danny were polar opposites,
although I hadn't known they'd have exactly the same taste in
women: Anna.

I thought it would save us all, that flat, and when the others
arrived we descended upon our new local pub feeling like it was
us against the world.

The smell of printing had left Fleet Street when I arrived, mainly
because Fleet Street had left Fleet Street, but I'd done my homework and read *Towards the End of the Morning*, half of Andrew
Marr's *My Trade* and *Scoop*, twice.

On my first day at the newspaper Gillian Anderson had got
me onto, I went swaggering through a shimmering marina of
mini yachts feeling like it was better than the books, if anything.
It looked more like Cannes and, behind the docks, the Tower of
London loomed with beautiful, brutal history; a world-famous
site, calm and solid amongst streets of beeping buses and the grey
commuters on Tower Hill. As I floated along, I wondered if this
was the day I'd meet the editor, be accidentally sent to a war zone,
foil reporters by leaving 'out of order' signs in phone boxes, or find
the centenarian Nature Notes writer sleeping at his desk as the
characters in my new favourite books had.

The paper had offered four days a week's work if I didn't go to the *Guardian*, but to my consternation, my main job when I got to the features section each day was to pretend to be on work experience. An atmosphere of redundancy hung in the air and the bank of desks I was told to sit on was crowded with the ghosts of expensive, more experienced writers.

'Don't tell anyone why you're here. Absorb everything,' I was told, so I read the papers as inconspicuously as possible feeling like a mole with no idea what I was looking for.

In the newspaper world, no day was the same and the lack of certainty appealed to my belief that I got bored fast. As I was dispatched to Waitrose for intrepid investigation (which brand of quinoa had the most salt in it, for example), I leapt from my desk with as much vim as a war reporter and, standing in front of hundreds of packets of grain, tried to work out the answer to the other question demanded by Gillian Anderson: 'What are millennials doing at the moment? What do you *do*?'

It seemed ridiculously hard to answer, but I'd already heard that ideas were currency, so I wrote it down and stared at the words, wondering how to get rich quick.

The fact I considered myself a bit of a chancer, and knowing I'd come in through the back door, made me feel so disposable I was essentially waiting each day to be fired, not realising I was as cheap as an editor's lunch and therefore semi-pointless to let go anyway. But knowing how many other graduates would kill to be in my place made me feel I could be replaced quickly and easily and the ingrained idea that we were supposed to have it all and make it look effortless worried me when I had no idea what I was doing. Imposter syndrome was high and heightened further by the fact I seemed to have landed in a press version of *Tinker Tailor Soldier Spy*, my role a secret and most people ignoring me entirely.

*

Still, it was better to be invisible on a national paper than at the *Truro Daily Express Online Bi-annual*, or any of the other end-of-the-world publications my mum had been suggesting might be more realistic places to start a career all summer. Invisibility is a good thing, I tried to pep-talk myself, not something that puts you on edge.

On top of that there was just the pure adrenaline of watching tomorrow's news being decided in conference rooms overlooking St Pauls, the deputy editor, a famous Fleet Street name, taking his place at the head of the table to slash and celebrate ideas that were carried to him like mice from the cats of each section. To his right, slouched a sidekick from online; online news booming in the wake of declining print sales and draping in glory anyone who could manage a laptop better than an editor triple their age.

Online was up first that morning, I saw, as a video projected cinematically onto a large screen behind the editor.

'A rat carrying a piece of pizza through New York has gone viral,' Online told the room, as a rodent dragging a slice of pepperoni through the streets was met with rolling laughter. 'It's raised lots of questions about whether he was carrying it home for himself, whether it was for family consumption or whether he was in fact a delivery rodent.'

The deputy pulled a face as the rest of the room remained hypnotised.

'I don't want to see that again, it was disgusting,' the deputy editor concluded, and the screen flicked to the next offering.

'Donald Trump and vegetables are trending online,' a pictures editor continued. 'This corn on the cob was compared to Donald Trump's hair,' they explained, following the corn with a picture of a potato, which did also bear a remarkable resemblance to the future president's face and won a laugh from the boss.

Then there was an affair between someone and someone else that was 'quite fun' one of the desks added, and Science reported that if you sit down all day you should fidget to live longer. In other news, a billionaire's whole family had been struck down by Lyme disease.

'How do you know if you've got Lyme disease?' asked Arts.

'The GPs are really going to thank us, aren't they?' commented a leader writer.

'Yes, and the hypochondriacs,' the deputy boomed.

'The head of the British Pig Association has just died,' someone said, looking at their phone.

'Now you're just being troublesome,' the deputy said.

'I swear he just died!'

'What, of Lyme disease?'

'Don't think so.'

Foreign reported that it wasn't a great PR moment for Isis, who'd released ten videos in the last week to try to dissuade extremists from returning to Europe on migrant boats, and the deputy asked who the goodies and the baddies were in a fight in Kashmir.

'Good news for Bay City Rollers fans,' the arts editor told the room when we finally got to features. 'They are reforming after thirty-five years.'

'Do you think they'll wear the trousers?' asked the head of news.

'And the wigs?' said someone else.

'M and S used to sell BCR knickers,' added the deputy.

'I don't remember that,' the head of news said.

Fashion offered *the sexy makeover of the midi heel*, AKA the MI5 heel apparently worn by back-office spies, and the rise of the biker cardie, to the sound of male sniggers, and we were done.

'What did you think?' my editor asked as we filed out an hour and a half later.

'Amazing,' I breathed, as though we'd just left the theatre. She snorted. Conference was the bane of editors' lives and as we walked back to our desks, I watched the reporters scan their superiors' faces to gauge the severity of the daily task; sly drips of sweat revealing they'd snuck off to the gym to pelt 5K on a tread-mill in an understanding that they'd not leave the office before 7 p.m. and would miss their children's bedtimes if they hit the gym after work.

Back at my desk, conference was helping the list I was making of subjects the paper liked and loathed, and I added 'rats/pizza rats' to the no-go list, which already included: trashy celebs (Kardashians), reality TV, non-British stuff, anyone parents wouldn't have heard of, drugs, clubs, vegans and J. K. Rowling.

On the approved list was: royals, posh (anything), millionaires, millennials, Michelin star meatballs, old stuff (if cool again – i.e. knitting, the WI), dogs, cat cafes, supermodels, Aldi and sex.

Later, when Prince Harry was seen tumbling out of a high-end club on Sloane Square and I was told to work nocturnally for a piece on the posh party scene, I saw how influence and celebrity made trends. Nightclubs plus royals were fine, just not clubs without them, I realised as my flatmates and I descended on Tonteria, where Will, Kate and Harry had all been spotted on previous nights. Inside the Day of the Dead-inspired club we were plonked on a table with a centrepiece of iced vodka. A miniature train running on a railway above our heads delivered shots while lingerie-clad women danced with men in gimp masks, and we agreed we could see why Harry liked it. How to party like a royal was summed up later in the week when I woke up after a night at a Russian vodka and caviar club opposite Kensington Palace with caviar in my shoes, feeling more like Princess Margaret than I'd ever imagined possible.

Being treated like royalty in the evenings made the squalor we lived in more disorientating. At home, I was woken up by a bailiff called Darren banging on the door, wanting to know why we weren't paying the council tax, despite the fact Welly had been receiving shares from the three of us each month. 'Oops,' he said, thinking he'd set up a direct debit but clearly not being taught much life-skill at his expensive school. I looked around his room at the boxes of leaflets and badges bearing the logo of his latest bizarre business idea and wondered whether we were paying for it. He was as lost as I felt, really, but the difference was that someone else seemed to be covering the costs of his identity crisis.

'He must get an allowance,' my mum said.

'Has anyone been given an allowance since the eighteenth century?' I asked her.

'Maybe stocks and shares,' she said.

After Liam I'd started seeing Sam, the bartender I'd dated in Leeds, again and it was just us and Anna and Danny in the flat a lot of the time as Welly went on culinary tours of pasta regions or attended fine art courses in Florence where girls seemed to meet him and throw themselves in the Arno. His confusion around who he was and what he wanted to do seemed to be mirrored in romance and he fell in and out of love fast enough to almost drown people. Other weeks he was busy setting up Ghanaian food stalls or some such, and I avoided asking if he'd actually been to Africa. He was a fit Tim Nice But Dim-type who made expensive boarding schools look like the most colossal waste of resources, and making the rest of us even gladder we'd gone to state schools where we'd been allowed to keep at least *one* foot on the ground.

Sam, who was commuting from Birmingham to see me, was doing well in piecing my heart back together for a second time and slowly I was learning that I didn't have to keep men at a distance. 'I love you so much I'd walk through a shark tank covered in blood with dogs biting my hands and lions chasing me just to look at someone whose friend once went to a shop where you'd bought a can of Coke,' he said, which was niche romance, but romance nonetheless. At work I'd had to edit a feature on a new dating app called Tinder, wondering whether it would ever take off but glad not to have to be on it and find out.

During degenerate weekends the four of us gallivanted around London feeling invincible but however late we got home, Danny's chubby Northern face woke me early on Sundays, grinning a few millimetres from mine. Three years in the making, this relationship with Sam, and we still couldn't have sex in the morning, I'd think, every time I saw Danny's face.

'What time is it?' I'd groan on those occasions.

'Eight thirty.'

'Jesus Christ.'

'I wake up early.'

'Well don't.'

He handed me a four-pint carton of semi-skimmed as Sam's eyes remained determinedly shut.

'What is it?' I asked him.

'White Russian. Mixed it straight in.'

I took a swig, then stuck my tongue out to air it, vodka rippling on my taste buds like high voltage.

'What time were we in bed?'

'Four a.m. or summit.'

I had vague memories then of Anna and I having a squashed bath in bikinis and sunglasses, while the boys sat scrunched on the floor beside us trying to remember the name of that guy from *SMart* whose girlfriend died coked-up in the bath. It might have been sexy if the bathroom didn't look like the peeling inside of a skip. In the bath, our limbs stuck out at Cubist right angles like the mangled limbs in *Guernica*.

Consciousness resented me in the aftermath. Our war: Monday morning. But having learnt to drink for confidence when I was a shy teenager, drinks had become magic tricks that made anything more exciting when we couldn't afford to go out, piling instead onto the sofa to drink cheap white wine and illegally streaming whatever show everyone was talking about, then tottering to Sainsbury's with Danny's Sonic the Hedgehog piggy bank when we ran out of booze. Alcohol was an activity in itself for a generation as broke and lost as ours but I was happy then, in a house of friends. We were a generation of binge drinkers obsessed with the moment because we couldn't see the future, but who blamed us when we were pitted against each other in every corner and denied permanence in every field.

Sam enveloped me in love after White Russian Sundays when fatigue made me dread work, despite the fact I loved my job and was proud of having started at the top paper in London, albeit on the bottom rung. The nervousness I felt at the end of the weekend was connected to the fraudulent feeling that my swanky office was nicer than my flat, I guess, and knowing that during the week PRs swirled me around heady London venues that I couldn't afford to visit at the weekends. I'd begun to wonder whether we were all just pretending in our twenties while we waited to turn into who we wanted to be, but it made me feel uneasy, waiting to fit into the scene.

Monday mornings were easier if Tailor – the most boring sub in the office whose nickname I'd devised from the 'personality' he tried to express in garish socks – wasn't in my Tube carriage. I could maintain the wonder, then, at huddling twelve-deep with the other commuters and squeezing myself into the space like toothpaste. Tailor lived two stops down the line and never failed to shroud a morning in negativity by telling me south London/London/the paper/journalism/life wasn't what it used to be. He most certainly didn't have the look of a man who would enjoy queuing for a one-dish pop up.

'Did someone spit on your shoes?' he asked during an early moment of our accidentally shared commute, staring at my Hotmail-blue heels after I took the one free seat in the carriage before realising it neighboured his.

'Oh. Snail trails,' I said, bending to smudge the slime in. I had the room closest to the 'garden' and woke up with curled, glittery tracks on my shoes each day.

He eyed me curiously.

'Thanks,' I said, flapping open the *Metro* with a purpose I hoped would inspire silence but never did.

'Did you see the story this morning about the minced teenager?' he asked.

'Sorry?'

'A man minced a teenager in Hounslow.'

'Good,' I said, looking back down at the *Metro*. Then had a brainwave. 'Hey, was the mincer a millennial?' I asked, wondering if it might count as a new trend.

'Not sure.'

To try to make myself feel less expendable I'd decided to ask The Editor if I could write news as well as features, which I hoped would fill empty, concerning days, as well as my empty, concerning bank account. During my first year in the job I was too broke to go to the Christmas party and too embarrassed to accept a generously offered payday loan from an older writer. Then when the other staff writer came back from an office Christmas sale and plonked a gift box on my desk, whispering, 'In case you need to give anyone anything for Christmas,' it was so kind that I went to the staff bathrooms and cried in a cubicle that was nicer than my bedroom.

We had to survive on so little in that city, but almost my entire family on my mum's side had been writers, so I hoped journalism ran in my blood. My grandparents had met at the BBC after the Second World War, and later wrote sixty books between them. In New York, my grandfather set up Visnews, a TV news company later bought by Reuters, and when my mum had gone into publishing, her brother had trained on newspapers and become a broadcaster for ITN, covering the Bosnian war. My dad's sister had run in similar circles on northern regional papers where she'd interviewed Scott Walker and Norman Wisdom, marrying a newsreader who worked with my uncle before the two sides of my family had even met.

Nothing comes of nothing, I repeated, guessing the email address

of The Editor and asking if I could come and say hello, which
was audacious, to say the least, but made me feel more like my
life was in my own hands, and less invisible. To my amazement,
he agreed. 'Are you like the scuttling editor in *Towards the End of
the Morning*?' I asked.

'More like Lord Copper,' he replied, and I thought: *Brilliant*.
Then: *Shit*.

'You're funny,' he said when I sat down in his glass office a
week later.

'In writing or in person?' I asked.

His eyebrows raised. 'Both.'

'Do you want to know something funny?' I tried. 'Guess how
much is in my bank account?'

'No.'

Damn, I thought, punchline ruined.

'I'd like to write news,' I said.

'Why didn't you apply for the grad scheme?' he asked.

'I did,' I said. 'I got the rejection email when I was sitting on
the features desk.'

'You can't go onto the news desk without training,' he said.

'Please may I have training?' I asked.

'Why didn't you do a masters?'

'I don't have ten thousand pounds.'

He considered.

'You've got your nose pierced.'

'Don't you like it?'

'I like it, but some of the people you might meet on news may
not,' he said conservatively.

'I can take it out.'

'I'll talk to Alan.'

I skipped back to my desk via the bathrooms where I threw my
nose ring in the bin and wondered how many hours it would take
the internal investigation to find my CV.

Then how long it would take them after that to realise I had bulked my lack of experience with references from big-name journalists I'd interviewed. Lynn Barber thought I was 'sharp'; Giles Coren that I was 'just the right amount of intelligent'; and Simon Hattenstone said I had 'balls'. All I knew was that asking for training seemed to have worked.

Two months later I sat in a basement classroom in the offices of Newcastle's *Evening Chronicle* listening to the advice that turtles in the Tyne were always news and thinking there was about a 10 per cent chance it would go down well in a London news conference. I put my hand in the air.

'Yes?'

'Please may I go to the bathroom?' I asked.

And they say my generation is infantilised, I thought, as I walked out the room and past a skeleton of a printing press that sat like the rollercoaster bones of a dinosaur in a room as glass-sided as a museum display case.

Newcastle. January, and I'd arrived in ice and darkness. The lesson: be careful what you wish for, I realised a month in, as I sat alone in the converted attic of a barrister for the Crown Prosecution Service listening to relentless shorthand tapes and finishing a bottle of white wine which made the symbols in front of me increasingly squiggly.

I'd been naïve enough not to realise that asking for training would send me out of London for a Press Association course that squeezed a year-long journalism MA into four crammed months of lessons, before exams. Whilst being taught how to find and structure news stories was clearly valuable, the government policy, journalistic law and shorthand I was required to have in blocks of school-style classes before becoming a reporter, were tough. But after meeting the Editor, I'd finally made it onto the grad scheme in a roundabout way that had started to feel just my style, or luck.

I had a two-year, full-time contract to show for it, which I hoped
would dissolve my daily fear of being told not to come in the next
day once I was allowed back to London.

In Newcastle I'd realised fast that the up-and-down nature of
house-shares made living alone seem dreamy until you're faced
with the void. The self-sufficient flat I'd found to move into would
have made me feel seventy-five if I didn't have to put my hand in
the air to ask if I could go to the loo and listen to *Roger Red Hat,
Billy Blue Hat*-style teeline tapes by night.

My mind drifted from the monosyllabic shorthand recordings
back to London, and I wondered what the others were doing that
evening. Before I'd left Welly had developed a habit of trying to
pull women in the kitchen at 3 a.m. on weeknights to a soundtrack
of pop filth with a coke-head friend from school.

'He's leaving for Sandringham soon,' Welly would say as way
of apology, which I wasn't sure was an entirely great thing for the
country, either.

At the time I resented going to work looking like I'd been out
when I'd just been kept up all night because of someone else's
revelries, but now I was alone, I found the emptiness I'd thought
would be idyllic hard to bear.

I picked up my phone and waited for someone to answer.

'Alcoholics Anonymous,' a voice said.

'Hello,' I said. 'How many days have you been sober?'

'Four hundred and two,' said a nice man on the other end.

'Can you tell me about it?' I asked, reaching for the bottle of
wine and unscrewing the top as quietly as possible so he didn't
hear me, while wondering if you could ever really know if you felt
as shit as someone else. I wanted to know if I was OK, because I
wasn't completely confident that I was. During the four months I
was in Newcastle, there was something akin to despair sitting in
me, more than I'd felt it in London, and sometimes it weighed so
heavily that I found it hard to get out of bed and into the classroom.

In lunchbreaks I sat in the pub with Mat and Alex, two of the boys on the course who'd become close friends, and we talked as cynically as journalists triple our age, which I wasn't sure was normal. Alex was an Action Man-type Scot whose place on the £5,000 course had been the 'dying wish' of an aunt who was still alive years later, and Mat wanted to report from South America, but knew starting in British news agencies would make it easier, even if they only paid £12,000 a year.

That morning we'd had a particularly farcical talk from the director of the course, a David Brent type who'd told us he always did well on door knocks because he was assumed to be unthreateningly inept enough to be invited inside, and so we were trying to laugh off the advice to appear useless over a pint. Really, we existed in a beery cloud of shot mood, but the head of the course didn't think mental health issues were a 'thing' so I hadn't bothered telling anyone I felt I was sinking into a mild depression. Being flung out of London and back into a patronising, school-like routine that curtailed my freedom made Newcastle feel like time in prison – but worse than that, because I'd asked to be put behind bars and had moved a floor above the prosecution. The saving grace were the boys on the course, who became great friends, and the Oxfam bookshop in Jesmond which I spent hours in every weekend, lugging back books containing different worlds to my attic like Matilda. But less irritating, I hoped.

When Sam visited we went to the coast and ate sausage sandwiches on the beach, but he was working in Amsterdam and I hated long-distance, which left me too alone in the week and had all sorts of unforeseen issues at the weekends, I realised, when we dabbled in some minor sexual experimentation and lost a sex toy inside me just before he had to leave.

'What am I supposed to do?!' I wailed hysterically, crying tears of the elderflower gin I'd drank half a bottle of because it tasted like squash.

'I don't know, Luce, but I'm going to miss my plane!' he said, frantically packing.

'I can't go to A and E *alone* with a sex toy lost inside me!' I whimpered pathetically, feeling like one of those men who had to tell nurses they'd accidentally fallen on a TV remote or a toy train.

By the time Sam had landed in Amsterdam, I'd fixed the issue and vowed never to be a sexual coward again; small things made internal loss more likely, I thought mock-profoundly.

I'd also decided to ask Sam to come to Scotland with me when I had to follow the other trainees up there for a six-month stint in the Edinburgh office, which now seemed safer all round. I knew I seemed like someone entirely independent but in reality I needed him as a crutch, which made me feel way too needy to be cool.

Knowing I was going back to London after my four-month prison sentence saved me from sinking into a deeper depression but halfway through the course, the idea I was returning to a home had shattered. I'd fielded strange phone calls from Anna, and then Welly, and finally Danny, in tears, who'd just been told Anna was leaving him after four years for Welly, and that they were going to move in together elsewhere. In Clapham, Danny sat in our empty house alone, in pieces.

'Just get here,' I said, and he got on a train the next day, while Sam flew over from Amsterdam. We took him out and got him plastered, the first step of any modern break-up. The fact it was partly my fault for introducing Anna to Welly hung in the air and I wished I could go back in time and not bring Welly into their life.

'I'm so sorry,' I grimaced, when Danny arrived.

'I thought he was after you,' he tried to laugh, sadder than I'd ever seen him.

'So did I,' Sam agreed.

'Christ, no,' I said, actually quite offended.

Welly and I had one night together when we first met and I'd woken up to find my underwear hanging off a 6ft wooden giraffe by the bed.

'Mushrooms are going to save the world,' he said, as I hopped back into them.

'Riiiight,' I'd said, downing a White Russian he'd mixed next to the bed (which was apparently a breakfast staple of boys in their twenties) and leaving.

'Way too Hugh Fearnley-Whittingstall for me,' I told Sam and Danny.

'Posh cunt,' they agreed in unison.

Danny changed profoundly after that break-up. He showed emotion I'd never seen in him before and now he'd let a barrier down, our friendship soared. If anything, I'd been a friend of Anna, but now she'd gone he started calling me when he was down or just to chat, and to my surprise, I realised over the years that followed that it was not Anna at all but Danny who would see me through life.

Their break-up affected me, too, much more than I expected. Seeing how years of commitment could be thrown away so fast, like the bags of their life he'd found in the bins outside our house as he'd walked to the train, was shattering and shook me. People changed, and maybe he and Anna had been a bad match, but it made loyalty seem so transient.

I felt so helplessly far away from it all in the months that followed, and pictured Danny alone in our empty house. He'd slept in my room ever since Anna and Welly had left, not being able to bear his old room any more, and I'd agreed to take Welly's after Newcastle, when Sam was going to move in with us to help with the rent. Danny was in charge of quickly finding us new flatmates in the meantime and knowing I wouldn't be able to meet them first worried me hugely, but we were desperate.

The disparity between my personal and professional lives raged again as I went back down to London for the British Press

Awards where I'd been shortlisted for Young Journalist of the Year. I sat amongst the great names of journalism in a glitzy ceremony, wondering when I'd start feeling things were going as amazingly as the décor, the champagne and the calibre of writer in the room suggested. The first person I'd walked into had been A. A. Gill, whose column I'd read for years, and who breathed the strongest coffee breath I'd ever smelt at me when I said hello. He'd already given up drinking, of course, and I wondered again whether I should.

Annoyingly, it appeared I needed to have already written a book in order to win that award that night, given that everyone in my category had, and I was reminded how much you had to achieve, fast, to be in the top tier of anything. I mimed a cigarette across the table at Caitlin Moran and we met Jay Rayner outside to commiserate with each other on our losses.

'The best person never wins,' Jay said supportively.

'You win *most* years,' I objected, as Caitlin, in a dress and Doc Martens, rolled our cigarettes.

I had the sense that I'd come a long way from Leeds, where I'd met them both, but not far *enough* by not winning, and I went back to Newcastle confused about when I'd feel like I'd got somewhere. My mood was oppressive up north, but I felt a responsibility to seem happy when I'd got everything I'd wanted, on the surface at least. So many of my friends were still struggling to get onto the bottom rungs of their respective industries and that made me feel unable to say I didn't feel great, actually, when they told me how amazingly I'd done.

Then when a war reporter I'd sat next to at the Press Awards was kidnapped in Syria a few weeks later, something changed in me again. Anthony's blue-and-black face squinted from the front page of *The Times* and I felt sick, sitting down heavily to read that he'd been shot, the photographer, Jack, locked in a car boot before they had fought their way out and escaped over the border into

Turkey. Anthony had told me at the Press Awards that he'd never been kidnapped and I'd tapped the table: 'Touch wood.'

It felt like smaller things mattered both less and more after that. As though my crumbling private life echoed in something bigger and uneasier, which made the domestic seem less important but more frustrating. I guess a public danger I saw every day in the news became realer, too, and I realised, for the first time, that journalists really were on a frontline, seeing and hearing the worst of everything and having to compute it for copy. That made the awards more poignant, but I'd started to see why so many journalists drank to cope.

Feeling my world vision shift, I blamed Newcastle for trapping me and counted down the days to parole. Then I got an email from a PR I'd known in London, asking if I wanted to go to Hong Kong on a press trip to watch the British leg of a global cocktail competition and I thought, *I really fucking do want to do that, yes.* If my job was going to lower me to such dark levels, I decided the other side of the seesaw must be the adrenaline-fuelled high life. Plus I needed a holiday. So I got the train back to London for the final time, booked a week off work and climbed into the blacked-out car bound for Heathrow where I was handed champagne in the business-class lounge.

Humid Hong Kong felt like another world as I stared up at the skyscrapers in disbelief, never having been anywhere like it, and we were just two hours into the first bar crawl when another of the journalists asked whether they should ring their dealer.

'You have a *dealer* in Hong Kong?' I asked, thinking this was surely how you knew you'd made it.

They were in their late thirties and I was just twenty-four, but gonzo journalism (if this was that) was not dead, I thought happily. For four steaming days we were taxied around Hong Kong's bars and restaurants and it finally ended on a sky-high rooftop with a magnum of champagne and a magnum of vodka, the bar guys thumping their chests in a rendition of Matthew McConaughey and Leonardo DiCaprio's *Wolf of Wall Street* song.

I looked at the city from that rooftop and felt like the whole trip had taken place in a fountain of booze on one long, hazy, druggy night of surreal heat. Then one of the PRs came up to me, shoved a wrap of cocaine into my palm and told me to finish it before we got through security at the airport, where I promptly lost my plane ticket amidst all the excitement and had to joyride around the terminal on a disability vehicle with one of the other writers, trying to find it.

During that trip I guess I thought I'd found the old Fleet Street: the hedonism and the drunken, hilarious glory that saved you from the black. This was the kind of life I'd read about in books before the world turned sober and broke, I thought, as I shut my eyes on the plane. There were still glimmers of grandeur in the world. You just had to look harder for them.

A week later I was crashing back down to street level in London where I realised Tailor was still sliding, as grey and defeated as a slowworm, through the doors of the press world ahead of me, and I was confused to find myself even less sure of things, despite having been trained. Now I was a reporter, news meant being dispatched anywhere at any time and I'd been told to keep an overnight bag with clean clothes and my passport under my desk as though I was Jason Bourne. It might have been good advice if I'd actually had a desk but hot-desking was another modern phenomenon that added a layer of anxious impermanence to our existence each morning as we scanned offices for where that existence was supposed to take place.

My suspicion that in Newcastle I was being regionally trained for a national paper became clear when I was given my first door knock late one Sunday night within my first weeks back.

'Michael who sorry?' I asked the night editor.

'Gove,' he repeated, uttering some more words that included: *leaked documents* and *disgruntled adviser* but not *The Thick of It* – again.

Perfect, I thought, when the editor had hung up, given that my first piece for the paper had been an attack of the education system Gove was in charge of. That, or very imperfect, I concluded, setting an alarm for 5.30 a.m. and getting up after a very bad sleep to cross London to Notting Hill where I stood yawning on a street that hadn't opened its eyes yet.

When the photographer turned up, I traipsed reluctantly to Gove's door, feeling helpfully inept, as I'd been advised in Newcastle, and extended one knock-shaped fist to the door only for it to move away from me and reveal Gove standing, shocked, in what looked like a fancy-dress Wimbledon outfit.

'Morning, Mr . . . ' I started into the slamming door. 'Shit.'

I looked back at the photographer. He shrugged. I knocked again. No answer. I walked back down the path.

'God, he really does look like Peter Brookes' cartoon version, doesn't he?' I said, in disbelief. 'That wet-lipped-shocked-toddler-face is uncan—' I mumbled, cut off by a 'fuck' from the photographer. I followed his gaze to where Gove was now legging it down the street in his 1940s tennis outfit, having snuck out the back door.

'Chase him!' he said. 'I'll get the car.'

'*Chase* him?'

'Yes, go!'

'Oh my God,' I said, starting to hobble-run down the street in my MI5 midi-heels, my handbag swinging maniacally under my arm. Was Michael Gove *really* running away from me in the street?

I sat down on a front wall to wait for him to ignore me on his return, which he duly did, claiming to know nothing about leaked documents and disgruntled aides, and then I went edgily back to the office to wait for instructions of who I should chase next. *Surreal*, I thought, shaking my head at my hot-desk.

The fast, impossible-to-predict nature of news suited my constant desire for change, but it also exacerbated my inability to sit still, something I saw in other news journalists too. Social media had made everyone a reporter, which was helpful in some ways, but meant developments bubbled constant and quick: online churnalism surging with tsunami strength.

As the three other graduate trainees fought over hard news, sniffing at anything that was deemed 'fluff', I lapped it up, relieved. *Happily* I paid people to spend time with me for a story on rent-afriend.com; set off alpaca trekking in the Isle of Wight (barely minding at all that alpacas bucked all over the place if you tried to walk them on leads like dogs); and went to Hackney to buy frozen mice to taxidermy at my kitchen table with a new kit that had sold out online.

Fluff was an antidote that helped lighten the impression that the world was darker than early Ian McEwan, I found. At the Old Bailey I'd watched the sentencing of a fifteen-year-old boy who'd offset his schizophrenia with marijuana and killed his own mother because he thought she was a witch. I'd scribbled the grim details from ambulance staff who'd arrived at the boy's home to see him giving what they'd assumed to be CPR, before realising he was trying to pull her heart clean out her body to make sure she was dead. The fact real life was stranger than fiction caused a blur of reality, totally. Nothing was too horrific to be real, I thought, as my world view changed in light of a frightening, savagely dark side I was being shown.

It was also the beginning of what would become the Me Too movement three years later and historic sexual abuse claims rolled in. Rolf Harris, then Max Clifford were amongst the first. Then I was sent to Southwark Crown to watch Dave Lee Travis convicted of one count of indecent assault, watching him holding court doors open for women anywhere near him as if he could change minds now.

It was during the hard, dark days that I missed the home Welly and Anna had blown up, even if I didn't blame them for prioritising love, which everyone did in their own way. I only resented that feeling strung out was harder to deal with when you lived with strangers. After emotionally straining days I didn't have the energy to talk to a revolving door of boys who burnt chicken in the kitchen and didn't 'believe' in rounds, or girls who cried constantly over 'Irish bastards' and emerged to make 'mug cakes' using vegetable oil that stuck to the mug and swam in your tea.

My sense of humour, I realised, when I was woken up to shouts of 'DIE, DIE, DIE,' from a gamer in the room next to mine and Sam's, was fading fast, and I instead wanted to scream. The friendships had given the flat a sheen of a home and without them it lost its glimmer, morphing back to the shoddy place it was, with its bathroom that smelt like a public loo, cracked windows that froze in winter and mice creeping through the kitchen like it was a Tube train track. All this for £2,500 a month and the threatened rise of rent from an impossible-to-reach landlord in France who banned improvement, I thought. What a joke.

It didn't surprise me at all to find that in 2014, one in five 16–24-year-olds had mental health problems, according to the Office for National Statistics (ONS), and 90 per cent of those aged 20–24 struggling with anxiety or depression were renting.

The impermanent conditions of our lease – the with who, what, where, how – made me avoid going back to my flat entirely, and instead I let myself be churned into the night when I left the office. Wine-and-dining PRs chaperoned me around the city to places I knew my card would decline if I had to try and use it, and I woke, hungover, to notes on my phone reading 'rotisserie seagull', wondering if I'd really been served that the night before. I'd once had to eat grey squirrel croquettes, so it wasn't impossible, and at the office I pitched, with at least 80 per cent sincerity, stories of

edible straws, or sea urchin sandwiches to the surprised delight of
the PRs who'd fed me.

Otherwise, I descended into pubs with colleagues or university
friends struggling up the lowest rungs of the ladders of law, TV, the
civil service, charity, opera houses or other newspapers and having
a depressing time of it, too. No one went home straight after
work in London because no one wanted to double the number of
commutes they did each day and the result was that you drank as
soon as you left your desk until last orders were called, looking
around you then, confused and wondering where time had gone.
My friends didn't want to go back to rentals either, but our avoid-
ance behaviours were hugely expensive, of course, which only
fuelled the anxiety when we looked at bank balances on the way
to 6 a.m. gym classes after little sleep. We just needed to let off
steam by night, and there wasn't enough space to breathe in the
rentals masquerading as homes.

I'd started using Sam heavily as a prop, but hiding in our small
bedroom was becoming claustrophobic in a way that made us take
it out on each other and I snapped, often, as he told long stories
about something he'd done at the studio.

'You talk about handbags more than Stella fucking McCartney,'
I'd say in one of those rows that's only amusing a week later.

'It's my job,' he'd say, as I raged that I just couldn't bring myself
to care about an interior shot of a pocket when I'd watched a sexual
abuse trial that day.

Afterwards I just wondered if I wasn't very *nice*; felt guilty;
resented my job for turning me harsh, if that's what was happening. Emotional fatigue from work was doubled by physical fatigue
from the late nights and it was getting to me. In those moments I
wondered if anyone was happy in London, given that most commuters had bags beneath their eyes the colour of five-pound notes.

Exhaustion took the shimmer out of the world and made the
Tube look like the waiting room of a euthanasia clinic; faces

relaxed into gloomy expressions before their features were rear-
ranged the other side for the day ahead. Ironically, I'd begun to
understand Tailor's moaning devastation in being transported
like cattle to the same desk for thirty years, and worried I was
quickly becoming him. I'd started counting the days until Sam
and I moved to Edinburgh in October – another upheaval but
another new start that allowed me to pin a hope of happiness
someplace else.

London was so confusing, being both the best and the worst
of everything and not seeming to offer any middle ground. After
Newcastle, I'd received an invitation asking me to attend a champagne reception with Her Majesty the Queen and HRH the Duke
of Edinburgh, which seemed . . . farcical. 'What the hell is lounge
suit?' I asked the card, wondering if I'd been accidently invited,
but deciding to book a day off work to find out, given it was on
real Fleet Street and I'd never been.

I was surprised to find I *was* expected, when I got there, and
was manoeuvred into a small line-up of young journalists where I
found myself staring down at Prince Philip as he stared up at me.

'Hi, Phil,' I said, having no idea how to greet royalty, obviously,
but immediately thinking 'Phil' might be a touch informal.

'You're tall, aren't you?' he said, squinting at me, as I realised
he hadn't heard.

'Yes,' I said, grinning.

'And what do you do?' he asked, as I told him which paper I
worked for.

'*Do you?*' he said, scrunching his face at me.

'Yes,' I said, finding the whole thing hilariously surreal. 'Are
you a fan?'

'Am I a what?'

'Are you a FAN?'

'God, no,' he said. 'I wouldn't admit to that even if I was.'

Two journalists down, the queen appeared to be having a more

placid conversation and then I saw the head of the Newcastle
course sipping champagne and remembered he was a patron of the
royally endorsed Journalists' Charity, which wanted to help the
new as well as the old faces of the industry.

'Why am I here?' I whispered, after leaving the royal line-up
to sidle up to him.

'You're the *future of journalism*,' he whispered back.

I snorted. As did he. Both of us knew I'd drank three pints with
the boys for lunch in Newcastle to cope with the lessons. How to
find planning permission stories for strip clubs being built next to
churches, for example.

'I don't feel much like the future,' I told him. I felt I could barely
handle myself from one day to the next and the idea that you lived
for the weekend, even when you loved your job, was hard to swal-
low. Surely that wasn't how we had to live?

Only noise relieved me from thought, so the disquieting quiet
of night shifts, where the office and London below drained of
life after the buzz of the day and the adrenaline that saw the
last edition sent for print, was toughest until I was finally taxied
home at 2 a.m. Through the cab window I stared at the city's
nocturnal face. Cash machines lit like glow-worms in the night;
suits sat with their heads in their hands at bus stops; and people
in summer clothes shivered home, presumably thinking what I
would have been: that they couldn't believe they were still out. It
felt like seeing a secret, hidden side of a city that turned chaotic
when the sun rose and when I think of that time I think of the
Ramadan breath of the cabbies who often drove me home and told
me about their lives as I watched the eeriest hours of the world
outside the window.

At the flat I climbed into bed next to Sam and pulled Alfie up
the bed to breathe into his warm fur with relief.

The grads had to work a week of night shifts every few months
and during the days in which I waited nervously to go into the

office at 6 p.m., I sat on Clapham Common with Alfie, watching everyone else whose hours didn't fit the mould. At first, I'd enjoyed the difference of the nocturnal pattern and went running during the day, until the music in my headphones became a ringtone and then an editor's voice demanding to know why I hadn't answered their emails. If you worked the nights, one of the editors thought you should still be on call all day, despite the fact no one could perform well if they worked 10 a.m. to 2 a.m. But 'that's how it was' apparently when she was training. I felt myself disengaging totally after those conversations, powerless to object to the absurdity of some requests, but also wondering if I was the only one complaining – was everyone else fine with never being allowed to switch off?

In an industry which didn't *ever* stop, I'd no idea how reporters were supposed to be given enough time off not to have a meltdown, but there was something about the night shifts which didn't help. All day you felt you had to be on top of the news enough to know what chaos you'd be arriving into at 6 p.m., and most reporters on the late shift secretly prayed nothing big would happen overnight. I'd once met someone who'd been working for a prestigious news agency during 9/11 and they could barely describe the horror of trying to cover a global news event alone, while the editor on shift fielded calls from every paper in the country.

Most people just carried on, knowing it was a tough industry and therefore doubting they'd get much sympathy. All you needed was a coping mechanism, we thought. That meant descending into bars with other journalists who knew what it was like, and filling the night with noise and drink and people. Yet during the solitary existence you had to live on the days before night shifts, it was easy to feel apart from the rest of the world. Everyone I knew had conventional hours, so I just dossed about on my own and felt completely separate from humanity by the end of the week. On those lonely days Alfie was a lifeline but we both had a strange kind of separation anxiety when I had to leave him to head to the Tube.

At the start of night shifts, or during Sundays in the office that cut into your weekend, I trawled the wires (where some of my friends from the Newcastle course now working for press agencies filed stories they hoped would be bought by the nationals) and thought the world looked even more ridiculous. Roger Moore lived in fear of forgetting to do up his flies, one headline said, and the fire service had rescued a drunken student who'd become stuck in a tree after a freshers' ball in Kent.

'Any calls?' the editor asked, coming back from conference.

'Er, yeah a woman phoned to ask whether it's true David Bowie has a new girlfriend because "the nurses won't tell her"?' I said, pulling a face.

'Oh, she's been phoning the news desks for a decade,' he said. 'Total nut.'

I imagined her in the huge, frightening, grey buildings of a now-closed institution a relative of mine had once been admitted to before it shut down and felt the world disjointed and unhinged.

Soon after that the summer drew to a close and at the end of September Sam and I left for Edinburgh, while Danny boarded a plane on a one-way ticket to Australia. He landed back home four years later, but by then Anna and Welly were already married.

Dear Lucy

Just seen the latest pieces – and they make me feel very old
indeed. I cannot see the point of *Gogglebox*; and as for the
sexting – hell in a handcart or the uplands of freedom? Don't
know – but really glad I missed it. I think I'd rather have read a
book and done piano practice for seven hours a day than spent
it flashing my private parts around the ether.

Thank you for your wishes on becoming a grandparent.
Everybody says 'oh how wonderful, you'll really enjoy it',
which is true but it does have its melancholy side because it
just seems another confirmation of entering a very different
life stage, with only a box at the end of it. Today I have to play
the organ at a funeral, which doesn't help the mood induced
as I enter the last month of employment. At my last lecture
ten colleagues turned up; students applauded, and I nearly
lost it completely but resisted the temptation to cast myself as
Prospero drowning my book.

Watch your liver in Scotland but have a good time,

Everleigh

PS The dress code of 'your' first wedding does sound modern.
Would I know a 'badass' shoe if I saw one?

3

Sunlight on Cold Water

In a dirty boxing gym off Holyrood Road I stared at Sherlock Holmes, who was trying to deck Harry Potter in the filthy ring in front of me. Holmes' cloak flapped unmenacingly as he danced towards a grown man wielding a wand, a wonky lightning scar of marker pen on his forehead.

'It's going to be a fight for the best character in Scottish fiction award this year,' the PR chirped next to me, in case we needed the stunt spelt out.

We did.

To my left the Gruffalo, dressed in a shaggy, decrepit-looking costume, waited for his turn to punch Potter and I realised I hadn't imagined Inspector Rebus smoking in the car park outside.

Welcome to Scotland, I thought.

After a small goodbye party with our friends, Sam and I had arrived in a bubble of hungover glee after a four-hour train journey from London and called the estate agent of the flat we were moving into, only to be told we weren't due for another day.

'What?' Sam, said, exhausted and standing next to all our belongings in Waverley station.

'Ummm. I may have ... '

'Please tell me you didn't get the wrong day?' he said.

'It's fine, I'll get us a hotel,' I said quickly. I knew one nice hotel in the city, having been taken on a date there when I was a student, but thought now probably wasn't the best time to share the specific details. Such as not sleeping with him when I realised he had a tattoo of a shark lifting dumb-bells on his bicep.

'Why are you so useless with dates?' Sam asked. 'It's so weird when you have to be so organised for your job.'

'I'm numerically dyslexic,' I joked, trying to kiss him on the cheek. He moved his face.

I got dates and times wrong all the time in my personal life: missed birthdays, double-booked friends, turned up at the theatre with tickets for the night before. For years I didn't realise that it was because I just didn't have enough headspace free to organise myself.

After we'd installed our whole life at the Tigerlily hotel and lifted Sam's mood via the minibar, we decided to go out and eat the most Scottish dinner we could find to celebrate our new city, feeling like we were on holiday.

'Irn-Bru!' Sam hollered, but after that, cullen skink and a deep-fried Mars Bar, Sam was bent double in the street. 'I'm not sure I'm going to make it back,' he said, as though we were English soldiers injured on foreign soil.

'You'll be fine,' I said, used to his hypochondria but then feeling my own stomach shift uneasily. 'Shit,' I said.

'What?'

'GO!'

We ran through the beautiful streets after that and two hours later lay on our £200-a-night bed in the hotel's dressing gowns with all the windows open, recovering from the kind of food poisoning I'd not had since Mumbai on one of those standard backpacking trips students fill long university holidays with.

'Well, *that* was romantic,' I said.

'Do you think it was the cullen skink or the deep-fried—'

'Please don't say those words,' I begged. 'I will literally throw up.'

*

Yet after our first, poisoned night, we loved Edinburgh immediately. It was a breath of wet air after a summer of sweltering
commutes where sweat rolled off the faces of passengers who
didn't have enough space on the Tube to lift a hand and wipe it
away, and it was invigorating. Here you could breathe; the space
opened my polluted lungs as I walked to work with Arthur's Seat
and the Scottish hills stretching greenly into the distance beyond
North Bridge, then down the Royal Mile and past the infamous,
murderous World's End pub. Our tiny office of six was above the
Scottish National Party's headquarters, amusingly, but even if
politics was still following me around (or me, it), the news here
felt more manageable in some ways, maybe because it wasn't read
crumpled into someone else's face on the Tube. In London, I'd
watched the ink disintegrate under hot fingers before the sentence
was out. The news was better, too: quinoa and Gwyneth Paltrow
were goners; whisky, grouse and wild stuff were go go go.

I was the last trainee to arrive in Edinburgh and every event of
social, cultural and political significance in Scotland's biggest year
was wrapped up in a way that made me feel that I'd turned up so
late to the party that the recycling was already on the pavement.
Medals at the Commonwealth Games in Glasgow were won; the
Edinburgh Festival performed; and all that was left of the Scottish
independence referendum was a hangover of Yes and No signs still
showing in window allegiance all over the city. Nicola Sturgeon
was to be the first woman to lead the country out of its despair.

Then, a week in, our editor died. Mac was famous for taking
the grads under his wing but he had emailed me before I arrived
to apologise that he was on an 'enforced absence'. He had cancer,
but said he was looking forward to meeting me as soon as he was
released from his 'confinement'. Until then, he'd always be on the
end of the phone, he said. Then he died.

I stared at his coffin at the first funeral I'd ever been to and
wondered about the man inside, feeling dejected that the person

everyone said *made* you in Scotland didn't exist any more. Then I felt pathetically selfish for even thinking that when the guy was *dead*.

'Imagine the drunkest you've ever been and times it by four. That was Mac in his drinking days,' someone said fondly, and someone else stood at the altar and said news ran in his blood, while I wondered if it really ran in mine.

I'd been waiting anxiously to meet Arla, the grad who'd arrived before me and with whom I'd shared a mutual loathing back in London. She'd joined a drink I'd set up with one of the trainees after I'd started on features only to ignore me for the entire evening, which was almost impressive given there were only three of us at the table, but had reminded me why I'd disliked girls at school.

Part of the issue, I thought, was that the paper usually hired two graduates each year, but had that year taken on three, then me, so the others were wondering who the hell I was and whether I diminished their chances of a job at the other end, I guess.

Stories about graduate trainees who *had* become friends, then been sat down at the end of the two-year scheme to be told there were only jobs for half of them hung in the recent past of the paper. 'Basically it was like, who wants the job?' someone told me, and then they'd been made to look around the room at the people they'd become close to and decide how much they'd talk up their own strengths and highlight other people's weaknesses for a contract. That made the friendships we were expected to form, and which eased the day-to-day stress of things, feel like war treaties that could betray you.

But in Scotland avoiding the enemy in an office of six was quickly impossible and now Arla and I lived only a street apart, too. On top of that, our male colleagues were pushing us together with the ambition of those setting up a blind date, so when Arla slunk into the office wrapped in a fur coat and sat down opposite me, I concentrated harder on my screen. That day a nurse had been dissolved in acid by a 21-year-old who'd been previously acquitted for attempted rape by claiming he was gay, I read (horrified with the world as usual), but the conversations about when Arla and I were going out had already restarted.

'Have you been to Cafe Royal yet?' she said.

'Nope,' I said, shaking my head.

'Oh, we have to go. I'll take you after work,' she said, as I plastered a smile on my face but wondered why it wasn't a question.

Then a bottle of wine in, we somehow realised we liked each other. A lot. I should have learnt from the Danny and Anna experience and from my friendship with Everleigh, that sometimes the best friendships were found in the people you'd least expect but I guess I still had a way to come with trusting that women weren't all like some of the ones I'd gone to school with.

'Sorry if I was a bit of a prick in London,' Arla said, as we crushed outside Cafe Royal to light fags in the pouring rain.

'You were a *massive* prick, yes,' I agreed, laughing. 'But it's fine.'

'Sorry,' she said, pulling a face. 'Probably just being insecure about who the fuck you were.'

'You were being insecure? Imagine how I felt?' I said, amused. 'You kept banging on about the wires and I thought you meant the one with Dominic West.'

She snorted and we went back inside to stand at the gold bar where we sunk two bottles that night amongst the steamed windows before stumbling back down Broughton Street to our flats. We gallivanted around Edinburgh together after that or ate Chinese takeaways on the sitting-room floor at mine. Sam became used to me waking up at Arla's and coming home to squirt contact lens fluid in my eyes before I walked back to work. She showed me, I guess, that girls were harder work sometimes, initially, but just more complex than guys, and more brilliant for it, and I loved her for that.

Christmas was a month away then and the city was dark most of the time, freezing Scandi-winds blowing us about and lights dangling on every street as fireplaces raged in many a mahogany pub.

Being adaptable enough to quickly make a life in a new city made me feel more powerful than I'd felt in London, knowing I was passing a macro test for reporters because we were expected to bowl up and find a story anywhere in the world. But it was also just undeniably slower paced, which made switching off in the evenings easier and kept you feeling sane.

Having Sam sloping along next to me also helped me feel more stable as we cruised Leith or bar-hopped around Inspector Rebus pubs I read about in Ian Rankin books, ate pie sandwiches and drove to the beach. Growing up by the sea had made me feel calmest around water and I felt like I breathed better in the salty air that whipped us as we stood staring out at the vastness of it all. Sam was Adidas shell suits and a camera slung over one shoulder, recording everything as his hair started to salt and pepper at twenty-six. He was launching his first exhibition on Edinburgh's barbershops and we toured charity shops for old frames for the prints he was putting together on our sitting-room floor in the evenings. It felt like a life after London. A home.

I had a project too. A big one. I was looking for a relation of my mum's who'd been missing for the past twenty-five years. Trauma had estranged Adele from our family, and I'd sat on the stairs when I was a child, listening to my mum speak on the phone to tenants at Adele's last-known address and with an ex-husband, trying to track her movements and find out if anyone knew where she'd gone. But no one did. I'd heard my mum telling my dad that she was convinced she would have been told if Adele had died and I'd wished I could help but, aged ten, had no idea how.

There was one view among my mum's relations that because we couldn't choose our family, we should be at liberty to leave it, but my mum felt it ran deeper than that. At what point did troubled minds want, but not know *how*, to come back to you? Or what if they thought you didn't want them to?

Then in Edinburgh, as I got used to the systems now available to me as a journalist, I wondered if I could find her on the electoral register that helped us locate people for comment. I just needed her name, but that was part of the problem. We didn't know if she was using her maiden name, the married name she'd used twenty-five years ago or any other, new married name we wouldn't even be able to guess. 'Adele' wasn't even her legal first name, but a nickname she'd preferred. To make it even harder, her real, full name was as common as Anne Smith, or Tom Brown.

Secretly I'd been wondering whether I should leave journalism and retrain as a psychotherapist, because a year in I was finding that news left me with too many questions, not about what was happening in the world, but *why*. I was quickly more interested in the mental states of the people in breaking stories, but there wasn't space for that in short, formulaic coverage, so on the side I was constantly reading literary accounts by every psychotherapist, psychiatrist and neurologist I could find about people who mistook their wife for a hat, thought they were dead, or led otherwise ordinary lives until one day something changed. Wondering if it wasn't the healthiest habit, I devoured books on Beachy Head, the famous Sussex suicide spot, Kay Redfield Jamison's manic depression; and the life story of Billy Milligan, whose personality split into twenty-four different people after childhood trauma.

In psychology I think I was looking for answers to the whole world because I couldn't help feeling mental health issues hung in the air, as well as in the background of my family, and I wondered, dubiously, if I could dance around them forever. What if depression was in my genes, too? By reading dozens of case studies in the books, I wanted to know how you could avoid snapping, like I had once before at seventeen. I wanted to be shown how to be 'normal', and know what 'normal' actually was. In the accounts of others, I was trying to get into someone else's head for five minutes to see what they felt like, so I could work out how I felt in relation to that. I had a strong desire to be 'fine' that was in constant battle with wanting to be *great*, as we'd been taught we needed to be. My fear was that I wasn't either, I guess, and so it wasn't just one woman I was looking for. I was looking for who *I* was in relation to the invisible women in my family I knew nothing about, wondering if I was like my grandmother Celia, who'd killed herself before I was born, if not Adele. I wished I could ask them questions about what had happened in their lives in order to better work out who *I* was, or would become, and wondered if I was just a third generation of a family whose introspection made them worry they felt too much, or too little, pushing them over an edge I didn't want to walk to. I think I wondered, subconsciously, whether finding out what had happened to Adele would give me some answers about what might happen to me if my mood didn't lift reliably enough.

I'd asked my mum to send me everything she knew about Adele and I stared at a timeline of her life, wondering how so many people could disappear each year, so many never to be found. I typed her date of birth and one version of the name she could be using into the search bar and wondered which one of more than 100 results was related to me, if any. Then I tried her married name.

'Fewer,' I told Sam, who sat staring at my computer screen next to me.

'What are you going to do now?' he asked.

'Write to all of them,' I said, getting a stack of paper and a pen.

It's an uncanny feeling posting a letter and willing it to reach someone you don't even know is still alive, but that's what I did when I got to the post box the next day, as though one would land in Adele's hands from pure hope alone. Technology meant I was able to look at all of the addresses on Google Street View and

I imagined the letters floating through their doors as Sam and I drove to the Isle of Skye for a holiday, the forests getting thicker and the fog closer as we drove until the sky looked like it was sitting in swampy pools in the space between the trees.

'It's starting to look like *I'm A Non-Entity, Get Me Out Of Here,*' Sam said, and it was. It was Celtic noir.

After the Highlands, where nothing but land stretched for miles, the idea of going back to rampaging, non-stop London disconcerted me. In Edinburgh we'd found a home in our flat on Broughton Street; a safe, private world that made the stressful public one I existed in so much easier to bear. In that flat there were no mice or snails or exhausting small talk with strangers. Instead we had sex on the sitting-room floor, just because we could, then opened prosecco and ate bacon sandwiches for dinner in our pyjamas.

The fact that the paper that had relocated me also paid my rent lifted a massive financial strain, and with our room in London sublet (illegally, as renters are forced to do), so much anxiety vanished. I didn't want to be driven by money; I just wanted to be able to buy a theatre ticket or dinner out without being broke for the rest of the month. Now that was possible, my mood soared with the freedom of it.

A senior colleague had told me he'd started, twenty years ago, on the same money I was on now, shocking us both. I didn't think it was a unique fault of the company I worked for, but part of a much wider problem that saw younger staff as cheap labour and forced us to be grateful for small salaries in light of a hugely over-crowded job market packed with clever, over-qualified grads. The other fault – of course – lay with landlords and an unaffordable housing market. If we'd been paid well, expensive rentals might not have been so devastating. Or if rentals were reasonably priced, the necessary, casual, badly paid shifts might not have broken us. But together they lit a bomb and, back in London, having to constantly ask my mum if I could borrow money until pay day, removed any idea I was doing well. A few years after we left Newcastle, only half of my class of fourteen were working as journalists, the rest having found the job instability and dreadful pay offered in the face of declining print sales unbearable and leaving for marketing, teaching and tech jobs elsewhere. Online journalism ran the world, now, with an increased workload and rates for freelance print journalists cut in half. Mat was now working as a freelance foreign reporter for the British nationals in Columbia, where commissions had plummeted from £1,000 to £100 and made stories barely worth writing at all. In the UK, freelancers who might have been offered £1-a-word were now paid half that, although 30- or 40-pence was more common.

I think I would have left journalism for psychology back then if it hadn't involved returning to such a destructive education system. I knew a career change could be done because my dad had done it: leaving school at fourteen without a single qualification and becoming a chain-smoking painter and decorator in Blackburn before thinking there must be something else out there and going to night school at eighteen. Eventually he qualified as a lawyer and owned three firms in London which still use his name.

But slogging through the education system when you've already done it once felt different, and I resented having been expected at fourteen to know what I wanted to do in my twenties and narrow my options by choosing GCSE subjects which then dramatically streamlined what I could study at A level, and even more so what I could study at university. I also didn't want to spend another £20,000 on higher education, obviously. The debt from the first round was bad enough and in the meantime fees had tripled.

I'm glad I stayed in journalism, but it showed how unsure and unstable I felt then, I think, the fact I nearly walked out on it all for the sake of a life which didn't make me live in the red, financially and emotionally.

Sam was mainly working in a studio in Edinburgh, but if he had jobs abroad, I went to Pickles, a tiny brasserie two doors down that sold pickled eggs in bell jars and had walls lined with jars of pâté, just to be around other people. I felt oppressed by invisibility and the quiet when I was alone, and I wondered if it was normal only to feel alive when you knew other people could see you.

During weekends I sat in St Andrews Square watching Christmas crowds milling about eating bright blue ice creams with frozen hands or sipping champagne at the nail bar in Harvey Nics. A guy sitting cross-legged on the bench next to me handed me a leaflet. *Two thousand architects and engineers reveal what you are not being told about 9/11.*

'Is this free?' I asked.

'Not for me, but free for you.'

'What does that mean?'

He turned away and I looked at the leaflet, which told me to watch a film called *The Anatomy of Great Deception*. Opposite, Jehovah's Witnesses fought with the conspiracy theorists for palm time and stole attention from *Big Issue* sellers, the truest cause of all. The world to me then seemed full of the lost and supposedly found, with their opposite, vying causes, each side adamant their epiphany would save you. It felt like a scam, the way a desire for happiness and safety was manipulated.

Maybe people just needed something, anything, to believe in, I thought, remembering a conversation I'd heard between two twentysomething boys dangling from the monkey-bar handles on the Tube in London.

'In the first year I did loads of drink and drugs, but in the second year I found Chrisjanity,' one told the other.

'Who's Chris Janity?'

'The church, fam.'

But religion was dead and the engaged attended church only to secure a godly setting for an Instagram op half the time, it seemed.

These days, we were the gods with congregations of followers online. But we didn't believe in ourselves enough either. We were faithless in all respects and not believing in anything made the world feel like it moved beneath your feet.

Later that week I walked home from work over North Bridge and shock hit me as I realised I had a front-row seat to an attempted suicide; a man running along the tiny ledge on the wrong side of the bridge and a woman who'd only just learnt his name trying to persuade him life was worth it. Two policemen followed her with a tiny stepladder in almost slapstick fashion, getting it upright just before he moved, and then dismantling it to try to erect it quicker somewhere else.

I called the desk and told the editor on shift what I was looking at, but he told me to go home.

'What?' I said, confused.

'Happens all the time, don't worry about it.'

Copycat suicides were a risk if we tried to write it, he said, and something rose in my body, like fear, about what that meant. That life being thrown away was so common it wouldn't even make the papers, and if it did, people would be reading for tips.

I looked around me on the bridge and saw a crowd had gathered, wondering how long a man's life would keep them in the rain. Then the woman said something that changed his mind, I guess, and he climbed back over the side into the arms of the emergency services. You could see then that he was a small, normal-looking guy with short dark hair, in his thirties maybe, but hard to tell. Someone you'd never have noticed anywhere else, and I wondered if that's why he did it. To see if anyone would care, or even notice. There was an atmosphere in the crowd, I realised after that, and it wasn't until I got home that I worked out what it was. It was anticlimax, I understood, as I went to the fridge and poured myself a massive glass of wine.

*

Christmas was nearing and in Edinburgh the market sheds in Princes Street Gardens went up, mulled-wine tourists toured, whilst the city remained less neurotic than London, less of a carousel.

Then in Glasgow, three days before Christmas, the driver of a bin lorry had a heart attack at the wheel and ploughed into the Christmas market, killing six and injuring fifteen in just nineteen seconds of screaming chaos. I stayed in the office with the news editor to feed updates of names and locations to Arla and another of our colleagues who'd jumped on a train to Glasgow to cover the story on the ground.

At first it looked like terrorism (the method eerily echoed in Isis attacks across Europe in the next few years), and the fact I was flying home for Christmas the next day seemed crass now that those who'd died weren't going to have one ever again. Knowing I'd be drinking prosecco with my family when those involved were about to have the worst Christmas of their life following the heartbreak in Glasgow made the story I'd been covering feel like it was on top of me as Sam and I left the disaster the whole of Scotland was talking about and flew home. I sat zombified on the plane as a woman with a huge engagement ring leant across her fiancé to ask another aisle whether they wanted fish and chips or Chinese when they landed. Had no one seen the news, I wondered? They ordered gin and tonics for breakfast and laughed like hyenas and I felt sick.

Later, I recognised the same feeling of anger and emptiness in a boyfriend who arrived back at our flat from Grenfell Towers covered in ash, barely able to speak about what he'd seen as he tried to cover the story for his paper. But at the time I didn't know if the problem was the world or me, and I felt numb.

Back in Scotland after Christmas I fell back into escapism through books and waited for my mum to hear from Adele, who'd have all of my mother's details if a letter ever reached her. Two had come back to me in Edinburgh, unopened and labelled return-to-sender, so the chances were diminishing but three more were still out there, somewhere.

When I was sent to cover the story of a missing teenage girl in Dundee it didn't occur to me that I wanted to find her so badly because I wanted to find Adele much more.

'Are you a private investigator?' the cabbie asked me, when he dropped me on the estate where the girl had last been seen, and whilst I told him I wasn't, I guess I'd become one in my private life, at least.

She turned up fine in the end, that missing girl, having been hiding at a friend's house to annoy her parents after an argument, but the fact I hadn't found her *myself* edged the relief with something blacker that I knew was linked to the fact that the returned letters made it feel like Adele was slipping out of my reach.

At weekends I ran away from my week on the treadmill, only stopping when a personal trainer called Robbie came over to tell me which members of *Cats* or the *Lion King* he was currently sleeping with. Shagging two members of the same cast of dancers using the gym *was* risky, he agreed, because they *did* usually find out, yes, and then he was sleeping with neither Rum Tum Tugger or Rumpleteazer. I left him with this epiphany and put my headphones back on to run another 5K, then sat in the jacuzzi and let the bubbles better me, grateful I could afford a gym membership thanks to not having to pay rent.

In the office I trawled the wires as I had in London, still morbidly fascinated with the world into which I had a glimpse of the worst and weirdest. A man had seen the face of Jesus in an Ikea bathroom door, I read. Dave, thirty-three, said: 'Jesus, as a carpenter, would like the prices at Ikea but I'm not sure what he'd think of the design. I actually went for tie backs for curtains, but they didn't have any so Jesus didn't help us there.'

My mum emailed regularly to ask how my days were and my

replies, when I look back at them now, have a coldness I don't remember being so flippant about it. 'Day pretty rubbish. Had to write a story about a 21 YO who went to a shooting range in Thailand on holiday and shot himself in the head. How was lunch?' I replied once. I think of the news now as a constant form of exposure therapy that made me see extreme situations as normal. Ordinary life seemed lifeless in comparison and essentially I was becoming the equivalent of a heroin addict who couldn't face the now-colourless world on a comedown less riveting than the high.

My move back to London was approaching and during the last days in Edinburgh I sat in Cafe Royal imagining the two Roberts, the Ayrshire painters I'd become obsessed with, drinking there before me, then leaving Scotland to 'make it', before ruining their lives on booze in Soho amongst some success. The idea that I'd spent so long waiting to arrive in London and now found it so unfulfilling that I didn't want to go back was confusing, because I couldn't picture life anywhere else. I didn't know where to try to find a home and my future, if it wasn't in London and I didn't want to leave our life in that beautiful gothic place. Edinburgh just felt kinder, slower and more human compared with London, and I knew I'd miss the Highlands, Arthur's Seat and the castle which loomed above the cold, cobbled streets.

On the morning of Hogmanay I'd been at one of the first gay weddings in Scotland, where I'd stood watching two men scattered in confetti on a grey Glaswegian street while lenses flashed, and I wondered if that was where my life with Sam was heading. I still smiled every time I thought about one of the grooms telling me he felt like Julia Roberts, and I wondered if that was what love was *for*, to fix all the darkness in the world. Is that why people got married, I thought, as fireworks exploded at midnight and Sam and I kissed on a cobbled street beneath the castle. It was my longest relationship yet.

Arla had left Scotland for London two months before me and was saving me a seat, she said, so I decided to text her to find out if the most recently employed news editor had smiled yet.

Before I'd left for Edinburgh the reporters were still taking bets on whether he had teeth.

Hullo Evvers,

Scottish exile over. Back in the *Great Wren*, as you would say.

I've been wondering if news isn't for me and keep having thoughts about studying psychotherapy. Or law. Took Sam to Edinburgh High Court to watch a case on a day off we had and he described it as *better than TV*. Certainly there was the same cast of heroes and villains but it felt a bit wrong to go for pizza and wine in the 'interval' as though it were a play when people's real lives were unfolding on the stand. Two already incarcerated juvenile delinquents arguing about a rape confession one had apparently made at the pool table. Still, watching it all, I thought: I should have been a barrister.

Do you ever feel like you could have done several different things with your life and wished you could have done all of them?

L x

Dear Lucy,

I guess I've never really thought terribly much about what
to do – I just went along with the next thing and fell into
academia. Actually, when I was in my late thirties (aeons
ago) I did become rather disheartened, and went to a free
appointment at a career consultants. After an hour's interview
the chap concluded that being an academic was probably the
right, indeed the only option.

   All good fortune attend you,

Everleigh

4

Towards the End of the Morning

Within a month of being back in London, I'd been thrown straight back into the melee of big-city life and Edinburgh felt every one of its 400 miles away and more.

Another tube-striking summer organised by the unfortunately named Mike Cash was inspiring as much sympathy from the exhausted and overworked as the drivers who started on £50,000 and at the top end earnt more than three times what I did. No one in that city would have said they weren't underpaid but striking wasn't an option for most so anger raged. TFL had made me two hours late to pre-dinner drinks, which was hardly a life-or-death appointment but I resented eating dinner at 11 p.m., mid-week, thanks to Cash, even if there were benefits to arriving obscenely late to restaurants, I now saw. Eating dinner very late was what the very famous did to avoid overwhelming attention. In Mayfair, I was now sitting opposite Drake, who appeared to be on a date.

In the capital, the dichotomy of glamour and depravity was unavoidable and it was even more transparent at these celebrity haunts where homelessness and stress sat on the street outside. Thin, addicted men rambled through the carriages of the Tubes, when they deigned to run, asking for spare change, and I'd once looked up to see Al Murray watching me, presumably thinking what I was thinking, that the world was suspicious of down-and-outs and confused as to whether money helped or exacerbated the problems. When the homeless man who'd just passed us lit a cigarette in the carriage, there was almost a sigh of relief from commuters who could now tell themselves they'd been right not to donate. *Wrong'un*, the cigarette said, in a world that looked for flaws first.

Judgement, when I knew so many of my contemporaries took cocaine as casually as they drunk pints, was futile and after Edinburgh, where I'd been away from the scene, I saw London for the city of functioning addicts it was.

Although could you really argue you were functioning when you had to take antidepressants or carry the 'pill in the pocket', propranolol, to block the physical effects of a panic attack, I wondered? It wasn't as though a lack of sleep and white powder was helping.

I wasn't at the pharmaceutical stage yet, but handfuls of people I knew were taking prescription drugs to cope with the effects of recreational ones, and washing it all down with booze. Drinking on top of a cocktail like that was sending some of them wild and a PR who'd taken me to a posh restaurant had gone loopy from the alcohol by the end of the night and climbed railings into a (un)gentleman's club before being removed through the front door. After that she'd run around Piccadilly Circus like a wildcat while I tried to tempt her into a cab, but the next day she couldn't remember a thing. Getting kicked out of pubs as much as men were was practically a feminist right for some of the women I knew, but this was an altogether different thing, and while I hadn't called the AA again, I knew I also still drank too much. Everyone I knew laughed at the paltry number of units we were advised to keep to each week and just lied on the GP forms about alcohol consumption when required. For my generation bingeing was too much of a coping mechanism to be rationed.

But the light and the dark was so stark in London, I remembered on Drake night. Earlier, in the office, I'd spent two hours analysing videos of Jihadi John beheading aid workers captured by Isis to help the crime correspondents identify him, then left work for a bar that had just been crowned best in the world by a drinks organisation. The PRs waited with Dom Perignon and ordered Dali-esque cocktails that arrived in giant gold ants or riding tall, silver Lego elephants, while Laurence Llewelyn-Bowen leaned at the bar in a lurid shirt.

'What's the story at Nobu?' I asked, that night (which turned out to be Drake, but we didn't know that yet).

'They're serving a beef heart on top of a new cocktail,' one of the girls said.

'Why?' I asked.

'I'm – not sure,' she admitted and I just laughed. I'd been on a press trip with one of them so we talked frankly enough to cut through the pretention and, anyway, I was back in a place of not wanting to go home.

Sam and I had returned to the room we'd sublet whilst we were in Edinburgh and so we were back in Clapham in a house of renters who'd changed again. They were always *nice*, and it wasn't their fault, but the flat just reminded me so much of the friends I'd originally moved in with and who these new people couldn't compare with because we just didn't have as much in common. Making a constant effort with people who'd never seen a prawn in their life, or freaked out when I ate rocket (in one case) was just too much effort after the exhausting days I had chasing the world at work. So I belonged to the night, and wherever it was going, my eyes paling with each drink but my PR friends armed with cocaine they had me rack up in marble bathrooms before I rejoined them at a table covered in ludicrously expensive black cod.

Who am I? I thought, almost amused by the high-end depravity of it, but liking the chemical rush that blocked my emotions and made me forget I was in court the next day to watch a male teacher at an all-boys' prep school be sentenced for child pornography.

Cocaine dinners weren't the height of professionalism, we decided that night, but at Nobu Boris Becker had got a woman pregnant in the broom cupboard, the story went, so surely anything went for us too. Really, it was all a game: the idea that I'd be having dinner in a sushi restaurant part-owned by Robert De Niro (bento boxes: £150) if I wasn't a journalist who could write about them, just part of it. When the weaselly, air-kissing manager asked if we'd like saké alongside the champagne and I told him I'd only had it hot, he almost fell over.

'Good God, *where*?' he practically sneezed.

'Oh, I . . . can't remember,' I said, thinking: YO! Sushi, Bristol, eighteen years old.

Everyone was an actor in this play called *The Scene*. It wasn't like Nobu's waiting staff could've footed a bill there either.

Celebrity was partly to blame for the war on vanity we found ourselves in, I think. Every generation grew up with singers Blu-tacked to their bedroom walls but now we carried them on smartphones in our pockets and documented our lives alongside theirs on Instagram in a way that made a highly competitive generation compare ourselves with even the famous. There was something so everyday about online stardom that it made it seem more achievable, touchable, I suppose. I'd once seen Miquita Oliver in a bathroom and asked her, half-cut, whether we went to school together, not realising I 'knew her' from Channel 4, then Instagram.

When I moaned about having to have social media accounts for work, resenting the veneers and the sycophantism and the chasing of likes in a popularity game I hadn't asked to play, someone told me it wasn't fun until you got 40,000 followers. But since when was it normal to have your thoughts and movements judged by 40,000 strangers? Did you finally feel you'd got somewhere then? My thinking was more aligned with a guy I overheard on the Tube likening Facebook stalking to self-harm and saying he didn't know why he did it to himself.

Normality, and the idea of privacy, was totally lost in relentless online realms, I realised when one of the PRs got out of her seat to ask Drake for a selfie and I started piling ginger into my mouth so I didn't gas him with cod. But before her body had turned halfway out of her chair towards him she was spun back down into her seat by a bodyguard doubling as a sashimi fan. She sat as stunned as a cartoon character, wondering what had just happened. We looked at Drake, who was now shaking his head at us, hands half raised like: 'What the fuck?'

'Do you think he's doing that at us or . . . ?' the PR asked.

'I'm pretty sure that's intended for us,' I said, under my breath.

'What the fuck?' the other PR said.

'Do you think we look wrecked?' I whispered.

'Surely rappers have cocaine for *breakfast*,' one of them said then, as we carried on, cringing over a rejection from one of the most famous men in the world, but confused as to why we were following, online, a man who would never speak to us in real life.

In some ways modern London had barely graduated from the pages of the Muriel Spark, Jean Rhys and Edna O'Brien novels I was reading. I didn't let a man buy my stockings, but we were still scraping rent together to pay for a room in someone else's house and sharing the space with a random clutter of strangers. We still drank gin in our rooms before we went out to save money, and considered selling our bodies for medical science. Not that I'd got into FluCamp when I'd volunteered to be made ill for £4,000. Maybe it was testament to some of the places I'd lived, but the idea of sleeping in a hospital bed for a fortnight while doctors injected me with flu and then watched me recover (they hoped) for clinical research purposes didn't sound *that* bad to me.

Meanwhile, single friends were still waiting for a man in the same way women had always waited, though they had dating apps to speed things up and could admit their sex drive was higher than his without being straightjacketed.

The idea that sex, drugs and celebrity were all part of a top-tier existence had remarkable staying power but there was a disturbing new attitude towards cocaine in 2015. Certain industries had a cocaine reputation, but I was now going to parties where the doctors were the first to order six grams for the room with the efficacy of booking blood tests. Personal trainers quoted studies that the class A was better for you than tobacco and booze and later, when I moved in with Polly for a few months and became a regular at a pub that sat like a lighthouse for lonely locals spanning all ages, I realised it wasn't just my generation either. It was much more to do with availability and a widening void of loneliness felt by everyone, everywhere.

Cocaine was powdered stamina for those who drank too much and an artificial ego boost that stopped you agonising over hard, inconsistent life. The fact we took a drug to sober us up enough to keep on drinking was almost blackly funny, given how much money was wasted on the enterprise, but it was all part of the new 'work hard, play hard' balancing act, which left you feeling everything *but* balanced as you partied harder to restore the natural order.

The truth was that babbling nocturnally on a drug that kept you standing made me feel more capable of voicing emotions that were harder to confront when I was sober, albeit in a detached way that made it seem like they didn't affect me as much as they did. Maybe I just liked it because nothing felt as frightening on a rush of serotonin. Anything seemed possible in a difficult world where reality often felt bleak. On Drake night, a notification popped up on my phone screen halfway through the evening reporting that four people had just died in a plane crash and the drug numbed me against yet more tales of death and despair, which was just a relief.

We were the generation constantly told we'd never own a house, which embedded a throwaway culture in which the traditional ideals were entirely lost, so threw our pay cheques at fashionable hedonistic consumerism instead and by 2019, London was snorting 23kg of the Class A *every day* according to a piece in the *Evening Standard*. The cocaine industry was worth £1 billion a year and what did we have to show for it? Mental health issues and knife crime.

I'd started running the 4 miles from Clapham to work to offset each evening's ruinous gallivanting and the spikey point of the Shard loomed higher and larger above me as I ran, a metaphor for what would happen that day if what I wrote wasn't liked. *Spiked.*

I slowed outside the Tube to sidestep the crowd and heard a woman telling her friend that she hated the Shard. 'What is the point of building all these useless erections? Aren't there enough in London already?' she said, as I ran past her and into the changing rooms at the station.

When I got to my desk, I opened my email and started typing a new message to Everleigh telling him I was wondering if I should leave London, which meant leaving the newspaper, too. My parents, naturally, were horrified by the idea and were quoting things about my *CV* but something didn't feel right. I wish now I'd realised it was just anxiety – something you could do many things about – but at the time I had no idea and thought it was the job and my flat.

I looked back at the news desk and huffed, wondering at what age I'd feel like I knew who I was. So far, I felt I'd just been making it up each day as I went along.

That day there'd been another terrorist attack. Open-fire on a tourist beach in Tunisia which had killed thirty British sunbathers. Death tolls already listed couples who'd been waiting months for the holiday; some celebrating fiftieth birthdays, others significant wedding anniversaries. Many had died shielding their partners from the spray of bullets.

Then more information came through and I was dispatched to Watford, thinking, as the Tube crossed London, that the widow

I was calling on had probably been lying on the beach worrying about tan lines before she heard gunshots. I saw so regularly how completely life could change in a second that I'd started to feel it was more likely I'd find myself in the middle of something, than not. Game Over seemed to hang on chance alone.

The police opened the door when I got there, telling me in a tone that suggested I took pleasure in being there that I should leave, so I walked back through the stifling heat to the station via Wetherspoons and sat feeling madly on edge, trying to resuscitate myself before I had to put on a face at home. Whatever home was when you lived with people you barely knew. Sam was always more relaxed about it than I was, somehow.

It felt ridiculous to dress up for work when you were door knocking the dead, I thought, as if the grieving noticed clean shirts and brushed hair, painted nails. I pictured the white sand stained red in Tunisia – and how much the people there would give to still be alive. The idea that the dead would sneer at wrinkles of age or the blue hue of tiredness under your eyes and not see life in the blemish, extra weight, or scar was obscene.

My evenings of vain celebrity seemed even more vacuous in comparison, I realised, as I finished my pint and walked back over the bowling-alley carpets to the street, my mood so shattered it felt like I was walking over the smashed remains on the way to the door.

The disparity of London was audible on the Tube as the train left the outskirts and the students who told each other they needed to start eating liver, because it was cheap, morphed into women who were thin for entirely different reasons. 'Are you lunching today or tomorrow?' they asked each other in central London, before the carriages slunk south and passengers changed again, a guy clutching his leg and telling his friend he'd pulled a muscle doing community service.

Conversation filled my head and I realised why the lonely sat on

Tubes for company as well as warmth; every stop a whole world
in London. A new plot unfolding distinctly at each station. I let
the lives of others fill my head, feeling outside it all, as a mother
in Chiswick worried Bertie wouldn't get his pen licence at school;
a student in Kilburn dreamed of an undercut and a moustache so
he could be that guy in *Stranger Things*, and en route to Brixton, a
guy in high tops drank Tropicana and said Tarantino was his best
friend in all the world.

Later I understood better that the mind sometimes glazed over
as a defence against anxiety, drawing the curtains and turning
the volume down, kicking out an unwanted guest who was too
loud. I didn't even use the word 'anxiety' to explain how I felt
then and while labels aren't always helpful, I think a label would
have freed me from an invisible problem I thought I only had to
be tougher to cope with. In reality, I felt too fragile, *inadequate*,
and fear had set in. A fear that this was it: life stretching on and
on and on in commutes and a daily hot-desking game of musical
chairs. I couldn't let go of this *What next? What next?* mentality
that made me race towards burnout. A faint sheen of ungrateful
dissatisfaction had been cast over everything.

Was it normal for the start of your life to feel like the end, I
wondered, as I had panic attacks in the flat at weekends and cried
so much I couldn't breathe. Sam walked me round and round the
Common until it subsided on those days, trying to make me eat
something on the way home, neither of us understanding what was
happening to me? Didn't I have everything I'd wanted?

I'd read online that St John's Wort was a natural remedy for
mild depression – if that's what this was – so I went to Boots
and bought packets of the stuff, plus bottles of Rescue Remedy
and Kalms, doubting herbal power absolutely, but desperate for a
placebo effect, at least. Moving so often meant I never registered
with a doctor when I got a new address, otherwise I might have
gone to a real one.

I just couldn't switch off any more, I realised, and I wasn't the only one. Phones we were too terrified to answer stayed gripped in our palms as we worried we'd be told we had to work all night as well as all day if we picked up. We opened email with one eye shut, dreading an onslaught of communication and yet feeling panic wash over us every time we lost signal, knowing being unreachable was not OK. Ever.

We thought in Facebook statuses and planned our next posts; filtered everything. *Look how fucking happy I am*, we said online, before we broke down behind closed doors. It had started to seem like a con. Everleigh had replied to my email about jacking it in to tell me it seemed a choice between safety and bravery. But what if they were the same thing?

As the summer drew to a close and I started descending darker mornings on the street into the Tube station, I'd decided to get out. Sam's hatred of London's expense was on top of me and if he wasn't spurring me out of some deeply existential panic, I was dragging him out of his black money moods. Being in our twenties was a hugely frustrating financial see-saw as we celebrated pay day with one night out and then had to stay in and wait for the next one. But we had tactics, I told him again: Kroni not Peroni; groundling tickets at the Globe and £5 bottles of wine at home before we went out. Sam didn't like the theatre anyway, so I went alone and watched people meander around the foyer like they were walking through a thick fog, seeming confused when the usher asked for their tickets and said the play was about to start. *We've bought tickets to a play?* their expressions seemed to say. I gulped back the last of the red wine and ordered a cheap, tinny refill.

I went out alone enough to know, deep down, that Sam and I had little in common, but I was trying to ignore it because I felt too fragile to lose him as a crutch.

In hindsight it's harder to tell whether he was part cause or cure, because the differences between us jarred, and I might have been happier in London without a boyfriend moaning about the price of a pint all the time. Instead, we blamed London and the flat to avoid blaming each other and imagined we'd be different elsewhere, like in Edinburgh. It felt like hope at the time, but it's always fear, too, that you'll break up and then realise you made a mistake. Turn around and find them snapped up by someone else. I know now that I don't give up quickly enough sometimes – but the truth is that walking away from relationships is harder than staying a lot of the time.

I tried to look ahead at my life and couldn't imagine it in London any more, I realised in a dark wine bar in Borough Market where I drank coffee on my lunchbreaks, knowing no one I knew would come in.

'How old are you?' one man asked another. 'I'm much older than you, see? Now I scratch my head and my hair falls out,' he said and I thought, *Imagine sitting at a desk until your hair fell out.*

Some days my mood was too black to get dressed and I phoned in sick, then walked to the Picture House to sit in cinema-darkness alone watching whatever was on, crying usually, regardless of the genre and purely for the release.

In the evenings, Sam and I were dreaming of life elsewhere more and more and I hoped the pursuit of happiness would be easier when we arrived.

'What about rural France! I can write a novel!' I said, one night, as Sam and I lay on our bed with laptops, planning *where.*

'We don't speak French,' he said.

'We'll learn by buying baguettes like they do in the movies,' I said, rolling away from my laptop and onto him.

'What about Amsterdam?' he said, more soberly but more sensibly, knowing he could get a job in the same Dutch studio he'd worked at while I was in Newcastle.

'All right,' I agreed, pushing myself up and straddling him on the bed.

'Really?'

'Really,' I said, and the next day I walked into the managing editor's office and quit.

Everyone dreamt of throwing caution to the wind, I saw after that, when the fact we were leaving became an excuse for others to tell of what they'd once wanted to do. Before stretching their faces into excuses for why they hadn't left yet. I knew most of them would always be waiting for another reason that they couldn't: desperate to dream, but too scared to fall asleep. But one day they'd scratch their heads and their hair would fall out. Then what would they think about the life they'd lived?

As for leaving, all it seemed to come down to was whether you leapt or not. So we leapt.

By the end of that year, one leap of faith had already paid off.

Adele had written back to my mum.

'Lucy found her,' my mum told a Christmas table of family whose eyes glinted with emotion and then a week later, we were gone.

Dear Lucy

I woke up this morning still thinking about your piece on renting (particularly pointed given Cameron's attempt to persuade us that he will move from a renting to a buying culture – ho, ho, ho). It graphically suggested why moving to Amsterdam, naturism or not, should seem a really attractive proposition. I do admire your courage in stepping off the production line.

I think restlessness is a condition of contemporary life, an expectation fuelled by the endless bombardment of stuff, especially via mobile phones. Though I suppose I did have a mini mid-life crisis when I thought about leaving academe. But I think that had to do with the sense of 'will it be ever thus' and a thought that one might break out before it's too late.

The late life crisis – which perhaps afflicts me now – is the sense that the end is all too near, and so many things will never be done. After giving my last lecture I did feel the end of the runway horribly in sight.

Perhaps the other question concerns the phrase 'have everything' – what is 'everything' these days?

Let me know how it's all going – and I'm not looking for salacious details about nudist enclaves, promise.

Everleigh

5

THE AGE OF REASON

Saying that Sam and I realised we were moving to a naturist camp from the very start would not *strictly* be true. But if we'd been in any doubt before we'd left London, pulling up to the giant pair of breasts above the entrance of our new home would have made it clear enough.

They belonged to a woman on a billboard behind the barrier to this secretive, outskirty area of Amsterdam we'd driven eight hours to and were designed to remind us that *under no circumstances* could swimwear be worn in the pool.

As the mist set behind us on the winding roads through the Hulkestein Forest in *Twin Peaks* fashion, I opened the door so Alfie could jump down, having last marked his territory in an entirely different country. I realised, with slight horror then, that his grey jumper would be more than our new neighbours would be wearing inside the resort.

I looked again at the billboard, then at Sam. He gulped. We hadn't even been to a nudist beach before.

We'd been sold on the tiny A-frame house on Airbnb, which was under £400 a month and welcomed dogs, before we'd noticed the disclaimer running along the bottom of the pictures that explained what exactly Flevo-Natuur was.

'For a respectfull [*sic*] 100% naturist stay', I read aloud from the website and we laughed our heads off.

I looked back at the screen.' "Bungalow on largest Dutch recreation park . . . for going fully undressed on all the ways." '

'On *all* the ways?' Sam cackled.

'Shall we just do it?' I asked him.

'Can we do it?'

'We might like it,' I said, without much certainty. But flats in central Amsterdam were as expensive to rent as in London, we'd realised, and I'd already quit my job. 'Do you want to be a naturist?' I asked Alfie, picking him up and twirling him around.

But now we were here, we stared at the double Ds wondering what the hell we'd just done.

'If it's so cold we don't see a single muff or knob in the entire month, I'm going to be livid,' Sam said, after we'd assured reception we weren't voyeurs and drove through the fog to find our new house.

'There are quite a lot of . . . statues,' I said, peering out of the window into the front gardens at a lot of well-hung stone. 'It's like one big filthy garden centre,' I added.

'That one looks like a Nazi eagle,' Sam said, propelling the car along to where our octogenarian landlord said he'd be waiting. We hoped in clothes. Which I now realised was not a given.

The main problem, however, seemed like it was going to be the pronunciation of his name.

'Jizz,' he said, shaking our hands as I tried not to look at Sam.

We couldn't have moved into a house on a naturist camp owned by a man called *Jizz*, I thought. It was spelt Gijs, but surely not pronounced *Jizz* here? I knew from the reading I'd done that there were three main rules of naturism: never use the word 'cult', never suggest it's about sex and always carry a towel (towels were a 'boy's best friend', because they hid accidental erections which violated rule two).

While Sam hastily offered to unpack, Jizz/Gijs walked me through the darkness outside to a tiny campsite shop to show me where our intriguing new community got supplies. Next to it, naturists of all shapes and sizes cooled their genitalia in the winter air outside a huge sauna and I stared through the door of an indoor swimming pool, feeling like Louis Theroux.

'It's very quiet in winter, you see?' Jizz said. 'Some people live here all year around, but now I stay just for the sun. My wife used to come too, but she says the lawn is not kept well enough any more.'

'Is that a euphemism?' I joked.

'What's a euphemism?'

'Don't worry,' I said, pretending to look at a packet of pasta and realising there were half a dozen penises and a 3D catalogue of bra sizes in my peripheral vision.

'You will see quite a lot of naked people in here,' Jizz said, almost apologetically. 'But the apple strudels are very good and Vincent bakes fresh bread every morning.'

I nodded in a way that I hoped suggested an interactive biology lesson with an inappropriately named grandad was completely normal, and plonked eggs and bread on the counter in front of Vincent, who was about to become my only friend in the country.

Running through my head was the fact there'd been nothing online about what kind of accessories you should pair with complete nakedness, but the men in the egg aisle seemed to already know: socks, sandals and, occasionally, a cropped leather jacket.

Back outside, I watched a man as rippled with fat as a ribeye steak loading his young daughter onto a bike with stabilisers and smiled like it was the most normal thing in the world. *Normality is protean*, I told myself, as I waved goodbye to Jizz.

'AS IF his name is Jizz!' Sam squealed when I got back to our new house.

'It can't be,' I breathed.

'He said Jiss! Or Jizz. Definitely.'

'How the hell am I supposed to write that?' I said, having already been commissioned by Gillian Anderson to divulge our new naturist life to readers and doubting his name would get past the subs. I was also highly sceptical anyone would believe me, and in the end just called him Larz.

'What did you see out there?' Sam asked excitedly, like I was Marco Polo.

'So much dick,' I told him. 'It's like an Argos catalogue of . . . bits,' I said. Bits that made me appreciate Sam again with fresh affection.

Despite the hilarity, it was exciting as we sat amongst our unpacked boxes that night, eating scrambled eggs for dinner, drinking the champagne someone had given us for Christmas and peering out through French doors at a rainbow of other colourful A-lines dusted with snow.

My mind flashed back to London, to someone I'd accidentally met when things were going badly with Sam, but I shut it off. This was our new life. A fix.

Preparing to tell our parents we were becoming naturists felt a bit like how I imagined coming out as gay might be like. But unlike sexuality, our new preference had arrived overnight and neither of us had ever imagined we'd have to say: Yes, you might have *assumed* we are textiles, but we are actually naturists. 'Textiles' was what naturists called people who liked clothes, and I was trying to get down with the lingo.

Yet unmoving British prudishness made us reluctant to even say the word 'naked' in front of our parents, let alone be imagined undressed.

'Are you pregnant?' my mum asked, sensing an atmosphere.

'God, no,' I said.

'Oh, fine.'

'We're moving to a naturist camp,' I said, glugging a glass of wine as my dad choked on his beer.

'Okayyyy,' she said.

'Basically it's cheap,' I said, as though that was the only explanation anyone needed.

'Of course it's bloody cheap . . . in January!' my dad bellowed.

'Well . . . why not?' my mum said, gallantly supportive as ever. 'We used to love the nudist beaches in Ibiza, didn't we?' she asked my dad.

'*What?*' I said.

'Although you probably don't want to know that, do you?'

We all agreed they'd postpone a visit, and after that telling people became quite fun.

'I haven't felt this interesting my whole life,' Sam confided after we started being grilled at parties.

People wanted to know what the rules were. Did you have to be naked all the time? Would you be extradited if you wore clothes? What happens if it snows? Is it a massive orgy? Is anyone attractive? The boys all worried about 'accidentally getting turned on' and everyone had a different idea about which garment they'd be most devastated to lose, depending on which part of their body they hated. I remember being very blasé about the whole thing but, in truth, the moment when we'd actually have to strip off felt like a long way away. Running to work every day in London had left me thin, but when the naturist piece I was writing about life there was published one friend asked if I'd been photoshopped and someone else if I had a prosthetic leg.

'How fat was I before?' I asked Sam.

These questions were both from women, which didn't seem hugely feminist, but I knew my weight fluctuated fast, saved only by my height, which stretched it out a bit, if I stopped running. It was an uncomfortable truth that I felt happiest when I felt thinnest, but the conversations we had before leaving surprised me, revealing that no one was happy with, or willing to say they liked their bodies, even if I'd have loved to look like them. What I'd least expected was how the men worried as much as women, and I saw that only the extreme hilarity that Sam and I were moving to a naturist camp gave both sexes the confidence to admit it under the guise that it was all a bit of a joke. Beneath it, there was just collective body dysmorphia.

On Instagram, the boys said they looked at the muscles of their celebrity equivalents, and the girls at the waist sizes of actresses paid millions to stay (often unhealthily) skinny, then looked in the mirror and felt sick. So we caned the gym, stopped eating, or did both, while also trying to excel at work and in relationships, despite not having a single calorie to spare to concentration or patience. Alcohol was seen as something that stopped you thinking about dinner and I realised my generation was frozen in competitive comparison of our bodies, too. Obviously, everyone felt better when they thought they looked good – the problem was what we thought *good* was.

Were my intelligent female friends really buying into the size zero look that was causing models to die backstage or collapse exhausted on catwalks? Did my intelligent male friends really believe they weren't good enough without a six pack? I knew from Muriel Sparks books in which girls described bread and butter pudding as suicidal and admitted they felt starving all the time, that women had always worried about their weight, but this seemed different. There was a suggestion now that eating disorders were worth it; normal.

Two of my friends had bulimia at school and one had even pulled me aside – aged twelve – to explain how I could do it, in tip-off fashion, but I couldn't master the trick luckily. I'd still somehow got the idea I should be calorie-counting at thirteen, which is shockingly young to me now. Probably all three of us were experiencing 'perfect girl syndrome', that pressure which pushes girls to believe they have to be everything all the time: thin, pretty, academic, popular, sporty, successful in a way that made us concentrate anxiety and ambition on our bodies instead. I fainted quite often, from too little food and too much sport, while my friends threw up or went to sleep after school, they said, to cope with searing hunger.

As I got older and realised metabolism wasn't a myth, I just thought what a huge shame it was that I hadn't realised I'd actually looked great at twenty-five, or twenty or fifteen or whenever it was I'd felt I needed to be thinner to be better.

When I read about Schopenhauer's breakfast (the psychological theory that we should eat a live toad for breakfast as we get older to ensure the worst thing that will happen to us each day happens first thing) I saw that the travails of ageing should mean we valued our youth even more, rather than just hate it when we have it. Then I wondered how many calories there were in a live toad.

But here I was in a naturist camp, about to turn twenty-six and wondering if it would make me like myself in the moment.

In Flevo-Natuur it was immediately obvious that being happy enough with what you looked like wasn't assumed to be vanity or arrogance, as it would have been in the UK. It was part of a larger understanding of difference, Vincent told me, as I stood in the shop some afternoons for the company. It had given him more respect for humanity, working there, he said, and seeing people walking around after a mastectomy or caesarean or with missing limbs. 'Some people are so overweight they have to come in side-ways through that door,' he said. 'And they're all naked. And not embarrassed at all.'

Living without materialism was unbelievably freeing, and god damn cheap, I thought, too, as Vincent told me all sorts of successful millionaires left their clothes in the sports cars they parked outside the barriers so they could be judged for nothing but themselves inside. It was ironic that you sought anonymity by stripping off here, I thought, and *enjoyed* the kind of invisibility that was feared in London.

The only person who was always dressed, aside from Sam and I, currently, was Vincent, I realised. 'For professional reasons,' he explained.

'How bad do you *look*?' I asked as his eyes widened in surprise. 'I'm joking, I'm joking . . . I know that's not the point.'

I liked the fact there was no 'too' anything here, even if elsewhere the bodies you saw walking around might have been deemed too wrinkled, stretched, scarred, overweight, lacking or missing bits entirely. Bodies weren't things to be loathed, I started to see, and I wondered how my friends and I would have grown up if we hadn't been part of a society so obsessed by and ingrained with the idea of physical perfection. I certainly didn't feel I needed to go running every day any more – partly because I was too scared to run naked alone and didn't know what to do about a sports bra – but I also wasn't giving myself a hard time about it.

Two weeks in, there was snow on the ground and the Shetland ponies were iced to the grass on the island in the middle of the camp surrounded by a moat of frozen ducks, which made abandoning textile life less enticing. Sam and I waited for the camp and our fears to thaw, spending the time exhilarated by our new game of anatomical bingo.

'I saw my first pair of tits today,' he clamoured early on.

'You saw mine this morning,' I objected.

'Yours don't count,' he said, pecking me on the cheek and the next day winning by a mile when he saw 'a man as bald as a coot!'

'Damn it, I only saw one bum,' I conceded.

In the kitchen the olive oil froze cloudily in its bottle and I lay on the floor in my coat, reading, while Sam donned Lycra and went out for long bike rides in the cold, returning after five minutes to tell me ecstatically that he'd just seen a man with a frozen erection.

'He was just walking on the island near the shop, next to the Shetland ponies!' he clamoured. 'It was sticking right out, like this, but it had been almost entirely engulfed by balls because it's minus three out there today! OK, bye, love you!' he said, setting off again.

As for the fact that living naked was a sexual thing to do, I was yet to see a single orgy, to the disappointment of my friends, and was far from achieving the all-over tan British Naturism said was a highlight. It barely rose above 0°C and sunk to -5°C at night and I threw the curtains open each morning to find blizzards of swirling snow in marble-white skies. Crispy grass stood like meringue peaks in the garden.

But after a fortnight still dressed, I felt like a coward so on Friday night Sam and I downed a bottle of white wine and threw all our clothes on the floor of the living room before we could change our minds.

'Now what do we do?' Sam asked, looking at me as I held a boob in each hand for warmth and he moved his hands to his crotch, like a footballer awaiting a free kick.

'Let's put our shoes back on,' I said, as we hopped about naked then stood back up to revaluate. We'd seen each other naked hundreds of times in the last two years, but this felt weird. Analytical.

'Is having pubic hair cheating? Like . . . clothes for the genitals?' Sam asked.

'Oh Christ, let's leg it before we bail,' I said, sprinting out the door in nothing but short chocolate-brown Ugg boots. 'God, things really waggle when you run naked, don't they?' I shouted behind me, heading vaguely in the direction of the pool.

'I'm getting slapped silly,' Sam agreed.

Arriving at the pool, we slowed to a walking pace in order to look less deranged and strolled into a swimming area as bubble-gum-blue as a mermaids' lagoon. Two middle-aged men floated like corks in the water, and we slid self-consciously into the deep end.

'This is a metaphor for our entire relocation,' I hissed as we submerged.

'It's like having a bath with friends we haven't made yet,' Sam stage-whispered over the sound system, which for some reason was playing Michael Jackson's 'Beat It' loudly above our heads.

Then I noticed a kids' pool where an large ginger Viking had laid siege. Her two long plaits snaked over GG-sized breasts in a plastic bikini top.

'Look at her boobs,' I whispered. 'They're fucking *massive*.'

But Sam had left his glasses by our towels. 'I wish I could see. Or maybe I don't. I don't know what I think any more. Just stop staring,' he said desperately.

'I can't,' I hissed.

On the other side of the swimming pool, towelled naturists were ordering dinner in a restaurant that overlooked the pool and I found myself accidentally checking out anyone who moved.

'I feel like a pervert,' I said uncomfortably. 'And why are they now playing *Justin Bieber*?' I hissed. We were at least half the age of everyone else there.

Our epiphany came an hour later after nervous communal showers when we ran home with the heat of the water on our skin and realised adrenaline must have inspired the birth of both naturism, and streaking.

'I can't believe I was laughing at a man in a towel yesterday,' Sam said, shaking his head.

'Tomorrow I'm going to take Alf on a naked dog walk,' I agreed, feeling the place transformed from a creepy forest commune to a bizarre spa in the space of an evening. I wasn't sure I'd like to be ordered out of my clothes by a member of staff wearing them, as summer rules stated, but who didn't like swimming naked, we said, shaking our heads as though we'd been naturists for years.

The next morning I tried to remember our new lifestyle vows and didn't get dressed after my shower. But after twenty-six years of pulling clothes on, the day didn't feel like it had started without dressing, I realised, cursing 10,000 previous mornings in prejudicing me against my new life. I went to the window to survey the day, feeling proud, nonetheless. Then noticed a neighbour come out of the house opposite.

'Fuck,' I said, moving instinctively behind the curtain before remembering this was my new normality. I pretended to be arranging them and waved. He waved back.

'Good,' I told Alfie, sitting down on the sofa, but then jumping back up. Another problem, I thought, now I was naked. Could you catch STDs from sofas? I wondered. Then I wondered whether octogenarians had STDs full stop? I was quite sure I'd heard about a chlamydia awareness campaign launched by Age UK for sexually liberated OAPs, so I decided to sit on my coat, before opening *The Age of Reason*. In it, Maurice was drinking hot champagne in a nightclub with a younger woman. I checked the time: 10.30 a.m. Way too early to join them, I thought with some irritation.

I'd been warned about drinking in the day by people who knew the loneliness of solitude and it *was* quickly hard to avoid. After Sam drove to his studio in Amsterdam every day it was just me and Alfie until 7 p.m. or 8 p.m. Vincent was not always working in the shop, and the remoteness of the forest and the fact everyone I knew was in London made me feel as marooned as if I was on a private island alone. I knew I'd have to cycle 40 miles in the snow to get into Amsterdam on Sam's racing bike even if I did manage to strap Alfie onto me like a baby for the journey.

Whilst I again felt the freedom of empty days void of office routine, I was also barely writing. In theory, you could freelance from anywhere, but in reality, the features sections of the British papers were largely interested only in UK trends that I now couldn't experience in person, and not working meant my new life had emptied of purpose. I'd also become too distracted by someone

I'd met before we'd left to form a single sentence of the book I'd imagined I'd feel inspired to write with all this *time*.

By late afternoon, a glass of white wine therefore eased the void and I'd apologised to Vincent for fulfilling a British stereotype when I'd starting plucking bottles from the shelf more frequently.

Instead, he told me to listen to the crash of recycling day. 'People here drink a *lot*,' he said. 'Many are very lonely.'

'Why?'

'Because their friends or relatives won't visit them. Because of where they live,' he said. 'Lots of people still keep this element of their lives very secret – so they're quite alone.'

I saw it as a slightly sad place after that; the idea that lots of people were that isolated because of their belief in naturism. I'd read that in 1932, *The Times* had published a letter signed by Vera Brittain and many other literary icons arguing that the 'suspicion' surrounding open-air bathing clubs where members swam and sunbathed naked was iniquitous when you could pay to see semi-nudity on stage. Why did the bathers have to secrete themselves in a wood, it asked?

Yet more than eighty years later here I was secreted in a wood and thinking not that the whole world should live nude, but that our attitudes were skewed if real bodies were still seen as vulgar, while over-sexualised pop culture was teaching another generation of children that their figures were something to hate, starve, hide and fear. Like I had been taught.

I put *The Age of Reason* down, realising I'd been staring out the window for the last twenty minutes and checked my phone again: nothing. But past 10 a.m. was good, I remembered. That meant he'd have got to his desk with a flat white, flustered, fired a few pointers for conference to seem helpful. By 11 a.m. it would be calmer, more coffee would have been fetched, tomorrow's pages starting to be arranged. Alone in the forest and without routine, I guiltily measured my life by the timings of a man I missed in London, telling myself I didn't care if he messaged or not, but knowing I did.

Bored, and noting a purple veil of cold had spread over my skin, my fingers snow white at the tips, I walked to the flaming oil barrel of a heater Jizz had assured us would adequately heat our new home, and turned up the blaze. I stood with my back to it, rubbing my arms warm. You couldn't get close enough, I thought, waddling backwards and screeching in pain. Alfie looked up.

'I've branded myself,' I told him. 'I've literally branded myself like naturist cattle.'

In the kitchen, I swivelled around to check the damage on my naked reflection in the window and saw a long, fat, red line burnt into one bum cheek.

'Oh, fuck this,' I told Alfie, going upstairs to get dressed so the day could actually start.

It was *highly* dangerous doing everything naked, I realised, noting that the splash of burning oil was still visible on my stomach from the omelette I'd tried to cook nude the week before.

When I came back downstairs, a message sat on my iPad. A picture of a playing card. Six of hearts.

Shit, I thought, *it's happening.*

6

LEVELS OF LIFE

Life is all about timing. Chance encounters that we'd never know existed if we'd arrived a minute either side. If what had happened had been a couple of months earlier, I wouldn't have moved the relevant chess pieces across the board to arrange a life in Amsterdam. If we'd never met, maybe I would have been happy there, rather than feeling that every mile Sam and I put between ourselves and London only measured how much further the car carried me from Tom.

Staying for him and agreeing to a cliché would have been too much of a gamble even for me – although a cliché never feels like cliché when you're in it; it feels like the realest thing in the world, and the understanding that that's what it is only comes afterwards, when you blame yourself for imagining it was anything else.

Tom asked me to meet him in King's Cross the day before I left and cried into me in the rain. It was New Year's Day and the rainbow streamers sprayed into the air the night before drowned like confetti on the grey slabs of Granary Square.

'I don't want you to go,' he said, eyes pale and full of tears. 'I meant it when I said I loved you – I know it's soon.'

We'd been talking, or whatever it is you're doing in the very early stages of falling in love with someone you can't be with, for only four weeks. It was the steeliest, wettest day I'd ever seen; pathetic fallacy always the first fallacy to arrive, I thought, ignoring the fact it's all fallacy if neither of you are single. He was one of my senior colleagues, ten years older, and possibly thought my leaving would be helpful. Maybe he thought, initially, that he'd get on with normal life married to someone else when I left.

On Christmas Eve eve, with London half-emptied for the holidays, we met in Green Park and he kissed me underneath the blonde arches of the Ritz then pushed me along in front of him through the crowd. Despite the rush of bodies, it felt like we were the only two people in the world as we walked through Piccadilly Circus beneath the giant, flickering screens to Leicester Square where the streets gargled with drunks, and sound leapt from Mr Fogg's like a jack-in-the-box as the doors swung open into the December darkness on the street.

In Soho we sat down to drink strawberry beer in De Hems, the only Dutch pub I knew, and he awkwardly handed me a history of the city I was leaving him for wrapped in thick Foyles paper, eyes blazing.

Given we could never go home together, I wondered if we'd do nothing more serious than kiss, although he had another plan entirely and later in the crepuscular light of Milk and Honey, I knew neither of us wanted it to end anyway. The bartender placed the first martini I'd ever drank on a tiny paper square in the candlelight in front of me and I tried not to gag on the strength. He reached across the table to run his hand down the V of skin left bare by my black dress, the same I'd worn to meet the queen, and moved to sit next to me, telling me he couldn't remember ever wanting anyone this much.

On the Tube home I read about historic Dutch drunks called water divers who got so pissed they wobbled into the canal and thrashed about in the brine before they were hauled out by policemen to sober up in cells. I wondered whether Amsterdam would feel like prison without Tom, vaguely resenting that my excitement about going had transferred into regret at having to leave him.

Then on Christmas Day he called me, and I remember the heat in my face as I listened to the excuses he'd made to leave the house.

'All I want for Christmas is you. And a hotel room,' he said, and I laughed, vocally leaning out of something I didn't understand in the same way I'd swerved our first kiss after the Christmas party, for several reasons, but mainly because he was *married*, and it had been a shock.

There was a vague question of: 'What are you doing?' in my mind. A question aimed mainly at him, but at me too.

'What do you do when you get married to someone you have nothing in common with and then meet the love of your life?' he asked before I left, and in the months after, as though it tortured him. At the back of my mind, it scared me that you could get something so serious so wrong and I wondered why he thought I could save him.

It also surprised me that I didn't mind his head-over-heels declarations. He was as melodramatic as airport fiction, and I suppose it convinced me I must really like him to put up with it. But I was drawn to the emotion of the language and a poeticism, which in the end became so poetical it turned to nothing, ironically, but was everything I was missing from Sam. Comparison was cruel, but I lived with someone who didn't want to go out and do anything, which made Tom, as he dragged me excitedly through the streets to everywhere he knew, more attractive and inspiring. If Sam liked me for what I knew, I liked Tom for what I didn't, and what he taught me, even if it was just how to drink martinis.

I wondered, like most people in these situations, if you really could love two people at the same time, but I was too worried that I'd fall apart without Sam to talk to him about Tom, and the rift it created between us, when we normally told each other everything, made the guilt weigh heavy.

As for the fact Tom had a wife, something has to bend in your brain to cope with the knowledge you're hurting another woman that tells you they're partly to blame – that sentence is horrendous to write, and sounds shocking, but it's also the truth. I might not have been able to do that without Tom exacerbating it heavily from the beginning and excusing himself by telling me frequently that his wife barely liked him, seemed to hate him even. I could see him get up from a desk across the office to take phone calls and come back looking stressed and unhappy, implying with a fake laugh that he'd been given a hard time for something *again*. A lot of the time his face crinkled with something close to tiredness and I began to notice his eyes paled when he was sad.

It's a coping mechanism in a love triangle for each of you to shift accountability onto one point of it. The idea that the person you love might be inherently bad is beyond the ability and desire of imagination. I guess we can't afford to see the person we've fallen for, or made our bed with, had kids with, invited 100 people to watch us stand at an altar and marry, as manipulative, cruel or false, because it's too much of a reflection on us and on our choice.

With Sam involved too we were a love quadrangle which balanced something and made it easier, despite the fact it only raised the number of people being hurt. A quadrangle made it Tom and I together against our relationships, although we avoided speaking about Sam or Tom's wife in a warped logic that *talking* about someone who wasn't there was a worse betrayal than what we were doing. He said it was 'kinder', and I agreed because he designed everything else, from the code names to the texted phrases that hid us in plain sight. I was Matt (the same name as his best friend) and he was Arla, and we'd have coffee soon – which meant *I love you*, he said, and that was that. When Tom gave me a necklace inscribed with the letters CS, I wore it all the time and told Sam I'd found it on the street, letting him believe I was just weird for wanting to adorn myself with lost property.

Later I saw that I gambled to win, while Tom gambled to lose and to feel alive in the process, but in the beginning it seemed like we were made for each other. We spoke the same, read, wrote, thought the same and I'd stopped believing that opposites attracted or worked after we met.

'You have the biggest eyes I've ever seen,' he said. 'Two people's eyes,' and I protested that that made me sound like something out of a horror film.

I remembered how embarrassed he looked when I'd swerved his first attempt to kiss me, and how I'd felt so sorry for him I'd put my hand in the pocket of his coat, wondering later if that meant it was my fault. That I'd started it. But we just sat there that night, clinging to the only place still open, and smoking a packet of cigarettes lying on the table, which he'd not done in eight years, he said. Everything spilled out of him and I wondered what it was about *me* that made him want to admit all of his past mistakes, but he said I was the only person in the world he felt he could really talk to.

'You're having a mid-life crisis,' I laughed.

'I feel like everything with you is amplified through a huge sound system,' he said.

I looked around us at teenage girls with rainbow lips and Fred Perry clones swaying like wave machines on their Christmas bonuses and thought Londoners were a determined bunch: squashed by life and sporting office skin tones, but roaring on the backstreets and letting the idea of a hangover walk them back to the bar to delay the pain.

'Have I ruined your idea of me?' he said, looking like a little boy, and I lied and said of course not.

After that you kid yourself an invite to dinner is just that, but of course it can't be just anything when one person's already started you down a different path. By agreeing, you go along with the idea of another narrative, I realise now, daring them to persuade you, perhaps. I just wanted to be near him, I think, because he made me feel alive in a way my own relationship didn't any more and I was curious about how it would play out, unable to imagine how it could.

At a restaurant in Bermondsey, we stood at the bar of the tiny, crammed tapas restaurant and drank cold white wine, ordered violet petals of octopus and blistered, bitter pimientos de Padrón from a small blackboard. Then he touched my arm and ran his hand down my side to my hip.

'I'm nervous,' he said, which surprised me, because he was so much older and I'd thought he knew what he – what we – were doing. 'I just – I want it to go well. It means so much,' he said.

Then I let him kiss me and I tasted the seawater tang of octopus on his tongue.

'You kiss with your eyes open,' he said.

I laughed.

We were both so nervous in the end, we went to the entirely wrong hotel first, but that became a funny story afterwards, part of our early, inept days. We left the right hotel room before midnight in a state of crumpled sheets and gin-and-tonic limes and he said, 'I love you – do you mind?' and I should have laughed then, too, because we were two weeks in. People didn't fall in love this fast, I told myself. Did they?

But he'd meant those words, he said in King's Cross, and they raced us so quickly into something else. Later I wondered whether I should have let him say them at all, but it *did* feel like the beginning of something, not the end, I agreed as I looked around Granary Square and found it ghostly and surreal without its usual bustle. It felt like there was nothing else to do but keep seeing each other; the excitement in the first stage of love is self-ish, desire all-consuming, and time with him swam around inside my head. I felt like I was walking about in a daze if he wasn't there, like we both died when we went back to our parallel lives and only breathed again, properly, when we came back together.

'What are we going to do?' I asked him.

'I'll think of something,' he said.

'I think Sam thinks this is it for us,' I said. 'Move abroad. Get married in a couple of years, have kids.'

But Tom was clinging to me and the words were muffled into the collar of my coat.

'Don't marry him,' he said, pushing his head into my rain-soaked hair and I just felt numb, which I guess he took to mean I didn't care as much.

'You seem to be taking it much better than me,' he said, putting one hand on the back of my neck and looking at me. Maybe he saw then how scared I was. 'I will find a way to stop you slipping through my fingers.'

'I want you to.'

'I will.'

After that, I let the escalator carry me down to the Tube and when I turned around he was still standing at the top of it with tears falling down his cheeks, and my optimism swirled away in the rain when I returned to ground level in Clapham. We didn't know when we'd see each other again.

Numbness stayed after that amidst the joy of the new in Amsterdam, and I lay on the floor listening to a huge playlist of songs Tom was adding constantly to in London and reading of freedom in Jean-Paul Sartre. Amsterdam was also my first taste of isolation and with only the characters in books for company, I thought about Tom even more. He messaged and called all the time from the office, which pushed me towards him and further away from Sam.

'Three or four courgettes?' Sam would say when we shopped for dinner and I'd say: 'I think I'm in love with someone else.'

Although of course I never did. I said it out loud once while he slept next to me and he didn't wake up. The rest of the time the words marched to the tip of my tongue and stopped. I was terrified about what would happen if I admitted I woke up every day thinking about someone else and wondered if my unconscious would betray me like nightmares had betrayed Jonnie when I'd slept next to him. I went to bed scared that I'd dream of Tom and say his name out loud.

'Tell me everything,' he emailed from his kitchen table in London at 6 a.m., reporting that he'd got up to comfort his crying child and was writing an email to me in the middle of an interview he was working on in case his wife came in. The detail of his deceit made me feel more guilty because it made his life elsewhere real, but I knew I was the only person he could tell and tried not to believe what I really suspected, that he was revelling in the secrecy which he thought made his home life more interesting.

'Mundane things are the hardest,' he wrote. 'Washing up last night's pasta dishes. Places are even worse. I see the ghost of us everywhere we've ever been. That spot in Queen's Wood where I kissed you and your face lit up like a firework. I walked through King's Cross the other day. Fuck. That was hard.'

Messages reading 'I miss you. I love you' came daily, then quickly weren't enough, losing meaning with repetition. Sometimes I drove into town with Sam when he left for work and walked around Amsterdam alone, learning the streets and wondering uneasily whether Tom was dampening my new life, or whether I just always wanted to be somewhere else once I arrived. I bought an old Nokia, the kind of burner drug dealers used and then quickly threw away, and texted Tom.

'Guess who?'

'You've got a phone?! This is that barmaid I'm seeing in Rotterdam, right?'

'Which barmaid from Rotterdam?' I tapped into the squashy keys, trying to remember how to text without touchscreen. 'This is Marta. The waitress from Antwerp.'

'Fuck. Yes. Of course. How are you Marta? Still on for Madrid next week?'

'Take Greta. We're over.'

'Please, Marta! She meant nothing to me. It was just an absinthe thing.'

'Fine. I've had a fling with absinthe myself – I forgive you.'

'Sweet. Are you still bringing the riding crop and peanut butter?'

I was in Waterstones on Kalverstraat and snorted out loud in the library silence.

'Marmite was our thing,' I replied, suppressing a grin.

'Oh yes. You're Marmite. Someone else liked peanut butter. Don't worry your pretty little head about it, darling. You'll always be my Marmite mistress.'

The vulgarity of the word 'mistress' made me baulk.

He decided we needed to see each other soon after that and took a job that would mean we could stay a night in Paris. Then a picture of a number arrived every day on my iPad and although I put off booking a train out of pure shame, I knew I'd go because my empty days made me crave the excitement I knew I'd feel boarding a crimson Thalys train and being carried across Europe towards Tom.

Paris was biting and snarling with January cold when I arrived, like the dogs dragged around by their homeless owners beneath the chamber-like roof of the Gare du Nord. Bright red letters of European cities twinkled like Christmas lights on the arrival boards: Lille, Strasbourg, Bruges and St Pancras, the last due in less than five minutes, I saw.

A wave of nervous anticipation swept through my entire body then, like fire through a forest. I scanned the station for our meeting place and saw the fat, dollar-green letters of Starbucks near the exit, perched like a row of pigeons in the rafters. Two dishevelled men, plastic bags slung over their shoulders like a catch of rabbits, curtseyed out of the way when I passed, and I realised I was holding my breath.

I'd felt all morning like I was standing in deep water, and pushing myself up on tiptoes to avoid the waves licking my face, two watery cans of Heineken somewhere near Brussels did nothing to settle my unease. A *Before Sunset* script lay open on my lap the entire way, unlooked at, and I stared out of the window instead. The film was what he always quoted was the reason to get off the train – or get on it, in our case – but I was only sure about us when we were together. Likening us to the characters in *Before Sunset* was a hyper-romantic, teenage way to think about it, I can see now, but I didn't question it at the time. Instead, I bought him the script.

The sound of badly bashed piano keys swung into the air from the concourse as I moved through it and someone lit a cigarette beneath a No Smoking sign. The station felt like the inside of a ghost train; edgy and nightmarish. I watched a woman with blood-red hair hold a tissue up to her bloodied nose, red spots already stained onto a white fur scarf, and realised everyone here was waiting: the homeless for warmth, the beggars for money, the ticket holders for trains where they'd sit, waiting to arrive somewhere else. I was anxious as hell and went outside to light a cigarette, then ordered a coffee and sat down alongside everyone else, to wait.

You spend a lot of time waiting in affairs, I thought, as I watched the crowds rush past a slanting sandstone house that stood like a disaster not an art installation in front of the station. Behind me sat a street of identical croque monsieur cafés, their tables dressed like jam jars with red-and-white chequered cloths; Paris's first line of defence before the real city behind it. Then I turned back to the crowd and he was right there, stock still and staring at me with a smile stretching out like a road.

'You came,' he said.

'So did you,' I said, as he leaned down to plant a kiss on my mouth, then he took my bag and off we went down the Boulevard de Magenta towards the Place de la République.

It was almost midday and crowds of workers sat at tiny tables lining the streets, ordering wine and the plats du jour, discussing their mornings. The square felt quiet and heavy with grey, Paris in recovery from the attack two months ago, when 130 people had been killed and another 400 injured by jihadists at the Stade de France, the Bataclan and at bars and restaurants in central Paris packed with Friday night drinkers.

In the middle of the square, a ring of flowers circled the base of the bronze monument as though Marianne had dropped a petticoat of petals, and the language of tragedy could be read amongst the stems. Scruffy men with downtrodden expressions and trollies of lives sat around her on benches staring ahead at nothing. Somehow they all looked the same, as though dirt had become them and masked who they used to be. Tom held me tighter then, like he felt the atmosphere too.

At Hotel Gabriel we left our bags unpacked on the bed and stood on the balcony watching the Parisians slowly smoke their way along the street. Silver skeletons of unlit Christmas decorations still hung in the air as though the holidays had drained them of their dazzle and no one could be bothered to take them down.

'Let's go out,' I said, too sober and nervous to stay in the room with him.

There really was an atmosphere in Paris that week: a static feeling, like the sadness and shock hung in the air beneath the lights. People were jumpy, nervous, more cynical and it seeped into you. It made it difficult to tell whether we were on edge because the whole city was, or because of what we were doing. What we'd already done and were continuing to do.

On the Rue du Grand Prieuré we walked past matching pairs of girls wearing long coats and messy buns and stopped at the sea-green façade of La Pharmacie where people were clearing their plates and sipping wine amongst lone men with serious expressions and espressos, reading *La Figaro* and *Le Monde*. Neither of us were hungry, but we wanted a drink to calm our quick hearts and thought we *should* eat something, so we ordered a bottle of wine and foie gras toast, white asparagus with coddled egg, comté quiche.

'We drink too much,' Tom said, at the start of the second bottle.

'I know. But we live in stolen time. It doesn't feel like reality,' I admitted.

'I want it to be over,' he said. 'I want to be happy and I need to be with you for that. I want a lifetime of conversation and surprise and adventure and . . . tender yet audacious sex.'

I laughed. 'Tonight the streets are ours. We must walk them and decide what to do.'

'I've booked an indecently romantic restaurant,' he said. 'How sure I am about wanting to be with you is the only unwavering thing in my life.'

Being there so soon after the attacks did something to us, I think. The atmosphere broiled us and brought us closer together. We were an hour late to the restaurant, because we went to bed and couldn't get back out, arriving at 11 p.m. with cheeks flushed with affection. I'd fallen by then, I think, and it all seemed perfect in the soporific light as we ate snails drenched in a speckled green sea of garlic and drank champagne.

'This is an old favourite of Marlene Dietrich,' Tom told me.

'No wonder.'

'You're smouldering,' he said.

'Stoppp ittt.' I grinned.

Back in the hotel we lay on our sides an inch apart with the sheets melted like ice cream at the bottom of the bed and he ran his hand along the curve of my side. I thought about decisions made every day that wreck and ruin, bring happiness, love, affection, devastation, joy, sadness; make you shout, cry, laugh, hurt, doubt and run towards someone, or away.

Fate, if you believe in it, is so linked with love, but we never think about the people it must have kept us apart from too, if it's responsible for intertwining us with others. If one link in the chain was missing, would I never have met Tom, and been happy elsewhere, I wondered, as I fell asleep.

The next morning was the first we'd ever woken up together and we walked the Parisian pavements to find breakfast, then sat down outside a cafe with outside tables glowing with heated lamps, not noticing the bunches of flowers pinned to the railings opposite us. Then I saw the gun shots in the sides of the closed restaurant across the street and horror jolted through me then, that death had sat down where I was.

The attacks seemed to paralyse some people and stop them doing anything at all in a way that only imitated life afterwards. Others it seemed to spur in the opposite direction, making them more reckless because what if we were next? Tom knew somebody killed in one of the London attacks and told me about her. I would have loved her, he said, and her me.

In Paris our situation felt more urgent, as if we couldn't delay too long because the new, profoundly anxious atmosphere in Europe made everything feel more fragile and momentary. Waiting for anything suddenly seemed ridiculous, and the idea of long-term unhappiness unbearable. It was ironic that terror fuelled love and lust alongside death and hate, but we had terrorism to thank for that too, I guess.

When the details of the next attack were so unguessable, they felt unavoidable and it instead came down to being in the wrong place at the wrong time. The gamble of life, the risk of everyday, seemed obvious, which in Paris had included buying tickets for a gig or going for a drink on Friday night.

Yet that year the attacks seemed to follow Tom and I around in a way that might have felt, in fiction, foreboding. In February, we met in Brussels and a month later, three coordinated suicide bombings at the airport, and a metro station, killed thirty-two people and injured more than 300. We'd toured the streets before the devastation hit, eating strangely cubed pig's head in À La Mort Subite, drinking lurid green cocktails in Goupil Le Fol, and looking as disappointed as everyone else with Manneken Pis. It didn't occur to us that the first place we chose to go translated to 'sudden death' but it must have been in our subconscious, how life was quickly lost, and you only had one shot while you held on to it.

Later I wondered whether it was absolving to reason that the changing sense of danger made us gravitate together, but I recognised something similar during the pandemic. Sex was a comfort; love, a crutch, and attachment a defence against a future unknown. When Tom and I were together it felt so right that it wasn't until the next morning, when I woke up without him and wondered where he was, that it really hit me that our lives ran parallel in different countries, with other people.

Maybe we fell in love too easily because we both needed it at the time, or maybe we were both looking for something and mistook each other for the cure. Maybe we were both lightweights in love, or maybe the freedom of travel that was available then inspired a freedom we sought to live with, a right we believed to be ours and refused to live without. But our constant goodbyes were fragile and it soon felt like our relationship was taking place in the interval of an increasingly bad play, where we snatched time at the bar together before rushing back to separate seats.

'The bad play being my marriage?' he asked.

He was beginning to look more tired, paler-eyed, as he had at work when things were going badly at home.

'More casual relationships can be bad plays too,' I said. 'They just have fewer acts.'

Two months in, Sam and I were unravelling fast. We'd left the naturist camp for a cabin in the woods in Soest in February and I was struggling to live with the lies. Getting into bed with him when I thought I was in love with someone else felt profoundly wrong for everyone. Tom hated it and told me he'd moved into the spare room. His wife was asking repeatedly if he was having an affair, he told me, but my name was yet to be mentioned. He denied what she knew was true at first, but I could hear he was falling apart. 'Our child is so *young*,' he said, over and over again, worrying they wouldn't remember him living in the house if he left now. He made me swear again and again that I'd never leave him if – no, *when* – he did.

The fact Tom was delaying telling his wife meant, in the meantime, all four of us were going mad in different ways and for different reasons, and I felt more anxious than I'd ever been, drank bourbon at lunchtime and waited, constantly, for updates. We spoke several times every day and I told him he had to make a decision, said I couldn't stay in Amsterdam arguing with Sam even more now we'd broken up. That had happened in late February – both of us feeling the relationship untenable, but him not yet knowing exactly why, and continuing to try to live together, because we had to, while Tom gaslit his wife in London. I knew Sam and I would never be properly over until I left – how could we be 'broken up' when we lived together in the middle of nowhere and had to share a bed at night, I thought? We used the words against each other in arguments that had worsened and then tried to get on as much as we could in the day, waiting to see, I guess, who would duck out first.

Being alone all day gave me too much time to think as I walked Alfie through miles of forest on sandy, heather-lined paths that wove between thousands of trunks. We rarely saw another person. Sam had taught me to make secret policeman – joints for people who couldn't roll cigarettes – so I took his small bags of New York Diesel or Blueberry 54 and sat on a log in the depths of the forest with Alfie, teasing the tobacco out of a Marlboro Light and then poking it back in once I'd mixed it with crumbled green. The warnings on the cigarette packets were in Dutch, so

I figured I was immune, being English, and smoking made time move more easily.

The woods were also a panacea to the streets of Amsterdam where Sam dropped me when I needed to see humanity. I went birdwatching of a different kind in the Red Light District, thinking I'd write a book about a murder there, until I read John Irving's book about a murder there. Instead, I just watched the men billowing about the windows like pay-as-you-go phones always out of credit, snatching looks for free. The seediness appealed to me for some reason, possibly because the girls in the windows were waiting, like I was, for a man, although here the men looked more like sharks as they floated past the glass and flashed their eyes sideways as they drew level.

'What if they wake up on a Monday morning and they just can't be fucked?' I asked Sam, wondering if Monday blues spanned all careers.

'Well exactly,' he said, quite seriously.

Touts called adverts for 'real, genuine filth' along the canal next to adverts for €11 beef stew and warnings not to capture any of it on camera. I felt lucid in the cold February mornings, listening in a way that picked everything up but the girls. At the time I thought I was looking for characters for a book, but now I think I just wanted to be around people after the extreme isolation of the forest. I liked the timings of the street, where at midday the early birds came off shift and the new girls took their glassed perches strapped and fastened like tightrope walkers in a way that made sex-pest tourists swing around the windows like mating apes.

It was 3D porn really, and by then most of the women I knew watched porn as much as men and didn't mind admitting it. I'd started flicking over it more in Amsterdam out of escapist boredom, unconsciously spell-checking the titles, laughing at the awful grammar and inventing a game, as I scrolled over a mass of sordid options, in which I was an A and R man looking for song title inspiration for his bands. 'Daisy Wants More' (The 1975), 'No Peeking Daddy' (Christina Aguilera, circa 2002), 'Girls and Cars – Scene 6' (The Vamps), 'Cum in my Mouth' (Missy Elliott), 'Nice Girls Like To Play Outside' (Justin Bieber), 'European Partybabes' (Pitbull), 'Old Man's Life Story Makes Young Nun Fornicate in a Chapel' (Nick Cave & The Bad Seeds).

Cabin fever blurred reality alongside the sleaze and bourbon lunches until something growled like a creaking door in the trees above me, making me feel like I was in *Lost* as Alfie slept on, unconcerned. It was snow-cold and the only other life I saw was clinging to a couple of undernourished blue tits, who hopped about outside the door until I flung bits of omelette at them. 'Fussy,' I said, when they didn't touch it, only realising how cannibalistic an offer it was later on.

The cabin's owner had left an SAS survival guide by a Gaggia coffee machine so I memorised chapters on emergency childbirth, den building and crocodiles in case I got lost alone in the wilderness, and there was a chapter on what wildlife you could eat, but it didn't mention blue tits. I stared through binoculars into the wood for life, but only ever saw a neighbouring cabin's two dogs, who they let shit all over the forest. Madness felt like having nothing to do and depersonalisation made me feel like Leonardo DiCaprio in *The Beach* when he loses it completely and thinks his life is a computer game. I wondered hazily if I'd pass the surreal new level I'd found myself on, or whether I'd be a Wisteria Lane housewife in a wood forever, cooking dinner for Sam when he came home, asking him about his day, drinking wine and tuning out. Nightly we carried on watching Netflix, had an argument, went to bed.

Meanwhile, Tom called me from phone boxes, telling me not to answer incoming calls that could be his wife. He said he could write a *thesis* on how to have an affair in the twenty-first century, and I wondered whether he was handling it better than me because he'd done it all before, or whether he actually *enjoyed* sending me recent examples of his 'spycraft'. I felt like I was breaking – but he had more to lose. Situations like those do something to you: switch something on in your brain that makes you feel like you're unhinging, sooner or later, and knowing that would have stopped me from starting, even above the guilt and the amorality. Selfish – but saving and protective, to appeal to the self. I just didn't think about myself enough back then and was strangely passive, in some ways, about what I was letting happen to me. And to Sam.

Decadent, awful, time stretched ahead of me and I tried to remember that Camus quote. *To come to terms with time was the most magnificent and most dangerous of experiments.* To endure it you had to be able to stand yourself, and I couldn't.

In March, Sam and I moved again, this time to an Airbnb farmhouse on the other side of town and that was when everyone found out. I was at the Van Gogh museum in Amsterdam with Mat and Tris, friends from Newcastle who'd flown over for an Interrailing trip, and we were trying to spot madness in Van Gogh canvas when Tom texted me to tell me he was leaving work for a 'summit meeting' with his wife. An intercepted text on Valentine's Day was the beginning of her discoveries. 'Why would your best friend send a message like *that*?' he'd told me she'd asked – saying he'd tried to pass it off as a joke.

'I'll call you after,' he said, and I shivered with anxiety for hours, unable to concentrate on anything. His parents demanded to see him after that and every time he spoke to someone new I waited to be called and told they'd changed his mind.

Mat, Tris and I left Amsterdam for Rotterdam, then Antwerp, Brussels, Bruges and Paris as we'd planned to and more madness seemed to unfold in each city. Tom's wife knew it was me by Rotterdam, having already guessed but been denied the truth by Tom. Then Sam found one of my two burner phones in the farmhouse and had packed my bags by the time we arrived in

Antwerp, telling me not to come back unless it was to pick them up and get out.

'I should have left you in London,' he said, which seared me with pain, but I couldn't exactly argue. Before we'd left he'd picked up a message from 'Arla' that said 'I love you' and after he threw my phone at me, I'd told him we'd kissed at the Christmas party, not thinking he'd believe me for a second. But he had. You fucking *lesbian*, he'd screamed, asking if I needed to get having a girlfriend out of my system? *No, no, no*, I'd stammered, describing it as a stupid mistake, but too scared to tell him *Arla* was actually *Tom* in case he refused to come to Amsterdam. We were leaving the next day and I wondered whether Tom had wanted me to get caught, then, to stop me going. He'd never not used the code words before.

Now it had all finally come out Sam was calling me everything under the sun and I apologised and said, in idiotic defence, that I'd not intended to fall in love with someone else.

'You're a twat,' he said.

When I look back on that time I think: why? *Why*, when I had someone who would have done anything for me, did I treat them like that? I could have left nicely – made Tom wait.

'This is what I was saying before about you wanting to be a part of an affair because it makes you interesting. All of the books you like are full of it,' Sam said and I wondered whether he was right. Whether I'd started to see life as fictional. A game.

Vulnerability was creeping in and I only felt safe or distracted enough to feel normal when I was moving, after that. With Mat and Tris I arrived in a new city in Western Europe every other day and in Paris there'd been Tom, who'd booked another Eurostar so we could work out what to do next.

His phone never stopped ringing that second time we were there because, despite his confession, I saw all he was doing was continuing to lie deeper. 'She's not here,' I heard him saying on the phone, as I stood on the freezing balcony of our hotel bedroom in an attempt not to hear, but failing not to. Sadness settled in my stomach like a stone.

It had been me that had told Tom he had to admit I was involved after his wife had worked it out. Lying to someone else's face when you were outright asked a question was different, I told him: it was not only cruel but it made the person feel like they were going insane. It was absurd to worry about the pain of another woman when I was part of the direct cause, but the idea he was gaslighting her on top of all the other dishonesty was my limit, I guess. Maybe I just thought too many women in the past had been made to believe they were losing their minds over the vagaries of men.

As we walked around Paris that second time, I doubted Tom heavily, but still felt I *needed* him, especially now I'd lost Sam, and we stood in Shakespeare and Company like the couple in *Before Sunset* after they'd lost touch and been reunited.

'I want to bring my kids here one day,' I said distractedly.

'Our kids,' he said, five minutes later.

'What?'

'You said *my* kids.'

'Our kids,' I said, trying to shift the darkened look on his face.

We sat by the Seine after that and he fell asleep with his head on my lap and I flicked through one of the books we'd bought and read a line about more lies being told in bed than anywhere else in the world.

Then I remembered the first time we'd been in Paris, where life seemed to sit easily ahead of us. We'd had dinner, that time, at an old record shop and spent the night talking a mixture of French and English with a small group sitting around one table, several of them in situations like ours.

'Do you love him?' a woman called Audrey asked me, looking at Tom.

'I do,' I said, everyone watching us, and he smiled.

Then Reno, the owner, pulled me up onto the shop floor and started twirling me around.

'Lucy, I have to take you to see my father's wine cellar,' he said. 'My last girlfriend was Polish and my parents didn't like her. But they would love you.'

'What about Tom?' I laughed, looking at him as he watched Reno waltz me about.

'He is married. Did I tell you I'm a great cook? And I have a Brazilian gardener who is also a great cook if I'm lazy.'

'Isn't she a little young for you, Reno?' Tom asked, eyes glittering like a wink.

'No one knows how old I am – so no,' he said, releasing me back to the sofas and our mess of plates.

'I think he liked you,' Tom said, when we left.

'I think I like *you*,' I replied.

As he slept by the Seine I knew he'd slide his wedding ring back on on the train and hide the photos on his phone, denying again that we existed and throwing us back to square one. I had nowhere to go now but back with him to London and to my brother's flat, where I was going to sleep on Charlie's floor while I worked out whether to stay in London to be nearer Tom, or just retreat back to Bath. I wondered how we'd manage being in the same city again, but had a feeling it would involve the same snatches of time it had at the start.

'What are you going to say?' I asked him as we got off the train in St Pancras.

'I know what I want to say,' he laughed darkly. 'I want to say, "Don't you see? I'm really in love." But I'm not sure that would cut it.'

I could've said then that that was exactly what *I'd* done, but I didn't. I guess I knew by that point that I was braver than he was, which he said all the time, but I'd not believed at first.

In the loneliest, most doubtful moments after our goodbyes I felt stupid for believing in us and believing he did too and would really stay with me. I knew he was too worried about being liked and tried to please everyone by keeping up the veneer of a life he didn't want to be his any more.

In London, I met friends and listened as they all gave me differing versions of the same advice, and I started to wonder if Tom and I were just both lost and unhappy and trying to use each other as a raft.

'No offence, but if he's not happy you could have been anyone,' my friend Libby said. She was a few years older than me, sick of men but still desperate to get married, and always a voice of harsh reason. 'You're the attractive option because you're much younger than his wife and you're still excited by the world. Everything is possible when you're in your twenties – you're relaxed and happy because you're not exhausted from looking after a crying child all the time and you want a load of filthy sex because you haven't pushed screaming brats out of your vagina yet. But trust me, once a cheater, always a cheater. If he was really serious, he would have already moved out. And older men get obsessed – trust me,' she added.

She'd dated a guy who was forty-six when she was twenty-two and now had a restraining order against him, I knew.

'If Tom leaves his wife for you and six months down the line you turn around and say, "I don't want this," you'll have a psychopath on your hands,' Libby added. 'Dan broke his restraining order again last week and the Met did nothing. They're fucking lucky I've not been murdered.'

We were sitting in a scallop-shell booth in a Pont Street restaurant near her office and she poured half her glass of wine into my empty one.

'Lucy. Everything will be OK. I'll make sure of it.'

'It really doesn't fucking feel like it's going to be OK,' I said. My hands had started shaking all the time, but she kindly said nothing as I trembled the glass of wine to my mouth.

According to other men, Tom needed an ultimatum. Gal, who

was closer to Tom in age than me, laid his hands on the pub table and told me I was fucking stupid to get caught; that he'd been having an affair for years because he needed more than his wife would give him, but that he'd never leave. 'Despite what they say, not all married men want to leave their wives. Go to Cuba. You have my permission. But then make him choose. And then get on with your life,' he told me.

Tom had booked us a week in Cuba in April, telling his wife it was an arduous-sounding cycling holiday he was writing about for the travel section, because she apparently didn't like bikes. We'd agreed that when we returned from Havana it was all or nothing. I never asked how he got away with paying for it without being found out because my name was next to his on every document he sent me, but they came from an email address he said she didn't know about.

In the meantime, friends told me to get myself set up in a flat he could move into if it came to it. 'But find out if he's still sleeping with his wife,' my friend Alex said. 'You're perfectly entitled to ask because if he is, he's cheating on you too and it's cruel and selfish. Plus it means it's not over with her, which he's saying it is.'

I asked him. He was. 'It pales into nothing compared to what we have,' he said, as though it mattered how good it was and not that he was still doing it. I felt sick. Of the lies and the fact that he was trying to have it all. I wondered if he really thought everything was about sex but sex, and sex about power. Over me, over all of us.

In London, I arrived at a house that smelt of hockey sticks, and Charlie just laughed as I told him everything.

'What's funny?' I said.

'It's just like a film, isn't it?' he said. 'Paris, Brussels, Cuba. Is Wes Anderson directing?'

'Feels more like a Tarantino,' I said. 'It's a fucking bloodbath.'

7

GIRL WITH GREEN EYES

'I can't believe you,' I hissed across the seat at Tom, who was sitting on our flight from London to Madrid, where we'd transfer to a plane bound for Cuba, with a perpetual erection.

'*Sorry*,' he whined. 'I thought we could join the mile high club.'

'No one actually does that in real life,' I whispered back. 'How do you think we'd possibly do that?'

There'd been six people in the queue for the bathroom ever since take-off, including several toddlers. The idea we could sneak in together was quite obviously impossible. He pulled a pathetic face.

'Is it even legal to carry Viagra into other countries?' I said, holding *Our Man in Havana* in front of my face like a spy.

'They're ... herbal,' he said, looking so sorry for himself I had to laugh then, and he smiled.

'Maybe at the airport, we could ... ?' he wheedled. 'I've never had sex in Madrid.'

I snorted and re-opened my book, knowing not much would have destroyed our high on that plane. We'd swapped turbulence in London for turbulence at 30,000 feet and switched our phones off.

While I stayed with my brother, Tom and I had been snatching a few hours or an evening together, feeling like there wasn't enough time to say or plan what we needed to. But now we had a week, the longest we'd ever spent together, to work out if after the beginning we'd had, we'd ever share a house and talk about boilers, a conversation I was shocked to realise was hugely appealing after a start like ours.

'Can you imagine?' he'd said, the night before, when we'd met at a pub near his office so he could give me the boarding passes and not risk them being found by his wife. 'A week. Sunshine. You. Me. Incredibly poor Wi-Fi.'

He put a guidebook down in front of me and flashed it open to show me the little dots he'd drawn next to the things we could do. The marina, Hemingway's house, café con leche – which was essentially just milky coffee but always sounded more romantic in another language. I looked at the boarding passes – 6D and 6F.

'We're together – I checked,' he said.

'Look at your *name*,' I said, reading it in full for the first time.

'Better than sounding like a gypsy fortune teller,' he said.

I choked on my pint. 'Is that what mine sounds like?'

'The middle two, for sure. Come inside, and let Mama Rose Annie reveal the secrets of your destiny . . . ' he said, grinning.

'Do you want to know what your destiny is? It's coming to me very clearly,' I said, telling him he'd find himself boarding the plane alone if he called me a *gypsy* again.

He laughed and leaned across the table to kiss me over a Penguin-orange book I'd pulled off the windowsill to read while I waited. I'd accidentally plucked one called *The Book of the Fallacy*, which was apt.

'How was it?' I asked, when he hugged me at the airport the next day, moving back to check the look in his eyes.

'Fine. I mean, you know – awful. She always says she loves me when I'm going away, which feels – tactical.'

By that time, I was desperate for it to be over, whatever that meant for us: the hotels had lost all glamour and I saw our rooms in them as private worlds that exploded when he left in a rush, his phone ringing on the bed with his wife's name while he was in the shower. Every time that happened, I just shouted his name until he came to get it, not being able to stand the feeling she was in the room. Only once I considered answering it myself – and sort of wish I had now – but I never did. 'Where does she think you are?' I'd always ask after those calls, and he'd give me the name of some friend, who's sofa he was apparently sleeping on, despite having told her the truth about me, he swore.

I'd started waking up to texts that were signed by his wife sent from his phone telling me it was over, then get another message from him, an hour later, saying it wasn't, apologising, calling me, turning up at my house, claiming they were separating. Feeling so batted about gave me panic attacks he left work to try to fix, sometimes, while I just shook and cried, feeling like I had no idea what was happening any more. I didn't trust him at all, I realised, and felt constant unease when we weren't together.

At the Waldorf one morning I'd run a bath and lay in the boiling bubbles eating biscuits from the tray by the kettle, then checked out alone and jumped when they called me by his name, assuming we were married, and wandering afterwards down the Strand in a daze. I gravitated that day towards the Dutch pub, ordering strawberry beer and sitting outside smoking until my table was full of London's other misfits.

'What are you doing here?' I asked a guy called Noah.

'A bottle of cherry brandy and my mother had forgotten to take the pill,' he said, as I laughed my head off, having meant what was he doing at the *pub*, obviously.

As we talked a homeless woman holding a sleeping bag stopped by our table and half-heartedly ran through a spare change request.

'Karen!' he interrupted. 'How are you?'

Noah knew everyone in Soho and I guess it hadn't changed much over the years, still being somewhere all sides of life gathered looking for company; somewhere you were still left looking after a homeless woman's sleeping bag while she went wandering down an alley to shoot up, as we now were. Noah thought London was already a dystopia years before the pandemic. A version of Neil Gaiman's *Neverwhere*, with London split into levels. Conventional lives with jobs and relationships taking place above an underworld of darker things and where people who'd slipped through the cracks survived, or didn't.

'Want to come to work with me?' he asked, as day neared evening and his night shift at Soho Books beckoned. He regularly had to chase businessmen with briefcases down the street after they tried to steal foot-long dildoes from the shelves, I'd learnt, which sounded kind of fun.

But we'd drank eight pints *each* and I needed to sober up, so I wobbled to Chinatown, to the Golden Dragon, the restaurant I'd been going to with my parents since I was a child, and sat at the back of the room in sunglasses trying to eat enough egg-fried rice to not fall over on the way home. Alcohol by then made my emotions more manageable, other people more fascinating, the opportunities of the night seem endless, the moment sparkle and run on.

What was going on beneath the tipsy surface of my life made me see London as a form of *Neverwhere* too. I was so lonely I formed five-minute friends everywhere, dropping in on Noah and finding him drinking cans of energy drink called Pussy amongst the books. Then I jumped around Soho between friends and unknowns, going anywhere offered, looking for something more than just a thrill. I think I'd lost all sense of who I was by then.

Later I realised big cities are dangerous places if you don't know who you are because there's nothing to hold on to as you're swept along by the current, twirled through rapids, thrown down waterfalls, trying not to drown completely. Sometimes I liked the inconspicuousness of it, but simultaneously I found the idea I was slipping through the cracks unsettling. I wore dirty jeans and a jumper of Tom's to avoid anyone thinking I wanted to be chatted up by being in pubs alone. Then it got later and Soho drunker and men told me eyes like mine must get me anything I wanted, and I moved on, feeling they'd not got me anything at all. Feeling like I had nothing and not wanting to be known. Being with someone who's never there makes you feel invisible in the end. Without Tom, I clock-watched time until we could see each other, and with him, counted down another goodbye now four, three, two hours away.

'Just don't think about it,' he always said, but that was impossible. I didn't *want* to compartmentalise in the way he seemed to find so easy.

Now I was back in the UK it was easier to get freelance writing jobs again, and working helped take my mind off Tom more than the emptiness of Amsterdam had. It also eased the concern over how broke I was from failing to be refunded for so many Airbnbs that I'd now never move into with Sam. Our plan had been to relocate every month to emulate a *New York Times* piece written by an American journalist who said a move a month helped her and her husband decide which neighbourhood in New York they'd most like permanence in. The naturist camp, the cabin and the farmhouse had been so fun in some ways and part of me still wished I'd be moving into the beach house we'd booked for June, even if I'd now prefer to change the company.

But that life was over.

In the weeks before Cuba, I sat in Charlie's local trying to write, if I had a commission, or just drinking to calm my nerves while I watched the lonely-looking regulars who made ageing look tragic because it so often took place alone. A crinkled woman limped like an injured bird through the door, her mouth shaping silent words as though she was talking to someone who maybe once joined her, and I wanted to ask her what she'd seen and whether it all got easier, with age, or only harder? I'd never felt more alone than I did with Tom, and felt weak and stupid for pinning the idea of happiness to someone who made me wait endlessly in exile. I saw a shadow of someone I didn't like, in those times.

'Are you ready to be called a homewrecker?' he'd asked once.

'What, are we in *EastEnders*?' I asked, half-joking but shocked, always, by his occasional crassness.

Why was I the homewrecker anyway, I thought, when *he'd* built the home he was now destroying, not me? He'd become obsessed by what he called case studies, listing all sorts of people he knew who'd left their marriage.

'I want to know exactly what happens,' he said, as though this small population study would allow him to control the outcome. It wasn't worth being one of the others, he said, who'd 'tried' to leave, but lost their nerve and had a crumpled sadness to them now over what might have been. But he was worried he wouldn't be able to afford to later on.

'Afford to?' I said.

'Financially,' he said.

I practically laughed then, thinking it madder than anything else that had happened so far, that you'd have to live with someone you didn't even like, and had nothing in common with, for the rest of your *life* because you couldn't *afford* to be happy. I was too young to know that's exactly what so many people really did do: become chained together by joint mortgages and childcare costs. His painting of his marriage as an expensive mistake tainted my idea of my own future completely. Everything I thought I'd believed in, like trust and loyalty, vanished when I was with Tom, and I started to see commitment as a trap.

I pictured myself in Brussels, waiting at the window of our hotel room for him to run across the square in the pouring rain, and knew there was a possibility that one day that girl would be someone else, and I would be the wife at home, wondering if my husband had kept his wedding ring on while he was away. It was catch 22 because if he left his wife for me, I'd always expect him to leave *me*, and I wondered if I'd have protected myself from such cynical views if I'd refused to become involved in the mess he'd made of his life. At the time I didn't feel young and naïve, but when I remember now that I was newly twenty-six, it's as clear as glass that I was in way over my head.

Havana was glazed with heat when we arrived and allowed ourselves to be hustled into a taxi to our hotel on the seafront, somewhere formally grand but crumbling, like most of the pala-tial buildings with their faded, Miss Havisham quality. The city smoked and swirled with dust, and people sat on desert-coloured streets watching the world with an un-anxious ease that was so un-European. There seemed to be a wild atmosphere always, like things could kick off at any time or break into dance, which they often did. Kerbside, the Cubans waited languidly for something to happen, rotating their heads like owls.

Tom and I couldn't believe we were there and went straight up to the swimming pool on the roof, ordering green cans of Cristal beer, and looking out over the jagged, gleaming, tin roofs below.

The whole city felt like a fallacy, really. A fallacy of liberation via a revolution that had faded its grandeur and made it harder to get shower gel in a shop. The impression of sin clung to the old Mafia haunts and placed girls on the knees of old men who bought them ice creams and paid for faked mutual desire. It was the per-fect setting for our week-long liberation; a city of sex in which we dreamed of a personal revolution. The sea, from that balcony, stretched its limbs with fishing-boat tights into Hemingway's marlin world.

'Daiquiris!' we agreed as we walked to Old Havana past tiny, corrugated pizza shacks and the fishermen dangling their legs over the sea wall.

'I've felt like we're in a cocktail shaker these last few weeks, waiting to be poured into a glass in Cuba,' Tom said, and we didn't stop grinning all week after that. There'd been an outbreak of dengue fever, so while they fumigated the city centre in the mornings we lay in bed, read, showered, went up to the pool and then went out in the evenings to drink rum with locals who dragged us through carnival streets promising a pianist from *Buena Vista Social Club* around the next corner.

We sat on backstreets eating fish and watching other couples smile and tip the troupes of musicians who circled like matadors everywhere, until the loved-up got bored of pretending to find the exaggerated attention charming, stole away their eye contact, hushed their conversations, and shook their heads at hats full of pesos.

Havana was a city of hustlers who'd all inherited Castro's notorious confidence, and the city was electric. The days flew by and then we flew home just as we'd learnt how to debone red snapper in torrential rain on the beach and navigate the streets between Don Quixote's statue and Hemingway's El Floridita. By that point we never wanted to leave the Buicks and Chevrolets that drove us along the Malecón to the Nacional, where Greene's characters drank and spied. After that near-perfect week, I couldn't sleep on the flight back to London because I didn't want time to go anywhere, knowing reality would hit us harder than the plane's wheels on the runway when we landed.

'Do you trust me?' he asked then, meaning, *Do you trust me to go home and tell my wife there's no way back?*

So I lied, and said yes.

It didn't take long for him to flip back the other way, of course, protean and scared. He said he needed longer, pleaded, said we'd only been together five months, said yes: it had been his idea to use

Cuba as an end point so things didn't stretch on forever, but leaving your family after knowing someone for *five months* was massive. I felt then like we should've cut our losses in Cuba, sensing how the mess would continue indefinitely if it was up to him. We should have drawn a line in the sand of our red-snapper beach, to save ourselves the pain of the dragged-out end.

'I thought you'd already separated?' I said instead.

'We're in the process of it, yes,' he said, unconvincingly.

They'd started marriage counselling, but only in order to separate in the kindest way possible, he claimed. But what he said he was doing, and what he actually was doing, didn't match up. I started answering the calls from unknown numbers I knew could be his wife, in case she wanted to have a conversation about what was actually going on, but after I said hello whoever it was hung up, and my life, as well as his wife and child's, continued to hang in the balance while he refused to make a decision.

When I argued that if he knew, he knew, he claimed he had dengue fever and couldn't leave the house and it became farcical how fickle he was, seemingly switching the course of his life on what was in front of him at the time. Maybe it was more boring than that: just a standard mid-life crisis. Or maybe it was the most tragic things of all: cowardice and fear.

When he recovered from his supposedly exotic illness we walked through Kensington Gardens talking about our situation endlessly, exhaustedly, and discussing how he could be a different sort of father to the one he'd imagined being; how there was never a right time to go unless you just did and made it work. He sent me pictures of him with his kid, as a test perhaps, and while I'm very glad now that I didn't have to take on someone else's child at twenty-six, at the time I was willing to, for *him*, I said, as we sat in Maggie Jones's like any half-serious adulterers would have, eating crudités because if you wanted to order wine, there had to be food on the table. Mainly we just slugged our way through a magnum of house white which they plonked down and measured with a wooden stick after, charging you per inch for what you'd drunk. We drunk it all, obviously, the angst of everything on top of us again now we were home.

Lauren Bacall he called me, on those days. 'She could drink most men under the table, too. Cigarette in one hand. A drink in the other. Industrial-strength pout.'

'I don't pout,' I said poutily, and he wove his hand through a timber yard of cucumber we'd not touched.

'We need to live together if we're going to do this,' he said, and I agreed.

When I picture him I still see dark blue shirts and dishevelled red trainers. Grinning, straight white teeth; a laugh that creased right up to his eyes and a walk that looked like he knew where he was going. Later I realised he knew no more than me where he was going, which made me wonder whether anyone really did.

Soon after that we moved into an Airbnb in north London for a week, so he could test the school run from a distance, and it ended in tears all round. Not just because we were waking up to the sound of the musician owner sweeping paintbrushes across bongos to a chilled techno beat but because Tom's wife called non-stop. I was never sure exactly what she knew, Tom hazy with detail, but he told me that he'd agreed with her that it was a trial run for them living apart. I'm pretty certain he would have failed to mention to his wife that he was living with me while he wasn't at home. In the end he told me she did find out so it was just another of the futile deceptions he never seemed to tire of.

As writing commissions started coming in more frequently, I was loving my job again, the sense of purpose easing the anxiety about the rest of my life as I was sent to join quidditch training on Hampstead Heath and to TV sets on Welsh industrial estates (mostly) to interview Maxine Peake and Matt Lucas, who were filming a new *A Midsummer Night's Dream* for the BBC, and

Frances de la Tour and Mamie Gummer, Meryl Streep's daughter, who were in Netflix's *The Collection*. Mamie was reading *Girl with Green Eyes* in her trailer, and when I read it soon after, it just reminded me of Tom. We'd managed to have one 'normal' evening cooking dinner in the Airbnb before all hell broke loose at his other house, his wife calling constantly and saying he needed to come back.

It was awful, but he wouldn't give up, saying we needed to make a real home together to make it work, and so I set up a viewing at a place in King's Cross owned by a photographer I knew. Tom bailed while I made excuses for him on the doorstep, then looked around alone with an ominous feeling about what his absence meant.

Later that day he called and said he just couldn't do it. Couldn't leave his child because he was being guilt-tripped to stay, he claimed, shifting the blame and playing the victim constantly now. I listened to him sobbing on the side of a busy road and said goodbye. Then went back to my parents' house in Bath feeling emptier than I ever had, knowing simultaneously that I couldn't stay with someone who didn't turn up to flat viewings, or call me back when I thought I sensed a change in my body after Cuba and bought my first Clearblue in Brixton, then a pint round the corner, so I could use the druggy bathroom upstairs to check I wasn't pregnant. Relief that I wasn't, when I saw the sign I'd been hoping for on the test, was edged by a secondary emotion somewhere near disappointment, I understood uneasily. It was reckless, but I think I wondered if Tom would take our relationship more seriously if I *was* pregnant.

It was Arla – the real Arla – that came to check I was all right, then, as I smoked with a shaking hand while I waited for her to arrive, and listened to the conversations going on around me so I didn't have to think about my own situation. Opposite me two early twentysomethings said they only cried in *X Factor*: 'You know that bit when they think they're leaving but they're actually going on holiday?' one said. Next to them a fortysomething told another that he'd taken a picture of his cock on Snapchat but couldn't work out how to send it to anyone. Two sixtysomethings discussed declining health: 'What's she got? Oh that's the worst one to 'av. My friend's 'usband's got that. My other friend's got it, too. Her quality of life is non-existent. She's in pain top to bottom, head to foot.' It was life laid out in decades, I thought, knowing thirty wasn't far away for me.

Then Arla emerged effortlessly at my table, grinning, and tanned as hell.

'Oh heyyy,' she purred.

'Oh hey,' I said, getting up to hug her. 'We are celebrating the fact that I am not pregnant.'

'Oh my God, I think I'm pregnant, too!' she said. 'I'm too scared to do a test.'

'Mine's in the bathroom upstairs if you wanna double-up,' I said.

'How's things with Tom?' she asked, when she'd got a pint.

'Shit,' I said, sipping. 'He says he feels like *"something out of Dante"*.'

'What a *writer*,' she drawled, laughing.

Seeing the ridiculousness of a man I thought had it all together helped, but it was the ease of communication, I realised, that made love, or what you thought had been love, harder to let go of, knowing the other person was just a message away. A text written and sent in ten seconds that said 'I miss you' had the power to ignite anything you'd managed to break off.

Willpower had to be absolute and you had to really, really know you were better without them. But I didn't know what to believe any more. The world just shook.

Dear Evvers,

I'm in Bath sitting at what my parents insist on calling 'the breakfast bar'. All I can see is fields and trees but it is an exceptionally miserable day. At least I have an excuse not to go running. Being a boomerang – do you know that's what we're called, the twentysomethings who move back in with their parents? – is very odd. There are lots of pluses, a stocked fridge and barely any midweek raves keeping me up until 2 a.m., but there are only so many episodes of *Gardener's World* I can tolerate, not having reached fifty, and my parents throw me some very concerned glances if I exceed two glasses of wine per night. My father fears for his rioja, he says. It's not easy for them either.

I'm just numb after S and then T and I miss Amsterdam's streets and the clanging bells of the trams and all of the tiny little pubs with their stocky blond bartenders. There was something very (physically) square about the men there. Like they'd grown up eating too many bitterballen. Sleeping on my brother's floor was an unwelcome throwback to the work experience days, Christ.

Incidentally I might be writing something on 'my quarter-life crisis' (apt) and was telling J, who stayed in Leeds, about it. Although she's engaged, owns a house now and is in a steady (if dull) job, she says she's going through exactly the same thing. She spends all day Googling jobs in London apparently. It just shows you that even the people who appear to have everything together often don't feel like they do, doesn't it?

L x

PS Keep wondering if my new Twitter followers (who all have names like NakedDave and CelluliteJanet) will leave me when they realise I'm not a real naturist.

8

The Long Day's Dying

When I went back home to Bath I found my mum wielding an air rifle in the kitchen. The one she'd confiscated from my brother fifteen years previously.

'BASTARDS!' she shouted, pointing it somewhere near the fields; 5ft 6 and a Phase Eight dress patterned in feathers hitched over one knee. The gun fired twice and I waited for real feathers to explode in the garden.

'Squirrels,' she said, when she saw my face. 'At the fat balls again.'

'Little shits,' my dad said, from the other room, bird-watching binoculars slung around his neck. 'Squirrel-proof? Bit of a con.'

Life at home had changed after the death of our last cat, a bird killer called Leroy we'd rescued from the RSPCA that sat on your lap once a year but mainly skulked nocturnally outside like Pete Doherty, resenting my brother's attempt to re-christen him Leanne Rimes.

'He just can't fight the moonlight,' Charlie said, pulling a face like David Brent.

Without Leroy, the garden was an aviary that's centrepiece was an elaborately large bird feeder under siege from squirrels.

'I'll Vaseline the pole again tomorrow,' my dad said, coming into the kitchen as I realised that my parents' house had turned Ayckbournian since I'd last lived here full-time five years ago.

I opened the fridge and found a pack of ham, then jumped up onto the counter to unpeel it.

'Canapé?' I asked my mum, holding out a pink wet oval.

'Don't be vile,' she said, reaching for a bottle of prosecco in the fridge door instead.

'I don't pop my cork for every guy I meet,' she said, filling three glasses.

'You always say that,' my dad said.

'Do I?'

'Yes.'

'Oh, well, welcome home,' she said to me, clinking her glass against mine, and I remembered how privileged I was to have a refuge, somewhere where my arrival was always seen as a celebration. After Tom, I'd decided to move back in while I reset.

I cheersed her and put the other hand on the counter, almost directly into a jug of meal worms.

'JESUS CHRIST!' I squealed, picking it up and peering at the golden, noodle-y worms, then shivering.

'Pheasant ladies,' they said in unison.

Our garden was cluttered with pheasants now too, apparently, but they were treated to slap-up meal worms instead of John Wayne in Phase Eight.

Unusually, my dad had picked me up from the station after things in London had fallen apart, which was suspicious, and made me think my mum wanted me to tell him about Tom in the car. She already knew most of the story and didn't like secrets, which made me glad to see one married couple still talked honestly, at least.

'How long's he been in the ... er ... office,' my dad asked on the way home.

'Oh years,' I said, accidentally clanging alarm bells.

'Why? How *old* is he?'

I told him.

'*How* old?' he said, swerving precariously on the dual carriage-way. 'And he's married with kids, I suppose.'

'Married with *a* kid yeah but . . .'

'*What?* I was joking.'

'Oh, sorry. He said it was an accident.'

'He tripped on the way down the aisle and landed with a ring on his finger, did he?'

'Apparently,' I said.

'Jesus Christ. Why are you telling me this in the car?'

'I thought I was supposed to.'

'Next time tell me something like this on dry land.'

'There won't be a next time.'

He scoffed. 'Do you . . . *both* need to move back here for a while, until you find somewhere else?' he asked.

'Thanks, but we're done,' I said.

I didn't know what my dad's view on divorce was, given he'd had one before he met my mum. All I knew was that we didn't talk about Gertie, his ballerina of a first wife. I think he'd mentioned her once in my entire life, which was the same number of times he'd mentioned a presenter on Radio 4 I'd found him listening to, before saying, 'I think I used to date that woman,' and walking out the room.

My plan in Bath was to recover, then work out what to do with life next and I knew I was lucky to have the countryside and my parents' house for rehabilitation. My brother and I had both needed it often as a break from London, rolling up on Friday nights wrapped in the sweet smog of a hangover on top of stress but knowing home would fix us before Monday.

'That *air*,' Charlie, who was twenty-four, would say without fail as soon as he arrived.

But he was right. It felt easier to breathe in Bath, where the slower pace of life meant we didn't race around. I thought of home as a recovery venue much like a Priory, although thankfully free, but was as unaware as my parents that Charlie also needed it more permanently that year, having been fired from his job in recruitment just after I'd left Tom. Or he'd left me. Or whatever had actually happened. For my parents, gaining two adult children back home in their sixties must have felt a little like being told they were expecting twins after a vasectomy, I imagined. But before he arrived home, Charlie had told me not to say anything, while he worked out his next move without income or severance pay, but still having to cover £800 a month for his flat.

'So you've been fired?' my mum asked, guessing immediately after he appeared in Bath.

'Um. I'd say it was more of a mutual decision to go our separate ways,' he said, euphemistically.

'Can't you just recruit yourself into something else?' my dad asked.

But Charlie didn't know what he wanted to do, so it was hard to understand which direction he should be ambitious in. All he knew was that he didn't want to work somewhere where part of the job involved fishing hammered MDs out of flowerbeds after they leant like the Tower of Pisa and finally fell.

Having met in London thirty years previously when my mum worked in publishing and my dad was still practising law, our parents were sympathetic to our plight. They knew how tough a city it was to live in, and on the back of the advertising boom in the 1980s (which advertised law firms for the first time), my dad's offices had been so inundated with business that he'd burnt out fast and hadn't worked in the industry since he was forty and had me. He'd sold his share of the firm when his marriage to Gertie ended and he was in the process of moving to a farmhouse in Cornwall with their formerly shared Great Dane when he met my mum. She'd seen his ad on the dating page of *Time Out* – although they left that part of the story out for two decades in the same way people who'd met virtually did, years later, when the newness of it felt embarrassing until it was the norm.

'That was in the days of letter writing,' my dad said, as I tried to spur myself out of heartbreak with the idea of a rebound, not wanting to at all, but knowing – with irritation – that they worked.

'How many replies did you get?' I asked.

'Oh. Twenty, thirty,' he said, literally describing the equivalent of 'likes' in the '80s.

'Did you meet all of them!?'

'No, no. I threw away the ones with awful spelling, or handwriting like a five-year-old. Then I was left with about six. So I called up the first three and met them. That was no good. Two just seemed to want . . . a fling, I think, and the third one was a bit odd. So then I rang the next three, and the fourth person I met was Mum and I thought, *Yes, that'll do*, and never called the others.'

'Sounds exactly the same as Tinder,' I said.

'Yeah, well, it is really. It's all just chance in the end,' he said.

Pinning so much on chance frightened me because you couldn't command chance at all and trying to grab the reins of my life, when it all seemed so out of my control, was a coping mechanism.

But my mum agreed, only having the conviction to leave a long-term university relationship when she was thirty-four, and going on a couple of blind dates, where she was *unconvinced* (she said politely) before meeting my dad.

'I thought Dad was rich when I met him,' she laughed. 'He'd just sold his company.'

'I thought you were rich, too,' he said. 'You said you were wealthy and your dad was a famous author.'

'I wouldn't have used the word wealthy,' my mum said.

'You did.'

'I probably said healthy.'

'"I'm healthy and my dad's a famous author"?' he said, disbelievingly.

'I wouldn't have said famous. He wasn't by then.'

My dad just looked at me.

They were dating for six months when my dad asked her to move to Fowey with him and she weighed up the options before joining him two weeks later. In that time, she'd had his handwriting analysed by a graphologist; wary of the stack of Ralph Lauren polo shirts in every colour my dad had still tagged and shop-folded at his flat. 'Very *American Psycho*,' she whispered.

We'd grown up so normally that it was hard to imagine their life once lavish. After burnout my dad worked less, and instead renovated the run-down houses we lived in, so we moved a lot, downsizing quite frequently, although he made them all look beautiful in the end: '70s wallpaper patterned with strawberries scraped off the walls, and avocado-coloured baths ripped out.

The farm they moved to in Fowey eventually consisted of chickens, ducks, some cats, my dad's Great Dane, two peacocks and two goats, who constantly but unsuccessfully tried to leap fences and broke their legs, causing my mum to sit in their stables and talk to them while nursing bandaged limbs and a pregnancy with me. They considered buying a pig, but decided against the smell, and the chickens quickly disappeared thanks to foxes.

It was a unique farm, in other words, but it was theirs and I have a couple of bucolic memories of being taken in the early morning to chicken coops to check for eggs (or massacres, maybe). We moved to Falmouth soon after, where my dad did a fine art degree at Falmouth School of Art a few doors down from our big house. He came home for lunch and threw socks into the tree in the front garden for me, then helped me climb a ladder, aged four, to pick them like apples from the branches. My favourite game.

After that there was a tiny flat next door, and then Cornwall behind us, no jobs and no good state schools, they said, and so Bath, with four more moves in that middle-class, academic city where I couldn't play in the waves. Instead, we walked about the fields and I decided very adamantly that I'd live in a tree if we were ever homeless, because then you could eat blackberries for dinner. At eight years old I thought we moved a lot because we were poor and I didn't understand why the dishevelled people begging in town didn't want to live in the fields and eat blackberries too. I didn't know that the renovations were how my dad contributed to the salary my mum carried us on.

Given the endless search for a home my life became later, it's strange to remember that I was worried about homelessness from a young age and, of course, we were never even close. My mum had watched her own father write himself famous and rich, but gamble and drink a lot of it away and he'd gone bankrupt twice when she was a child so she was careful with money. I haven't got a single memory of the actual house moves, so either my parents managed them superbly or I blocked them out completely. I still have to write a list of everywhere we lived in order to remember all the houses, and because my friends were usually left behind, too, I expected the people in the new locations to never be there forever either.

When I got back to Bath and thought about the London rental scene I'd descend back into as soon as I left my parents' house, I wondered if everyone resented their twenties as much as strawberry wallpaper. The main differences between my generation's experience and that of my parents seemed to be that the landlord didn't cook you dinner or give you a curfew and increased the rent every year. No one was arguing that it wasn't harder to get on the property ladder now, but everyone had slummed it, and heartbreak was always the same, even if you were essentially going through two break-ups simultaneously, as I was with Sam and Tom, which felt as grim as it sounds.

'Everyone's twenties are shit,' my dad said, describing it as a rite of passage while my mum lamented 'the brown rice years'.

'It wasn't really until you were a few rungs up the ladder, maybe owned your own flat and had two salaries to put towards a mortgage that you could start drinking scrumpy and eating crisps in a pub,' he said. 'Until then everyone just made the best of it, went out once when they got paid, then recovered the rest of the month, trying not to borrow so much that the next pay cheque was wiped out before you even got it.'

But there were big changes too, of course. In my generation co-buying a house was prioritised over marriage by couples who didn't have to marry to live together and couldn't afford a wedding *and* a house anyway. Women could prioritise their careers, freeze their eggs in their thirties to buy time, then get a heavy mortgage while they waited for a man, knowing single parenthood was less stigmatised if they needed, or wanted, to do it alone. Dating apps had made love and commitment fickle and less necessary, in some ways, although we were made desperate for something real after years of tiresome liaisons. By thirty, sexual freedom was turning to fatigue.

As my dad had worked out via his *Time Out* ad, first dates often didn't go *hugely well* anyway, even if Tinder did make a great international tour guide, as my brother was finding. Having not been single in the app era until now, I listened and learnt, increasingly envious of Charlie's new tactic to travel the world alone and find a local date to show him round when he got there. I knew women often got murdered for trying to do the same thing.

Not that it was always as glamorous as it sounds for my brother either. In Boston he'd persuaded a Tinder girl to come on a whale-watching tour but they'd barely been talking for half an hour before he went to the bathroom and got locked inside, the crew begging him not to sue the company after failing to kick the door down. Three hours later, and not having seen a single whale, he was released back at shore after they'd taken the door off its hinges, and found his Tinder date had disappeared. 'Went for lobster rolls after that, so – her loss,' he said.

My parents listened in horror to his tales of failed international romance and modernised the evening rule of no phones at the dinner table into: 'No Tinder at the dinner table', presumably in an attempt to save him from future disaster.

After London, life in Bath did seem slow and empty as we tried to get used to my parents' new life, which had changed to suit empty-nest syndrome years earlier and now included cinema dates and Moscow Mules at the neighbours' house.

We were just two of 3.4 million millennials, according to the ONS, who'd fled back to parents' houses in 2016 and were grateful for the option, even if the political and social differences between our generations were clear to both sides. My dad now referred regularly to a new friend called Jacob, who was everything he'd been looking for, he explained. 'He comes to the door once every four years, says hello, and fucks off again,' he said of our local MP, Rees-Mogg, while the rest of us tried to believe he was joking. It certainly had a satirical effect when my dad referred to Greta Thunberg as the 'Scandinavian witch child' and my mum told my dad that *he* was the only person who'd have been burnt at the stake.

Studies were looking into whether boomerang kids were ruining their parents' health by interrupting their new freedom, but that didn't seem to be a problem here. 'Are you able to forage for yourselves tonight?' my dad would call on their way out the door and, soon after, we could practically hear the Moscow Mules clinking next door, my brother and I lying on the sofas eating crisps and ham and feeling weirdly rejected.

My dad admitted two boomerangs really did make the ship creak, but wanted us to know we always had a refuge if we needed one, having once needed to go home himself and been told there was no room by his own parents.

'Was it that small house in Blackburn?' I asked.

'No, they had a hotel in Cornwall then with *fourteen* rooms!' he said, still annoyed forty years later.

Having to return home as an adult ignited so many ideas of failure, though, and my brother and I both felt it strongly, I knew. The

failure to move out and look after ourselves well enough to stop
our parents worrying about us, number one, but smaller failures
about not being able to keep a job, afford rent, stay in love, and
stay abroad, in my case, made us both feel lost and more helplessly
infantile than we'd have liked. Charlie now got a lift to work with
my mum and a packed lunch, too, and called his old school friends
as I fixed my eyes on London, thinking I'd only temporarily failed
at that. As the search for a job and a room began again I wondered
when my restlessness would cease, hoping I'd one day be able to
ride the desired shock of the new into something more stable and
calm. I found it hard to tell whether I was running away from
something or towards it most of the time.

Break-ups always feel like failures, and I felt suffocated by
betrayal after Tom; the hole in my heart making me feel stone-
cold and self-destructive. Two weeks after I'd come home, his
confession that he couldn't leave his child ringing in my ears, he
was saying that he couldn't *stay* and wanted to flat-hunt again.
'You're joking?' I replied, to his am-dram emails, bored of the
pretty words he'd promised there'd be something more concrete
behind. 'I did that, remember. You didn't turn up.'

I missed him all the time and hated wondering what he was
doing and how he was, sprinting around the break-up lanes, as I
now thought of the winding country tracks around my parents'
house, to run another man out of my mind. Then I sat in the fields
with eyelashes mascaraed with tears, distraught at how brutally
Tom had rocked my idea of who he was, but also who I was, what
love meant and what promises and honesty equated to.

Knowing he'd started lying to me too made me feel so stupid
for thinking someone who omitted things, or glazed over the
truth so completely and compulsively, could ever find an oasis of
honesty in anyone, as he claimed he'd found in me. I was angry,
then, wondering if he really thought I was moronic enough to
believe him anymore.

I hadn't spoken to Liam since I'd left him in Brighton the day we'd broken up, but I craved talking to someone who knew me and messaged him to say I wasn't sure I was alright, then found FaceTime ringing on my phone with his name. After he'd listened to what had happened he said he was worried I'd learnt to chase stories too much, bypassing my own happiness in the process. Is that what I was doing, I wondered? I hadn't felt like I was, but I didn't know what to feel any more. I just felt used.

Exes often help in break-ups, I thought, when you've lost all idea of identity, and need to feel known by someone you don't have to act for. The numbness I felt made me want to drink in the same way I did in London, where you could escape things by surrounding yourself with a crowd, but that was harder at this Priory version of home, my parents increasingly more sober with age, arguing they were too old for hangovers, and had suffered too many for one lifetime, anyway.

They preferred alliterative reasons to drink now, Charlie and I realised, Wednesday Wine Night the only acceptable evening of merriment outside the weekend.

'What about . . . muddled Mondays?' I asked.

'Tanked-up Tuesdays?' Charlie said.

'Thirsty Thursdays is genuinely a thing,' I said.

'Smashed Sundays!'

'We're allowed to drink on Sundays,' I said.

'Oh yeah.'

'You live at home now,' they said, which won every time.

The emptiness was exacerbated by alcohol, but I'd become so used to managing my emotions with it that I felt I still needed a drink to act as a block. That was entirely different to the way my brother drank, I saw after we'd both moved back there. Charlie lamented pre-drinks gone past and climbed trees with boys called Dave the Rave and Louis the Gooch with crates of beer to play Possum, an unsurprisingly Australian invention that's only rule was that you couldn't leave the tree before finishing the cans. He binged like all of our generation, but socially and as a game.

I drank wine in mugs, so as not to worry my parents, I told myself, but secretly I wanted my drinking to be invisible, too. I'd glued myself back together on the surface, but beneath it, I was a state. I also felt the weight of the past in relation to alcohol, knowing my mum's parents had both drunk heavily, in polar ways. My grandad drank socially, loudly, surrounded by people, but constantly and with anger running alongside it, fuelled by the Second World War he'd joined at sixteen that had left shrapnel in his body, and presumably more in his mind. Celia, the grandmother I'd never known, drank quietly, secretly, hiding empty whisky bottles around the house, after divorce, and my mum came back from university to clear the empties and try to make her eat something, calling doctors, watching her being taken away, then going back to Leeds and trying to pass exams, be normal. I wanted to be as strong as she was, but worried I wasn't.

I just didn't know how to start dealing with any of what had happened and thought of drinking as a way to forget, momentarily, the tumbling sense of loss. The end of Tom had left wide open the real void he'd been distracting me from: Sam, who I'd spent the last three years with, but known for seven and was now gone.

Yet in the emptiness I started to see how little I really knew about my parents' lives before me and realised it was a rare opportunity to start a dialogue I'd previously not been old enough to know how to broach. Being home, I guess, showed me how I'd been more fascinated by the company of strangers and conquests, but asked nowhere near enough about the two people I should want to know everything about.

My dad was particularly enigmatic: eloquent, but without much interest in being so, and growing up, my brother and I had learnt to read his mood on canvas, coming downstairs as kids to find existential new paintings which asked: Would you say you were made to feel valued and important?

We looked at each other, then back at the yellow letters on blue oil paint. Beneath them were three tick boxes: Yes, No, Maybe.

'Mum, is Dad having a breakdown?' we asked then.

'Oh – no. *Honda* wrote to him,' she said gravely. 'He phoned them up and was apparently not made to feel at all valued or important, and then they wrote asking if he had been made to feel valued and . . . '

'The AUDACITY,' my dad said, creaking the floorboards on his way into the kitchen.

With two authors for parents, my mum was used to living with moody creatives and fell often into an observer role, that I'd picked up to some extent. She was good at not minding when his 'studio' (the garage) moved inside for the winter and covered a small sitting room with oil paint and the occasional passive-aggressive canvas. She liked less that he moved her watercolours of Venice from prime-time viewing spots in our gallery of a house to a millimetre above a skirting board behind a door that never opened, my dad arguing that watercolours were *not* art.

At twenty-six, I'd started to understand that my parents were the two people who could help me understand who I really was, and I felt like a professional interviewer who'd failed to question her own genes, which was kind of hypocritical. With my dad, who didn't talk about the past if he could avoid it, it was about just being there to glean the memories dropped unconsciously into conversation, I saw, when I came downstairs one morning to find him blaring Shostakovich in the front room.

'What's going on?' I asked.

'One of our relatives just died,' he said.

'Really?' I said, knowing it couldn't have been a close one. 'Should we be . . . sad?' I asked.

'Not really,' he said. 'He spent the last four years of life thinking he was Prince Charles, which isn't a bad way to go.'

Being there to hear their memories – subconscious stories they didn't even realise they were telling – made me aware of how much I didn't know, and aware of how much history was lost if you didn't ask to hear it.

More than anything that time at home taught me what a direct, complex mix of my very different parents I was and how that had made me feel cut into polar opposite traits that were sometimes difficult to manage side by side. I was extremely social but sometimes socially anxious; introvert but extrovert; kind but impatient. As opinionated as my dad – but listened as much as my mum.

'What is an existential crisis?' I Googled. I was pretty sure I was having a huge one. Tom had given me a book on existentialism for my birthday and I flicked it open to read his dedication for the hundredth time. 'To the best existentialist I know,' it said in the front, but I felt unknown to myself then, and so lost trying to work out who I was in a room filled with Beanie Babies and pictures of my life so far. A literary map of London Tom had given me hung on the wall next to Sam's photographs of Edinburgh's barbershops and the film poster for my grandfather's most famous book: *The Long Day's Dying*.

I missed Sam more as I tried to work out life alone in the time warp. We'd been texting each other, lonely in our new, separate lives apart. He in Amsterdam, and me having stepped on a viper on the snakes and ladders board we'd played life on, and been thrown back to the beginning.

'Shall I come and see you?' I asked Sam, still needing to get my stuff back.

'I dunno, Luce,' he said. 'Can I think about it?'

'Of course.'

It was heart-wrenching to know he didn't want me anymore, but I couldn't blame him. I'd wrecked our relationship utterly and wasn't yet sure whether he'd want to salvage a friendship. Then the next day I woke up to an email telling me to come if I still wanted to.

'I'm looking forward to seeing you again,' I read. 'Even though it's very dangerous and my heart is going to break again when you leave. I'm sure it's better to have something nice for a day instead of never.'

I held my breath as I quickly read the rest in order not to cry.

'I dreamt about you last night. I'm sorry that we took each other for granted and looked down on each other and pushed each other away. I'm sorry I can't cook as well as you and I'm sorry that I couldn't change when you asked me to. I miss you.'

Then I cried.

I still couldn't believe we'd ended like we did, but I knew that getting back together, even if Sam agreed – which why would he? – wasn't what I wanted either. I'd loved him, but I knew we weren't right for so many reasons neither of us could change. And shouldn't have to.

I thought of it as goodbye when we met less than a week later, Sam waiting at Centraal station, looking more hipster than ever. Before the sadness arrived, we just laughed and felt happy, almost, at being reconciled. We walked to the ferry at the back of the station to cross to a bar he'd found on the water since I'd left. Amsterdam Noord stretched out backwards behind it and an August wind blew hard off the river Ij.

'I'm so sorry,' I said.

'I know,' he said, pursing his lips. 'You and Charlie both texted me to tell me you missed me this week. I miss you both. Maybe you slightly more.'

Break-ups often involved so much more than just the two people who'd been in it, I saw: the families either side; the neighbourhoods of local pubs and restaurants you'd loved when you were together. Everything changed when it was over. Even the takeaway menus.

We walked through Amsterdam along the canals I'd often walked alone when we'd lived there together, and went back to a bar on the Neinmarket opposite the clock tower, an old haunt we'd found early on. Sam dropped my bag on the floor and went inside to order Jupiler beers as I lit a cigarette, listening to a thin, precocious young woman opposite jabbering in Dutch-accented English to her friends about the Brussels attacks.

'What happened was really bad, but when it happens just before your exams you're like *really, guys?*'

'I'm just so desensitized to it,' said a long-haired girl lighting a roll-up, who thought she was cooler. 'Did you go out at the weekend? Me neither. I feel like, you know, I care less than when I was eighteen, when I was like, maybe younger in my head, you know? Like – I'm more concentrated on my work now and I've probably already had all those experiences of going out anyway.'

I snorted and felt their heads turn, as mine turned away. Imagine thinking you'd seen everything by twenty, I thought, or whatever age they were. I was only twenty-six, but I felt so much older than them as they discussed a world I knew they'd barely seen yet. I wondered if the cynical view I had of it, now, was Tom's fault for involving me in the problems you faced later on in life, before it was my time to. Had I really thought I could handle the complications of someone else's dissolving marriage, I berated myself, knowing I'd not realised until afterwards the extent to which I was in way too deep.

Tom had been stalking my Instagram account, too, and was sending vitriolic messages having guessed who I was in Amsterdam to see.

'I haven't done anything wrong and you're going to fuck your ex-boyfriend?' he texted.

You haven't done anything wrong? I thought. *Are you joking?*

But the stream continued:

'Are you getting back together?'

'How many times?'

'Why are you doing this to me?'

It's always telling when you realise people make everything about themselves because you could be anyone really. You're just a screen for narcissism's projection.

'We should have stayed in Edinburgh,' I said, when Sam got back with the half pints the Dutch insisted on serving. 'We were happy there.'

'We argued *all the time* in Edinburgh,' he said. 'I loved you more than anything, Luce, but I don't know where the picture of our blissful past comes from. We argued every time I came to Newcastle, too. But when I thought about those arguments more recently, I realised we were always two bottles of wine in. I knew our drinking was becoming a problem. I thought that would tear us apart. If we'd stopped and found it wasn't that, then maybe that would have been telling, quicker. Maybe it would have been different.'

I felt like crying so much of the time I was with him, overcome by guilt now we were looking at each other again and crippled with sadness about the end that was my fault. His laugh still exploded as he loped along next to me, but I could see the pain in his eyes and the way he still pushed his lips together when he was trying not to say something. 'It's really fucking hard to get over you, you know?' he said, and I cried for real, then.

Sleeping next to him still felt so normal that it felt like nothing had changed while I was there and I had to force myself to remember it had as we got stoned and ate peanut butter out of the jar in the new flat he'd found with three Greeks in IJburg. I admired him so much for staying and couldn't believe that what had happened to Danny and Anna had happened to us now, too. I knew Sam was trying not to ask about Tom, but he knew me too well not to know something was really wrong.

'You know, if you were going to leave me for a man ten

years older, you could have picked a James Bond type,' he said, trying to laugh.

'You looked him up?'

'I had to.'

Another knife in the side from social media, I thought, which at no point in the course of a relationship ever actually helped. Before you got together with someone new, you could now scroll through a show reel of idyllic times spent with an ex – when they were liked, of course – and compare yourself unfavourably with all of it. The knowledge that people only posted the best bits, and not the screaming rows or the boredom somehow incomprehensible in the face of jealousy and self-doubt.

Tom was fuming because he said he'd stopped posting pictures of his other life while we were together and thought seeing Sam on my Instagram was a betrayal, despite the fact he'd still not left his wife and expected me to hang around on the side even after we had broken up. The hypocrisy of it was astounding but helpful, despite the pain, in showing me how much I didn't want to be with him.

I'd also been right about Sam, I saw, regretfully, who was so lovely but made me wonder if I thought I'd loved him so much because he'd adored *me* so confidently when I'd needed someone to. The old annoyances vibrated around us that weekend: I was too impatient and he was too slow; he wanted to stay in and I wanted to go out. We didn't have books or art or the news in common to talk about when we did either.

'I love you but you're fucking hard work,' he said, when I got the train back to Schiphol.

'I love you too, but you are so fucking annoying,' I said, and we smiled at each other sadly.

We'd see each other again and in the future we'd call when we needed to cling to a buoy in the middle of rough seas, but we'd tied a bow on our life together after the initial savage fallout after Tom.

I flew back to London, relieved I was meeting Mat in the airport and flying straight to Berlin to stay with Tris, who now lived there. I needed another city of booze and drugs and noise to distract myself from the consciousness I loathed and when I got home, I vowed, I would go back to London and start again, regardless of the fact I was still heavily bruised from the last fight in the ring.

I'd had an interview in London at a big tabloid and it looked likely I was going to be offered the job; so then I'd just need a room, I thought, with a sense of déjà vu. The fact I'd only left the house in Clapham six months ago seemed absurd. It felt like years since I'd left London for Amsterdam, but the price of chasing adventure, I now saw, was that I'd become a commitment-phobe who craved permanence. How was I supposed to find stability when I was scared of sitting still, I wondered, as Mat bowled towards me over the concourse.

'Oi, oi,' he called.

'At last,' I said. 'Let's get airport drunk. The last time I was here I was going to Cuba with Tom,' I added.

'Lucy, Lucy, Lucy,' he said, having got me through the first leg of the European break-up drama and now about to get me through the void of having neither of the men involved.

Dear Everleigh,

Have you ever been to Berlin? I just got back and had to queue
outside a club called the Berghain for TWO AND A HALF
HOURS. We'd heard gothic looks helped tough entry, so
Tris wore eyeliner and a beanie that made him look a bit
like a leukaemia patient. All I had was a black jumper that
said peanut butter on the front in Dutch. Mat had forgotten
anything black, so wore a lumberjack shirt. An hour in I was
quite sure we were going to be rejected by the four doormen
of this unique apocalypse when a girl emerged from the club
in a swimsuit and sat on a rock eating chips. I think she'd been
in there since Friday. A woman in front of us was wearing a
dog collar attached to a lead held by her girlfriend, I presume.
It was 8 a.m. on a Sunday morning. Clubs are church here, but
thank God we were turned away at the door. I think I thought
I was quite cool before joining that queue. Could not have been
happier to find I am not.

L x

Dear Lucy

I'm pleased to say I've never been to Berlin, or a nightclub. We saw Berlin on a television programme and were very clear that it was not a place we would enjoy in the slightest.

May the gods continue to bless you,

Everleigh

9

NEVERWHERE

When I arrived back in London it was the height of summer and there was a fairground atmosphere in the streets. Hysteria almost, at the relentless political nightmares and atrocities in the news that constantly flashed on phone screens; horror buzzing and beeping with different ringtones everywhere.

There was Trump and Clinton; Boris Johnson and Brexit. 'Sir Shifty' papped on a £100 million superyacht while BHS workers were interviewed about surviving without a pension now Philip Green had sold the company for £1 to a serial bankrupted ex-racing car driver.

A couple of teenage Isis fans had beheaded an 83-year-old priest at the altar of a church in France. Not even his church; he was just covering someone's holiday, apparently. Channel 5 had accidentally aired a *Postman Pat* episode in which he appeared to be stamping on a Quran and another lunatic near Tokyo had gone on a stabbing spree in a care home, wanting to rid the world of disabled people. Shootings in Munich and Berlin followed Paris and Brussels.

In politics Corbyn was accused of killing the Labour Party while features desks asked whether Theresa May was the new Cara Delevingne, and the *Mail* tried to prove Trump's daughter was a prostitute. Then Bernie Ecclestone's new mother-in-law was kidnapped in Rio and the papers boiled like Central line commuters transported in heat above the legal limit for cattle.

Every time something huge happened, a shimmer of shock rippled through the office of the paper I now worked for and incredulity was drawn constantly on the faces of my new colleagues. Every day had started to feel like April Fool's Day but the fact the PM was singing to himself seconds after announcing his resignation was beyond ludicrous. Yes, Cameron looked like a C-3PO made of ham, as Caitlin Moran had noted, but the fact he seemed so pleased to be leaving the country in the shit after the Brexit vote was totally unnerving, regardless of whether you rated him or not.

On top of all the other ineptitude, Everleigh emailed to say the papers were quoting the entirely wrong play on the back of the Michael Gove/Boris Johnson backstabbing. 'The meeja seem to be paralleling Gove's pulling the plug on Boris with Iago which is surely absolutely the wrong play; wouldn't envious Casca stabbing Caesar in the back be a better parallel?' he said. I emailed back to say Gove's wife, who was now one of my colleagues, had been described as 'away' in her last two columns.

Political chaos just made me feel like I was watching a public breakdown after my personal one. It was highly unsettling, but I'd learnt in my early twenties that three things helped broken hearts: alcohol, books and time. Or was it that booze exhausted time and books extinguished thought until you could sleep off another day? I never worked it out, I just knew alcohol made it a hell of a lot easier and escapism dropped the curtain on an act you'd had enough of. When it rose again, the stage and the audience were easier to bear.

In my new flat near Kew, I woke to a stabbing sensation and fished a hand further down the bed to locate the sharpness, throwing the screwdriver onto the floor. I checked my phone: Saturday. No missed calls. Relief and despair both settled in me then as I swung out of bed and opened my door to find my new landlady's dog waiting for me on the other side.

'Oh, hello,' I said, reaching down to stroke Marie Antoinette.

'Where's Lottie?' I asked her, as she followed me down the hall and I noted the tobacco clouds floating in the sitting room, which meant she'd been here recently.

In the kitchen I peered into my empty cupboard. Eggs. Only. Again. I cracked two into a pan then stood at the stove eating the scrambled efforts with a spatula, feeling myself watched.

'You want a duck fillet, don't you?' I asked, as Marie Antoinette's ears pricked, and I put my saucepan down to rifle in a cupboard of treats more stocked than mine.

I held a dried duck fillet in my hand and sniffed it. Could people eat these, I wondered? Raising it slowly to my mouth, I extended the tip of my tongue to the treat and flicked it around my mouth for tasting notes.

'Bloody hell that is rank,' I told Marie A, handing it to her, then taking my saucepan to the sitting room where *Inspector Morse* (which she 'watched' when Lottie was out) blared from the screen.

'Who's going to die next?' I asked her as she curled into a ball next to me and went to sleep.

Having arrived back in London after a two-month recuperation in Bath, I was resurrecting my old life but had learnt fast that live-in landlords presented a different set of problems to regular flatmates. Lottie was a friend of a friend with a spare room and I'd been enticed by the fact that I didn't have to sign a contract. After my experiences with living situations so far I was reluctant to tie myself down anywhere, knowing how life could flip without warning, but I'd also lost the ability to imagine it full-stop more than six months down the line.

Owning the house meant it was the live-in landlord's territory totally, I now saw. That meant I didn't say anything when I realised Lottie smoked more than the Industrial Revolution inside or left her job to become a professional dog walker now she had an income from me. Instead I flung my curtains open each morning to find the cast of *Lady and the Tramp* shitting all over the garden and just hoped she wouldn't go out and leave them all with me, as she had once. Really, honest flat viewings should involve a 24-hour stay, I thought, when I realised a TFL alarm clock started in my bedroom at half five and continued every seven minutes until midnight; the Tube trains hitting the track like bullets at the end of the garden: tur, tur tur tur tur, tur tur tur tur, tur tur tur tur. I lay in bed counting the rhythm I now knew off by heart and thinking it could be worse, given I'd viewed the flat so drunk I couldn't remember what number it was when I moved in.

'It's all right actually, isn't it?' I asked my mum, looking around my new room, as she eyed me suspiciously on move-in day.

Possibly the hardest part was that Lottie often left the back door next to my room wide open all night by accident, which meant I slept with a screwdriver in my bed in a half-hearted attempt at self-protection, wondering if I'd wake up with someone in my room.

On other nights I jumped awake thinking Tom was there or in the garden, because he'd insisted on seeing me after I arrived back in London and then later, when I told him I never wanted to see him again, turned up at the flat while I hid behind the sitting-room curtains and Lottie told him I wasn't in. Maybe my mind was exaggerating what he'd do, but he'd also proved he wasn't going to let me go easily and I cursed myself for being lonely enough to have once let him stay over at the new flat, which meant he now knew where I lived. One night I'd had 40 missed calls from him and streams of relentless communications were common: 30 or 40 texts, plus emails and messages on social media, until I blocked him, finally.

Lottie's was a good place to be broken-hearted, because, in her mid-forties, she was so overwhelmingly bored by men that she never brought a single one to the house the whole time I was there.

'I haven't had a lover since the Bahamas,' she told me every few weeks. 'I've been proposed to nine times. But I couldn't stand a husband getting in the way of things. I'm too used to living on my own and doing things my own way. Aren't I, Marie A?' she'd say, flinging a duck fillet onto a shaggy green rug on the living-room floor that looked like fake grass.

It was only when she worried about money that she slightly changed her tune, wandering into rooms cackling into her phone about needing a rich old man with a huge pension, then lapsing into laughter that gargled hoarsely in her throat with a chain smoker's cough. Love or money, I thought. As usual.

I found peace by the river during that time and ran along the Thames from Kew to Chiswick feeling the world begin to right itself again. But I was jumpy, too, because Tom was refusing to leave me alone, and had emailed a senior editor at the tabloid I now worked at asking if I'd started yet. Claiming he needed to talk to me about something I'd done for him in my last job, I saw, when the email was forwarded straight to me. Then he guessed my new email address and I was jolted with shock when his name popped up on my screen in my first days trying to impress a new desk.

I forwarded the emails quickly to the personal address I'd blocked him from, deleted them from my work inbox, and then sat, as soon as I could, in a bathroom cubicle reading them shakily on my phone, feeling like my life was being wrenched backwards just as I was righting the present.

I'm so gutted about us. I know you said you didn't mean it when you said I was the love of your life. It was a silly, puppyish phrase to use. But I've never felt that way about anyone and I believe the same goes for you. I fucked it up. I'm so sorry. X

PS I know these unanswered rants are annoying to you and humiliating for me. But I don't feel I have anything to lose now. And they make me feel slightly better. Selfishly. I was just so used to being able to tell you how I felt about everything. That's one of the things I miss most.

PPS I've not given up hope. I know you'll think that's deluded. I should stop wallowing and get on with things. But there it is. As you once said, nothing this important ever came easy.

PPPS I'm in Amsterdam. Yet another place that's freighted with meaning and will always be. I find it very hard walking around London. So many fucking memories. That park by Embankment where we drank prosecco. Cycling from Koko to the station with you behind me, drunkenly complaining. We drove past the end of your road the other day on the way to Richmond. I couldn't explain why I started crying.

'We', I noted.

At the height of my distrust, I'd become so desperate for the truth I'd called a private investigator and might have employed them to find it out for me if I'd had £2,000 to pay the apparently necessary four spies to follow him. That seemed a bit *much* all round. Instead, he admitted enough of it, in the end. That he'd never moved out, that they were not separating, and that was enough for me never to go back. I hated him and everything he stood for after that and felt unbelievably lucky not to be as tied to him as his wife was.

But the emails were constant and harassing and I'd started looking over my shoulder as I walked home in the dark from the Tube, feeling followed by a jumpiness that was caused by more than Tom. At home, I waited for the doorbell, scared he'd turn up again, remembering what Libby had said about older men losing their minds when you tried to leave them.

The screwdriver was a silly idea that allowed me to get to sleep, clutching the metal under my pillow in case any man wandered through the door left open by Lottie, but I couldn't escape Tom in unconsciousness either. Overnight I dreamt I was swimming with my eyes open at the bottom of an electric-blue pool and felt chlorine searing the whites of my eyes as I tried to look up towards the people standing at the sides of the pool. The water made their shapes quiver and blur and in the dream my eyes closed, and some of the shapes tried to fish me out from the bottom and I finally recognised Tom, standing near the back, doing nothing. Letting me drown.

For distraction, I threw myself into my new job, where I was writing a list of subjects liked and disliked by the tabloid's editors, as I had done during my first weeks on the broadsheet before it. It wasn't dissimilar, but here they hated millennials and were more interested in watches. Amazingly someone had decided that I would make a good health editor, so other hot topics included Raynaud's, UTIs, osteoporosis and plus-sized models with dental phobias. Basically anything that bothered the readers, who were mostly over sixty.

The fact I'd been employed as a health editor caused the same reaction amongst everyone that knew me. 'You?' they'd say, before lapsing into what I professionally considered quite unhealthy levels of hysteria.

Both readers and PRs called daily to suggest features on piles, prostates or athlete's foot which made me avoid calls from the switchboard first thing when I was hungover, in case I threw up. Yet taking the job had meant I'd had a pay rise of £13,000, which helped leaping out of London to Amsterdam and back again seem worth it, knowing I'd have waited ten years for a similar rise if I'd stayed where I was. My saving grace, I considered, was that I wasn't proud, and could therefore write about anything for the right money, as long as I'd had a Berocca first.

The routine of office life was making me more sure of my sanity than the forest isolations of Amsterdam and the money cushioned the hours I spent in it, so life felt easier all round. The downside was that my niche new area of expertise meant I could only give medical advice to sexagenarians, and my conversation in the pub after work often plummeted into statements about how everyone should be taking vitamin D between October and April.

The pub was a safe place to be, because I was guaranteed to see none of the other health editors, and it didn't take long each week for the two good friends I'd found in the office – Amy, a fashion editor who could have been scouted by *TOWIE*, and Emily, a Vogue-smoking 24-year-old PA to one of the editors, to suggest we descend onto one of the paper's haunts where white wine helped me forget the obscure ailment I'd been reading up on that day. The problem was that Amy was usually going on holiday somewhere our cruise-obsessed readers might catch something I now knew about.

'It's forty degrees in Mauritius, *I can't waittt*,' she'd say in sing-song Essex, flicking a perfect curtain of glossy hair over her shoulder.

'Your main concern is probably ciguatera,' I'd tell her in a form of health editor Tourette's.

'Ciggy-what?' she'd say.

'Ohhhhh ciggy,' Emily would say then, picking up her pack of Vogues in one hand and the wine in the other in preparation to move into the smoking area.

'Yeah all right,' I'd agree, giving up. Happily.

I'd made looking surface-level fine a talent back then, but in truth I was only fine around other people and I didn't want to be on my own in the evenings because I was too worried I'd ring Tom. I knew he'd leave whatever he was doing in a heartbeat to see me, but then what? It would be the same shit all over again, I told myself.

Knowing he was metaphorically unreachable in the same city was horrible, and to avoid my head filling with memories that might persuade me to text him, I went out, where company and booze acted as a diversion from the fact I felt broken without him. That's what we always did when something was wrong before 2020: dressed up and went out.

But it was dangerous when you weren't all right underneath, I realised, waking up mid-week at Libby's (I thought) after I'd agreed to buy her a drink in Notting Hill when she got fired.

'Please tell me you have straighteners,' I whined, peeling my eyes open and seeing a room that wasn't mine, before I looked across the pillow.

'Who are you?' I asked the woman in bed next to me, then looked down and realised I was wearing a Victorian nightgown. 'Are you a Good Samaritan?' I asked, quite seriously, as she burst out laughing and I wondered in quick succession whether we'd slept together/how I'd got here/whether I was still in London.

'I've been lying here awake for ages, worried you'd *freak* when you woke up,' Polly, she told me her name was, said then, before telling me the rest of it. She'd been cycling home late from a restaurant in town when she'd noticed me crumpled at a bus stop and thought how hammered I looked, before U-turning her bike and coming to check I was all right. 'At that point I realised you didn't know where you lived, didn't have Uber – and you told me to call someone named Tom, but he didn't answer,' she said.

'Typical,' I said.

'So I thought you better come home with me,' she added, as I just stared at her across the pillows and she explained how she'd waited for the bus, told the driver where to let me get off, cycled ahead and then retrieved me back off the double-decker and walked me to hers. 'I put you in the spare room,' she said. 'And gave you that,' she added, pointing to the Victorian nightgown. 'I was writing you a note explaining you were safe and in Hammersmith when you crawled in here and asked if you could sleep next to me.'

'Jesus *Christ*,' I said, wincing with embarrassment. 'Thank you very, very, very much,' I added, before explaining who Tom was, and why I was such a wreck.

I was still drunk, I think, when I put her name into my phone,

because, once we became friends and after I'd moved in with her
a year later, the phone screen told me it was *Good Samaritans Ltd*
whenever she called. I was known to all the regulars in her local
as the one Polly had picked up at the bus stop and I didn't mind
at all, knowing someone much more dangerous could have found
me. I felt like I might owe Polly my life.

'One *tiny* thing,' I said, as she handed me a towel so I could
have a shower. 'Realising, of course, that you've done more than
enough already . . .'

'I have straighteners,' she said.

'And is there *any* chance I could borrow a dress to wear to work?
I'm a health editor,' I added, and I don't think I've heard anyone
laugh louder than she laughed then.

For a couple of years after that, the fact I'd woken up in the bed
of a (straight) female plumber after a night out was just a funny
story, and I wasn't mortified in the slightest as I told friends, and
heard them repeat it to others.

Polly wasn't all right either, I worked out later, but her guard
was up all the time too in a developed defence against the world.
I think I thought talking about *what* had happened, meant I was
dealing with it, but I can see now that I never actually talked about
how any of it made me feel. I guess because I felt like crying a
lot of the time, and didn't understand why, and knew kindness or
sympathy would open a dam.

It took a while for me to realise how similar Polly and I were:
laughing everything off, always talking, but the same silent sort of
emptiness beneath the act, which we never addressed. We argued
that our friendship proved London wasn't an unfriendly, harsh
place to live, as though we were persuading ourselves, too, with
the words. In the middle of it all was the local pub I met her in,
when I carried her dress back and bought her a drink to say thanks
for – well, all of it. The Loneliness Arms, as I thought of it later on,
stood like a lighthouse opposite the bedroom I'd woken in, always

full of lost regulars seeking shelter in the void. I knew there were pubs all over the city acting as rafts for those who felt as alone as we did, whatever the reason.

Perspective now allows me to see that night differently and when I imagine a girl, any girl, crawling into the room of a stranger because she can't stand the idea of being alone even in unconsciousness, I can see how splintered and vulnerable I was. The sadness of that scene makes me want to cry; panic surges at the idea of how precarious it was; of what could have happened, again. Where was Libby? And why hadn't Tom answered a call late at night that clearly implied I needed help? I think angrily. I knew why obviously but it meant I was left on a dark street, out of it, alone. Lost in a city I lived in, quite literally. Thinking about that makes me shiver and I feel like the luckiest girl in the world to have been found by Polly.

I wrote off another of my nine lives that night, and I reckoned I only had a few left. People said I needed to be careful, look after myself, but I barely cared at the time what happened to me – and what I felt was so much deeper than just heartbreak. I just didn't have any idea how to unravel what it was and still thought men were the answer to the pain other men had caused me.

When the apps became ubiquitous you could barely escape dating, hook-up culture and pseudo-love even if you wanted to. Libby had *twelve* dating apps on her phone, simultaneously reading a book called *All The Rules: Time-Tested Secrets for Capturing the Heart of Mr Right*, and advising me about rebound culture – which she thought was the answer to my anguish after Tom.

'The men are way better looking on Bumble but Tinder boys talk more,' she said. 'My new rule is that they have to speak first after we've matched. That's what the book said should happen. Apparently men feel more successful if they make the first move because of their history of hunting and so it's more likely to go well.'

'Hideous,' I told her.

Soon even Lottie was coming round to the idea of dating and it was hard to escape it at home as well as in my social life. Having become the informal custodian of half the dogs in west London, she'd realised the garden pound had massively freed up her working day.

'I was thinking that now I have all this time on my hands it might be quite nice to have a lover. I haven't had a lover since the Bahamas,' she said with a sigh. 'I tried Match.com but they said I had to pay £49.99 a month and I'm too tight. I'm so fucking tight.'

When I mentioned the apps were free, she was keen for a tutorial, so we sat in the garden and I watched her scrolling through Bumble in disbelief as a lot of older attention flooded in. Partly because she couldn't work out how to change her age from thirty-three, having made herself a decade younger on Facebook (which it linked to) for a joke.

'This one is genuinely quite fat,' she'd say, holding her phone screen out in front of her for me to see. 'But, fuck it, I'm no skinny malinky myself . . . This one looks like a cheeseburger . . . Oh God, this one likes kale shakes.'

She eventually matched with a cowboy who was visiting London, then quickly got cold feet, but by that time I'd agreed to go out with a Montenegrin who drank straight vodka through the entire evening and told me his cousin was the most wanted man in Europe. When I got home I told Lottie he'd referred to everyone he knew by the initial of their first name for their own safety, and mine, he'd said, and after that I didn't see her on Bumble ever again.

The only other Tinder date I've been on in my life happened not long after that, and confirmed her decision as well as my own not to use them. Carlos was a professional Brazilian tennis player turned Deliveroo driver now he'd arrived in London with little English. He would've also made a perfect case study for how porn had changed young men's beliefs about sex, I thought, as I was flipped around the bedroom every twenty seconds, after date three, trying not to yawn.

'You've watched too much porn,' I told him after.

'What?' he said.

'Nothing,' I said, deciding to call it off, and then receiving a dozen YouTube links to Charlie Puth and Selena Gomez singing 'We Don't Talk Anymore'.

That felt a bit much after three dates, but I was glad his English was improving enough to understand that no, we didn't (and indeed wouldn't) talk any more.

Over the next two years I kept moving, looking hard for meaning and a home. I left Lottie's for the flat of a reporter I'd started seeing at work, not only because it meant I got a lift in but because he had the kind of luxury flat without a mortgage you couldn't say no to, and was also looking to distract himself from hard life by going out and getting wrecked, which suited me down to the ground. We said I love you, not because either of us really meant it (I think) but because we wanted to hear it back and for a year we were accomplices in the quest to disengage totally via hedonistic pursuits.

Christmas came and London dazzled while remaining weirdly warm and I was dispatched all over the city to buy half a dozen frozen turkeys for the health desk from supermarkets and various posh butchers. Which was the healthiest, was the question burning my editor's lips and I cast my most apologetic look into the Uber driver's mirror from the backseat as I was ferried around with the bowling balls of poultry I needed to collect in order to run the tests that would get her an answer. Filing expenses for £300-worth of turkey has been my weirdest expense to date.

I had twenty-four hours off for Christmas and raced back to Bath on Christmas Eve before arriving back in the office on Boxing Day at 6 a.m. to find carnage in the news room. Empty prosecco bottles and tiny sandwich triangles flung all over the place. I was writing an email to Everleigh from my desk when Carrie Fisher died – the death of celebrity quicker than an email that year and a game of *Top Four Celeb Deaths of 2016* raging in the office. David Bowie, George Michael, Terry Wogan, Alan Rickman, Prince, Victoria Wood and Caroline Aherne had all died that year. When I asked Everleigh who his top four were he said celebrity deaths left him 'rather unmoved. Unless they are younger than me which increases *Schadenfreude* but also marks my own mortality. I'm more moved by the death from pulmonary embolism,' he wrote back, adding that 'old JD was right: "every man (and woman)'s death diminisheth me."'

Soon I was turning twenty-seven to a delivery of prematurely ageist gags myself, and knew I wouldn't stay much longer with Oscar, the reporter I was still living with.

'"One year nearer the grave, but cheer up, here's a bit of glitter." That's just not funny,' I read out loud, as he chain-smoked on the balcony. 'Next one, "You're getting old, motherfucker." Slightly funnier given the audacity,' I commentated, then saw my brother's handwriting. '"Happy 27th. You're now as old as Jim Morrison was when he took a heroin overdose in Paris!" Right – excuse me while I go and top myself,' I said, downing my glass of champagne because Oscar didn't believe in prosecco.

For months I'd been smoking late at night on his balcony and staring past the London Eye to the lit city beyond, wondering who else was out there. Wondering where happiness was.

Then Polly's lodger moved out, and I moved in, waking up for four months in the bed I'd shared with her opposite the lighthouse of locals, while she moved into the bigger room downstairs, and thinking life was a curious game, really. Oscar and I barely discussed the fact that we wouldn't see each other anymore, we both just knew it was over when I left.

But I still saw relationships as a cure for anxiety rather than the cause and also wanted someone to curb my enthusiasms, I think, and give me a reason to stay in, rather than go out. Relationships were quieter, often, I'd realised, and the idea I'd find a home through affection was intricately woven into my whole being as well as my lifestyle by then. They were also a way to escape expensive rental properties and private landlords where the idea it was *your* home never seeded. Both the boyfriends I lived with during those years owned their flats and wanted a woman to help make them a home, but I did wonder if not having to pay rent made me a kind of twenty-first-century prostitute.

Intimacy was a relief and an escape from the stress caused by my ingrained, learnt ambition and long office hours. If I wasn't going to bed next to someone else, I could barely sleep, as though being alone overnight was too much on top of the pressure. Before I worked at the tabloid I'd also never worked in an office where so many people complained daily about their jobs, and it was hard to stop the atmosphere of negativity seeping into you.

The brutal, famed Editor of twenty-six years, was open about the fact he believed reporters wrote better running on adrenaline, which made shouting and screaming common. Rumours of how he ran news conference filtered down to features, where we were told he had remote-control cars with the editors names on and drove them around the room as they talked, reversing or smashing them into things if the idea being posed for the next day's paper was, in his eyes, a car crash.

I don't know if that was even true but I'd once got into the lift with the Editor alone, and realised he even *breathed* like a bull as he raged silently behind me. His editors ran on fear, which was off-loaded onto inferiors, and meant no one looked like they enjoyed being there. Even the health desk was so tightly wrapped in stress that anxiety disorders surged, severe over- or under-eating was common, moods unreliable. I never could get my head around the hypocrisy of newspapers running mental health campaigns while destroying the well-being of their own staff, and I wondered if I was on the unhealthiest health desk on Fleet Street or if it was just more to do with a working culture that rinsed its employees until retirement? One of the chain-smokers I saw out the back of the tabloid's office looked like he was going to drop dead any minute.

My life as it was, was not *it*, not what I'd be happy to call 'my life' by the end of it if nothing changed, I thought, and I was restless, knowing only I had the power and inclination to fix it.

Then after I'd been in the role some time, my boss tried to fire me which made me cry in the meeting because I'd been trying fucking hard to be cheerful in the face of all the awfulness and I moved to general features where I was given virtually nothing to do as a form of punishment for leaving the health desk. My old boss and my new boss were friends, and the old one now sat seething in front of me, seemingly irritated that I'd won a game of chess I hadn't wanted to play by asking a more senior male editor for help in keeping a job at the paper. I just didn't want to be turfed out on her strangling whim alone but the unpleasantness increased, of course, and being paid to be a writer who was barely allowed to write made leaving inevitable another year on.

I made the dive into self-employment then that so many in my generation are forced to do by industries that say they can't, but actually just *won't* offer us the safety of a contract. Going freelance was terrifying and caused my work and love lives to entangle again, the cushioning of a new boyfriend's flat the only way I could cope with the anxiety of not knowing when I'd next be paid, and by whom.

When I left the office, realising I wouldn't now have a pension that would tint any short-term unease with the idea of long-term security scared me, but worrying about being seventy when you're living hand-to-mouth in the present was just futile and exhausting. Despite dreading I'd never reach financial freedom, I just had to ignore it to get through each week.

Yet six months in, freelancing was going brilliantly and jumping ship from a job that made me depressed was, with hindsight, so obviously the right thing to do. I was writing far more interesting features for *The Times* than I'd been able to at the tabloid, the latter preferring me to add price tags to celebrity yachts or watches as though I was writing a high-end Argos catalogue. I wrote interviews for the *Sunday Times*; trend pieces for three different features desks at the *Telegraph*; case study features on female bodyguards; millennial wives marrying men triple their age (partly for hard-to-come-by security, no doubt) and plus-size male models who gratifyingly had the same issues women did for a different features desk of the *Daily Mail*, which had a brilliant editor who'd known me since my early days in journalism. *The Sun* mainly wanted me to write about filthy references in kids' TV programmes, and *Grazia* mainly about fashionable water bottles. I was flown all over the place for *EasyJet magazine* to meet nuns in a convent in Ronda making saccharine pastries with a secret, centuries-old recipe (but who were more interested in my boyfriends), then to Berlin to stay at a bohemian millennials-only members club before boarding a plane to Mallorca to train at Rafael Nadal's tennis academy.

To my amusement I also had time to accept the perks now I ran my own schedule and didn't have to be in an office all day. Yes I *did* want to go to Champagne with Jools Holland to visit the Krug house he was currently working with for an event, I told a PR, and a month after that trip I sat on a train departing London Victoria drinking more champagne than I'd drunk in actual Champagne while Jools 'conducted' the luxury old vehicle through the countryside and pulled us into closed old stations to listen to some of his favourite new musicians perform on the tracks. 'Is that Jodie Kidd?' I asked someone, looking across the platform during the oddest but most brilliant day of my life.

It was complete freedom, being a freelancer, even if I got paid less than a ticket to any of the luxury events I was invited to write about, and the rush of adrenaline I refound that year made the world feel so exciting again. I got up at 6 a.m., read all the papers and pitched ideas to all the editors I knew, proud I appeared to have made yet another comeback after yet another failed attempt at office life. Life was all about comebacks, I thought, as I ran on the treadmill at my new gym like I was in the movies (I imagined) and waited for one of the editors to come back and tell me to start writing something.

Another year passed, like that, but at home I knew the wrong man was an untenable as a crumbling flat share, and refused to stay with one just for a roof over my head. When you moved into other people's homes you knew you'd always have to be the one to leave, but I was determined to find my own home somewhere more permanent. Did feminism not mean I could make it alone, I wondered? I was beginning to wonder if real life wasn't just like *The Lobster*. Where was the hotel I could move into, single, until I forged a new relationship and was allowed to move back out?

London felt a violent place to be young, amongst the excitement, and I'd begun to feel my generation was charging at the future with the same ambition generations always felt in their twenties, but hitting brick walls everywhere, in job and housing markets even before we looked at love.

After the Brexit vote it felt like the UK was reeling and there was an edgy division between Leave and Remainers in the same way I'd found existed between the Yes and No sides in Edinburgh after the Scottish independence referendum. During Brexit, allegiance to either side was fierce and splitting, both believing the other imbecilic for not being able to *see* how wrong they were.

Generational conflict raged and mine was just made to feel even more separate from the older population who'd largely voted to leave Europe and for selfishly electing living conditions they'd not have to endure as long as we would (we thought). Were they still even working? Did they ever want to work abroad? Did they want to travel as freely as we did? We doubted it, and that made us feel screwed over, yet again. Not only had we been denied the now positively cheap-looking house prices and loyal job security previous generations had basked in, but we now had to live in a country that wasn't part of Europe when we thought of ourselves as European as much as we did British. That made it feel like our identity was being denied, too.

No one I knew wanted closed borders and so the vote was jarring and resentment seethed. We were woke snowflake traitors; they were paranoid racists with extremely out-dated views, the thinking went – stereotype and generalisation thriving in the atmosphere of hate. The fact that there were still war veterans in the older brackets of the population was hard to get my head around, because we were indebted, always, but when was it going to be our time to fight for what *we* believed in? What we felt we were being denied was a feeling of belonging, even in our own country, and that has a hugely detrimental impact on anyone, anywhere. I hated how it was essentially segregating the generations, especially when I had many older friends. My rule had become not to talk about politics with anyone over sixty, because it risked exposing too much difference between the now oppositional forces of young and old. Our response was to reject older values even more than we already had, and in that anger a new counterculture felt like it was forming.

A year later I'd be sent Brexit speed dating by the *Telegraph* because political difference had been discovered as a modern cause for divorce. But if political opposition was destroying marriage, would it also ruin my friendships with people like Everleigh and my friend's dad Peter, I wondered?

When I'd decided to cut my ties to men I didn't want to marry, and stop ricocheting around the Tube map into other people's lives, Peter's house was the natural choice for a home.

We'd got to know each other while I'd stayed with my friend Hugo from Leeds during university holidays and since then Peter had been watching my migrations with what he described as 'mild horror', occasionally emailing to ask if I was 'still sleeping' in Hammersmith, Camberwell or Kew. I found the lack of the word 'living' particularly bleak. But since moving to London I'd moved eight times in the city alone, before you even considered Newcastle, Edinburgh, Amsterdam and Bath. Including the temporary shelters in those cities I'd moved house fourteen times in four years.

By the time I wanted to leave the pinball life of twenty-first-century prostitution behind, Hugo had moved to New York to work in a juice bar and fall in love with Californian actresses and Peter was experiencing empty-nest syndrome for a second time in his big house in south London.

'Look after my dad,' Hugo said when he left and then Peter emailed to tell me my room there was still free if I agreed to a three-hour moving-in tutorial (wine included). Agreeing, I crossed the river from north London in a van driven by a removal Rastafarian, listening to his YouTube conspiracy theories, and wondering what boomerang life without shared genes would be like.

'These places sell chicken as big as a cat's leg,' the driver told me, gesturing at the chicken shop streets, where takeaways pumped poultry with water, he said. 'I feel sorry for the youth that don't know the real size, innit?' he asked, and I agreed.

I was starting to feel a little sorry for the youth, too.

Dear Lucy,

Just back from a lovely five days in Venice. I was reading a historical detective novel by one Antonia Hodgson – enjoyed it, and then discovered that she was a graduate of Leeds School of English – one I certainly don't remember teaching. I didn't teach Naga Munchetty either, though did manage to make Holliday Grainger cry by refusing to sanction an extended absence to pursue her acting career (got that one wrong, then).

Keep smiling despite (or at) Trump, who looks like the first president who will rule by Twitter – something ghastly appropriate in that. Was ever such a one elected to such high office?? It's enough to make one agree with Churchill.

Best wishes,

Everleigh

PS Twenty-seven! But then, I'll reach my threescore and ten next year.

10

I MAY DESTROY YOU

When my plane hit the runway in Madeira and screeched to a stop, there was an almost unanimous release of worried breath, the landing strip so tightly bordered by sea on all but one safe side that it felt like an accomplishment to hit land, not water. The airport sat like a precarious hyphen into nothing at the very eastern edge of the tiny Portuguese island, already named after the man I was there to ask residents about: Cristiano Ronaldo.

I'd been flown from London by the *Times* sports desk to write a special report following allegations that the striker had raped an American nightclub manager in Las Vegas in 2009, then paid her £288,000 to sign a non-disclosure agreement. Kathryn Mayorga, then twenty-five, now thirty-four and just one year older than Ronaldo, claimed he'd invited her and a friend back to his penthouse suite after meeting them in a club, and suggested they use the jacuzzi before attacking her while she got changed. Ronaldo always vehemently denied the allegations and argued only that sex with Mayorga was consensual and in 2019, criminal charges against Ronaldo were dropped for lack of evidence but when I landed in Madeira the world was looking on stunned while his lawyers claimed that a pay-off was no confession of guilt.

In Madeira and then Turin, where he'd just signed a £99 million contract at Juventus, I was investigating what female fans, particularly, thought about the claim, which felt a little bit

like asking what both cities felt about their god, I realised, when
I arrived.

Octavio the photographer picked me up and gave me a tour of
the island where he had grown up alongside the Ronaldo family,
whose influence was visible everywhere, and who mostly all still
lived there, his mother in an unostentatious villa overlooking
the sea, his sister running a trashy Eurovision-style boutique; his
brother the CR7 museum.

I tried to imagine accusing someone of rape, then coming into
this traumatic *Alice in Wonderland*-style hell where even the door-
knobs in his hotel were modelled on his hands and felt my own
anxiety rising. Ronaldo's face looked out from every street and
when you couldn't see a mural, you only had to look harder. He
loomed everywhere and when a bus pulled in front of us, he stared
straight into my eyes from the poster on the back of it.

They were synonymous: Madeira and Ronaldo, but the CR7
motto – 'To be the best, you need the best' – reminded me of the
rumoured $1 million team he'd hired to fight Mayorga's claim. As
with all rape trials, it was her word against his. But whatever the
truth was, I doubted she'd be able to breathe in Madeira with his
image on every street.

Outside of tourist season, the October disquiet gave Madeira
that year an atmosphere almost of guilt, but in reality Ronaldo's
fans weren't going anywhere and few addressed the fact the allegations could be true. Even if they did talk about it behind closed
doors, the island inhabitants weren't going to address it in public
because they had too much to lose.

Not only was Ronaldo's legacy the main source of tourism to
an island that looked lost and empty without it but he was their
identity, too.

Everyone on the island had a claim on him, and their hero wor-
ship made them believe they knew everything about him, quoting
how much he (allegedly) paid his brother, a former addict, each

month to keep clean, and reciting a list of ex-girlfriends and where they used to meet – stopping, I noticed, at what they were interested in doing in the hotel rooms. It was a Catholic island after all.

Seeing him as a part of a national identity made Mayorga's claims an attack not just on Ronaldo but on the whole of Madeira, because they were the same thing. Later I arrived in Turin and saw he was now part of their identity too. The anger that an outsider like Mayorga was shining a new, less than flattering, light on the golden boy god they wanted sole claim on was exactly the same as it was in Portugal.

Madeira was prejudiced, but it was also disorientated. The replies to my questions about whether the accusation could be true clutched at everything that could be held up as 'evidence' of innocence. They ranged from 'he's a family man; he bought his mum a house' to 'he wouldn't need to because he could get any woman he wants'.

The very people who'd told me rumours about him claimed other people were always 'making stories' about him. Others evaded the question completely, saying it only mattered what he was like on the pitch or flipped it straight back at Mayorga without seeming to care whether she'd been raped or not. 'She accepted the money so it's disgusting she'd talk now,' someone actually said to me, although the most jarring comment was from a nineteen-year-old waitress called Ava who served us lunch, and told me Mayorga must have given *some* permission. 'A lot of people are crazy about him. He's number one and he gets a lot of girls so he doesn't need to do anything like that,' she reasoned, as I just watched her, remembering being the same age, which felt a very long time ago now.

It was rattling to see how ill-equipped so many people still were to talk about allegations of rape and how warped the ideas of who could commit it were. Did they really believe that you could only commit that kind of crime if you were unattractive, and therefore, on the flipside, that rape was understandable if you couldn't rely on good looks? Like: 'Can't persuade her into bed? Just force her then, yeah.' Those were comments that echoed the sentiments of so-called Incels – involuntary celibates – who were real, terrifying groups of men who claimed a lack of attention from women left rape their only option.

I didn't like where that line of argument was going, or suggesting it could go, but the family argument was also absurd – could you only be a rapist if you disliked your mum and didn't buy her a house when you became a multimillionaire?

Perhaps most awful to me was how women wrote the claims off quicker than men, as if they had more *right* to disqualify the experience of another woman. That surprised me and made me wonder if the men were just too scared to say what they really thought about Ronaldo, Mayorga and about the Me Too movement in general. But the female judgement was just so damning and tribal. The idea that Mayorga would invent a horrific rape and put herself through the mill of public speculation for cash made me at first think the women who wrote it off the fastest had no experience of it themselves. Later, I wondered whether they had too much experience and just couldn't bear to address it.

The British women I found holidaying there were more thoughtful, which made me think about the cultural shifts in the UK and the US following the Me Too movement the year before, but their responses were Britishly awkward, understanding that accusing Ronaldo in Madeira was like accusing the Pope in Rome. I didn't blame them for not wanting to start the fight, but it was still collusion in some ways. Is there a time and place for these conversations? Or should it always be the time and place? Surely the awkwardness involved in accusing someone was why famous men in the public eye – and many others – had got away with abhorrent behaviour so long.

We left the harbour and Octavio drove me up the hill to Santo

António, a parish on the middle of the mountain, so I could see where Ronaldo grew up in a blue house without a bathroom. We got out of the car and stood in a small car park lined with banana trees looking onto a tiny children's football pitch. The site of his house was demolished years ago, some islanders saying it didn't reflect the right image of the now superstar; others saying it brought unwanted attention to a poverty-stricken neighbourhood. Either way, his 'rags to riches' story was a huge part of his charm, American Dream-like in its aspiration, and I imagined it must make you feel untouchable when you came from nothing to be handed the world.

Shrines everywhere were scribbled with '*O nosso idolo*' (our idol) and before we knew Ronaldo had been acquitted it was becoming obvious to me that the question of whether we could still support accused cultural icons was hanging in the air behind the story. When Michael Jackson was accused of child sexual abuse, people asked: *Can we still listen to his music, even though . . . you know?* Could we, or should we, separate the artist from their art? The feeling was that it was all a bit *awkward*, wasn't it?

More deeply, the Ronaldo story was resonating with me on a personal level, too. When rape victims hear the word 'rape' they don't always associate it with themselves – however strange that might sound – and so I hadn't considered when I took the commission and started the investigation that I was one of those people. I'd written about a lot of my personal life, but I'd never written about rape, and at this point – in October 2018, more than seven years after it happened – I'd only told two, maybe three people in the whole world, none of whom were the police.

Despite the second reaction (Anna's) being so supportive and sensitive, the first, from another friend, had been so immediately dismissive that I'd decided to just not talk about it, and in time it was so blocked I didn't think about it for years. If it did flash into my mind, I could get rid of it before it did any damage, not

realising in the slightest that it was doing a lot of damage by sim-
mering there, undealt with.

So in Madeira it was surreal to be told for the first time, to my
face, what people thought about historic sexual assault allegations
made by women against men. One fan said to me, 'Nine years
later? To me that's strange,' while another asked sarcastically if
Mayorga had forgotten? I knew that it was impossible to forget,
because I'd been trying to forget for years without any real success.
The memory never went away even if you didn't ever speak it, and
I guessed that if Mayorga was telling the truth, that she'd cemented
over it until it tore her apart.

My experience wasn't part of the story, and my opinions as an
investigative reporter weren't relevant, but it was making me think.

When I arrived in Turin a few days later, I saw the fans there
resented the claims as much as they did in Madeira, and a transac-
tional air of 'we're going to get what we paid for ... even if he is
a rapist' hung in the air, a larger comment perhaps on how people
could still be bought and sold.

I'd never been to Turin, so I dumped my bags in the hotel and
went walking through Saturday markets selling collections of
antiques, silk scarves, second-hand clothes and everything else you
could think of, feeling excited both by the independence and about
covering such an important story. In the centre, heavily security-
guarded Juventus shops were already packed with fans waiting for
the 6 p.m. kick-off, and I sat down to order a slice of pizza and
a coffee and lit a cigarette, watching striped football shirts swim
about the streets like Black Jack sweets.

I stared at Ronaldo's face on magazine covers everywhere and
tried to work out what I thought about Turin refusing to break
their adulation for the footballer. 'Utopia became reality' when
Ronaldo joined Juventus, one publication said in a 26-page love
letter to CR7 that called him an 'epiphany'.

'*Nauseating,*' I said aloud to myself. The sports pages of the local newspapers were as OTT, and imagining the city's horror after they'd rolled out the longest, reddest carpet they could find for Ronaldo only to discover a very modern nightmare walking it two weeks later was almost blackly funny.

After I arrived at the huge stadium later that day and took my seat in the press stand, I was told by an Italian journalist that the local press had asked themselves whether they could backtrack, before launching a 'keep your hands off Ronaldo' campaign that was anything but impartial. That said too much about power, I guess.

As we talked, Ronaldo ran onto the pitch below me to the sound of Guns N' Roses and the crowd went wild. The whole stand behind Juventus' goal had been given to Italian school children who waved flags at their hero and I thought of them as the next generation who'd have their ideas about sex, money and power influenced by the outcome of celebrity trials like Ronaldo's as they grew up. I didn't want them to believe that you could get away with anything if you were famous, or more simply that women could be mistreated and then accused of making it up.

After the match I'd waited in the press pit to see if Ronaldo would give interviews and started adding my description of Turin to the story in Madeira so far, only realising when I left the stadium how dark it was, and with horror, that I didn't know if the buses were still running into Turin. The car park had emptied, a few drunk fans ordered greasy food from floodlit burger vans, the taxi ranks were dead and Uber's app showed a ghost town given that 41,000 people had left the stadium within the last couple of hours.

Trying not to panic, I walked dead streets in the direction of town, guessing it was probably over an hour's walk if it had taken forty minutes on a bus, and not knowing whether it was more dangerous to keep walking or flag an unbooked cab in the middle of nowhere. I'd been jumpy for years and imagined the worst whenever I walked alone at night, sprinting home from last Tubes and arriving at my door out of breath. Only once had there been a man in the shadows, around a corner, waiting, but that was enough. My imagination was overrun. I didn't believe it was just my imagination – I thought it was the modern, abusive world we had to live in and so I was fight or flight all the time.

I was so fuelled by adrenaline by the time a taxi pulled up in Turin that I remember that journey like I'm in the cab now watching the streets in the outskirts like a hawk and simultaneously staring at the blob of the car on my phone screen, not knowing the city well enough to know if I was being driven somewhere I didn't want to go, but desperately trying to recognise something. I talked the whole way there, because I thought maybe if he liked me, and I seemed human and not just a random girl he knew nothing about, I'd have more chance of arriving at the hotel. When we did half an hour later, I was so relieved I thought I could cry and I tipped him everything I had.

When I got to my hotel room, I wondered if I'd really just tipped a cabbie for not assaulting me but knew, essentially, that I had because I didn't think it was a given he wouldn't.

I lay in bed that night with the light on, exhausted, with darkness running through my mind. What would we choose to wear out if we knew the outfit would be ripped and ruined forever in an attack, I wondered? Would we shower and do our hair, and put make-up on and let ourselves feel that heady anticipation we feel before we meet friends at a bar, a restaurant or a party? How much would we pay for something to happen that meant we didn't go? You'd take FOMO obviously, but I'd have taken a car crash, in hindsight. Probably something even worse, I thought, as I finally fell asleep with the light on.

I was twenty-one, almost twenty-two when it happened to me. It was New Year's Eve 2011 and I was back home for the university

Christmas holidays, kicking about, and then agreeing to spend New Year's Eve on the coast, where a friend was throwing a party at a rented house overlooking the sea.

I'd never been to a 1920s-themed party so I was fizzing with excitement. My mum and I found a vintage shop in Bath stocked with elbow-length lace gloves and a hairpiece that would count, we thought, as twenties, above a black velvet dress. I borrowed the fox fur from my dad's antique dealing days, too, knowing the other people going were private-school types who would make a Bullingdon Club-style effort.

Another girl I vaguely knew from Bath and I got the train together that morning, and we talked about classy house parties on New Year's Eve being an amazing way to avoid a chaotic city crowd, or buying tickets for places you wouldn't be paid to drink at on any other night. My friend picked us up from the station and took us to an incredible house on the cliffs with white walls and so many bedrooms, then we walked down to the harbour and had a pint at a fisherman's pub. The sea blew savagely wet as we walked and the light faded, the night already keen to set in by 4 p.m. Then we went back to get changed, admired each other in the kitchen and drank champagne. One of the girls drew a beauty spot on my cheek in eyeliner and we had dinner, danced around.

Then I blank.

When I next open my eyes, it feels very late, and they roll to the back of my head in the way only hard drugs can make them. The fox is gone, and so are my gloves but my dress is hitched to my waist and there's a man on top of me, moving up and down, his face a monstrous blur. I don't know who he is. I lose consciousness again.

Time dies.

In the morning, I wake up and I still can't move, so I try to rotate my vision and see he's still there next to me. I don't know what room of the house we're in, and I don't know how I got here. The last thing I remember is standing in the kitchen

drinking Prosecco somewhere in the middle of the evening. I try
to move again, and he puts his hand on me, shifts as if he's going
to manoeuvre on top of me again and I can't remember if I tell
him to get off or push him away. I only remember that he *laughs*.
He says, 'You were much funner last night.'

Something like cold panic spreads through me then and I know
that my entire body is telling me to get away as quickly as possible.
I now know it's one of my friend's old school mates, someone I
remember barely speaking to that night. But someone who boasted
about having ecstasy on him, something I don't take, because I
don't like waiting to see how it will kick in. I never like waiting,
for anything. But I know above all else that I've taken a hard drug
that caused blackout and I know I wouldn't have agreed unless I'd
either been offered it at the point in drunkenness when no one
should have offered me anything, or unless I'd been spiked.

In the bed, I find I still can't sit up so I start sliding my legs onto
the floor and scrabble around for anything that might be mine,
hearing voices somewhere further away, then realising we're in the
attic room, at the farthest end of the house, where no one would
have seen anything.

I don't remember how I managed to get down three flights of
steep steps without falling or crying or collapsing, but I did, and I
barely remember what I did when I got back to the ground floor.
I think I just sat frozen until we could leave, and no one asked if
I was fine. They probably thought I was so hungover I couldn't
speak, but I don't know how the look on my face couldn't have
said so much more than that if anyone had really looked at me.

We had to travel back up country together after that and I just
remember wanting to get home and away from that house as fast
as possible, as though I'd start breathing again when I was alone,
and I remember the look of absolute guilt in his eyes as he looked
at me halfway through the journey. He said nothing about the
night before and neither did I.

I can't remember the days after that, in which I must have been coming down from whatever it was I suspected he'd given me and it all seemed a blur – I hadn't suffered much trauma in my life before that, but I knew children, especially, dealt with it by sleeping. The mind is supposed to try to fix itself when you do that.

The whole thing was just so immensely confusing in the fog of recovery that followed. Had I actually been raped? It was easier to think that maybe it was consensual (as if I wouldn't be sure) but when pictures from the night were shared two days later I felt the nauseous panic I'd felt in the morning after all over again. In every single photo he was right next to me, or staring at me as I walked away from the group, or from the other side of the party. I don't know why, but he'd targeted me. So I decided to tell my friend, thinking he might know what to do.

'Yeah, he's always been a bit ... weird with girls,' he said. 'I just have the feeling he's going to be really successful one day,' he added, like a fucking idiot, and my opinion of him changed forever that day. I thought he was the most stupid person I'd ever met and as dangerous as his friend, in some ways. But of course I blocked all that, too, because it was so tangled with the trauma I needed to shut off. That I felt I had to if I was ever going to carry on doing anything, really. I remained friends with that guy – the one who'd not cared that his mate had raped me – for a while, which was possible only because 'nothing' had happened to me, but now I think about telling him with almost as much regret as I have about going to the party in the first place. Because if I'd told someone else, they might have helped, and it wouldn't have felt too late to go to the police.

Instead, his reaction persuaded me it wasn't a big deal and so I shut up, and the destructive course that put me on for a decade began, shrouded in guilt because I wondered all the time whether he was just doing the same thing again to some other girl.

Before Madeira and Turin, if you'd asked me if I'd been raped,

I would have said 'no', and believed that to be the truth. It was that blocked. It didn't start bubbling out of me when my plane hit the runway in London either, or anything as epiphanic as that, but at the beginning of 2019, it did become something that I was confused to find I needed to tell close friends. After a few drinks had loosened me up enough to actually say the words, that was.

Maybe it was the trip to Madeira and Turin, or the Me Too campaign exactly a year before it, that helped me accept my own experience in a way I couldn't before. But when I said the words, a pressure lifted which in turn made me start to believe I could confront it. For years I couldn't say the word 'rape', and I hated the word 'victim', feeling that if I used that then I was one, and didn't want to be. 'Survivor' seemed dramatic and made me think of Destiny's Child bopping around the screen in skimpy khaki. And 'shame' – well I didn't like the idea I should feel shame, either, and didn't realise for years that that's exactly what I felt.

I felt the language had even flipped too far the other way, I realised, as I stood outside a restaurant in London a year later and heard a woman in her late twenties telling her friend that she'd 'basically raped' a guy they knew in the smoking area of a pub the night before. Presumably she meant she was all over him, but clearly she had no real appreciation of what it meant, otherwise she wouldn't have been so devastatingly flippant. There were some benefits to women being more able to say the word more easily, but *none* to them turning it into a joke.

Then later, in lockdown, a friend I'd swapped the horrors of our stories with texted to ask if I'd seen *I May Destroy You* and I watched, with difficulty, when I realised the series was based on Michaela Coel's own experience so close to mine, recognising the desire not to use the word 'assault', the reluctance to make it a memory, the flashbacks, emotional numbness, self-undermining, the distrust of tiny things, but also of friends, and men in general. I had to drink through it, to watch, but the way my head kept turning away from the screen and the amount I cried as I did watch, showed me for the first time how traumatised I was, which actually helped.

The series looked at how close friends often don't discuss rape even with each other, and I knew that was happening in the social circles I ran in, too. In the two years following the Ronaldo story, I quietly told a dozen friends, and eight had told me they'd also been assaulted. Two thirds. Then the conversations we were having started rippling through crowds of girls we met in pubs or parks, like the subject was becoming unstoppable after having been squashed for so long.

A female friend had been hit and raped by a boyfriend in her hometown after she'd broken up with him.

Another female friend had gone home with a boy after a night out and consensually had sex, but in the morning he'd forced her to again. 'I told him I didn't want to, but he did it anyway. Then after, when I was obviously pissed off, he said, "Sorry, I thought you were playing hard to get." Who plays hard to get at 7 a.m.?' she asked me. No one, I confirmed.

Another female friend drank faster and chain-smoked if the subject came up but said 'not now' every time I asked her if she wanted to talk about it. She texted to ask if I thought she should say something when her boss described her law firm as 'raping' a claim.

Another couldn't eat pasta without thinking about the guy who raped her at her flat after she invited him back for some food.

Sami had been hassled by a guy at work for a date, and told him she wasn't interested four times. She'd woken up next to him after a staff party when he'd taken advantage of the fact she'd had a few drinks and needed help getting a taxi. The guy was a lawyer and supposed to be in charge of upholding public trust and confidence.

Ruby had her virginity taken without consent aged fifteen by the 'popular' boy at school.

Someone else had been groped on a bus by a middle-aged man

who sat next to her, then followed home regularly from school by a group of men of the same ethnicity as the man who'd groped her until she finally told a teacher and was banned from travelling independently. She didn't know if the men's ethnicity was a coincidence, or whether they were working together in a pack.

That girl's friend was a performer and told us she'd had her leg lifted balletically by a man in the pub while the other groped between her legs. Her male friends watched, shocked, but didn't do or say anything.

Women weren't the only ones talking either, and one of my guy friends confessed he'd been raped by a man he'd met on Grindr in a hotel room abroad, not telling anyone because he assumed he'd be told it was his own fault for inviting him there.

Someone else had only been a child and I was the first person they told. They wanted to know whether my opinion of them had changed, now I knew. 'Of course not,' I told them, seeing they were still worried it was a result of something *they'd* done. Suggested they wanted it, somehow.

But mostly the stories did come from women, and when a couple of them spoke, they told their stories in the sturdy disassociated way I recognised as meaning they hadn't yet addressed the fact they knew they'd been assaulted. More often they told their stories with tears in their eyes that made you hold their hand, and then they gripped on. The horrible realisation that I'd only talked to maybe a third of my friends was with me all the time after that. What the hell was the figure going to be if I asked everyone I knew, and who was still trying to deal with it alone?

An equally astute screen portrayal of sexual harassment was *Bombshell*, in which Margot Robbie's character asks herself: *What did I do? What did I say? Am I weak?* Because you do do that. Blame and doubt yourself savagely, and silence feels less dangerous all round, despite the fact it is the *most* dangerous way to cope. For you. And for every other woman.

The only similarity in the experiences of those I did speak to was that no one – not one – had been to the police. They, like me, wondered whether they *really had been* raped. For years, I told myself I might have taken the drugs willingly. Maybe I'd wanted to mess around upstairs. What if I was accusing someone who hadn't done anything wrong?

But it always came back to the same thing. I was unconscious when he was having sex with me. And you don't have consent if the other person is unconscious. When I doubt myself, I remember that, and I know the truth, with relief, and feel my doubt replaced by anger. The truth, of course, is that if you have to wonder whether you've been raped – you most likely have. We know what consent feels like, especially as adults, and we know what it doesn't look like, too.

'I'll kill him,' my last boyfriend said when I told him, as did some of my more law-abiding friends, and part of me wishes he was dead, which is uncomfortable, but normal, I'm sure. Unlike some rape victims who have no name or face to throw their loathing at, I knew exactly who he was, where he was, and what he did for work – which is a joke in itself, given what he did to me. That information simmered with possibility.

When I watched Netflix's Epstein documentary and heard the women who said he had abused them speaking, I realised that most rape victims just want acknowledgement. Those women wanted to look him in the face and say: I know what you did to me. In the same way I wanted this horribly arrogant, privileged, apparently upstanding member of society to know that I hadn't, couldn't or wouldn't forget either.

Most of us will never get a 'sorry', because to give one offenders have to make an admission of guilt that they know could be used against them. So they continue to do the wrong thing, deny it to themselves, get away with it, possibly try it again someday, because morals bent once, bend more easily again.

But if the person knows that you *know* – well, you can tell yourself it's less likely to happen again, I suppose, even if the rapist won't admit what they did to themselves or anyone else.

It sometimes still makes me cry when I think about the young, completely carefree 21-year-old who didn't know how her world was about to unravel on that New Year's Eve. Who didn't know yet that other people could be that bad. Maybe I'm lucky to have got to twenty-one without seeing that darkness, because I know other people who had to see it much younger, and it can't not change you.

The bar for male behaviour had been set so low by a man at the start of my adult life, that I think I was able, afterwards, to put up with so much more from shitty men who didn't treat me like I deserved to be treated a lot of the time, purely because what they did was never as bad as rape. But what was, except murder?

Unfairly, but with some justification, I therefore didn't expect very much from men in my romantic relationships with them, which maybe made me stay longer with Sam, who was wonderful and safe, but who I had little in common with, and then put up with Tom's compulsive lying and deceit. Two years later it was possibly why I didn't leave another older, misogynistic boyfriend when he slapped me in the face during a row. I never forgave him, and I didn't respect him ever again but – well, I'd had worse, and we had a holiday booked. I should have left, because the relationship was ruined the moment I felt the force of his hand on my cheek at my friend's wedding, of all places, but I stayed another year, partly because I was freelance and desperate for the security of living with him. During that time he talked about walking me down the aisle and I thought, *In your fucking dreams.*

The comfort I still felt like I needed from men complicated things and created a hugely complex well of emotion it was hard to get my head around. I guess the truth is that bad relationships seemed safer than being single, not that I believed relationships saved you from rape, but because I somehow felt more protected from other men when I was with one. Not having someone to call and tell that I was on my way home worried me, because what if something happened en route? That's how women had learnt to think.

Worse is wondering all the time how different I'd have been if I'd not gone to that party. I'm almost certain that I would have found relationships easier and been easier to be with myself. I don't think I would have agreed to move in so fast with most of the men I've lived with, to try to make myself feel more protected, and I don't think I would've been waiting all the time to get hurt and been unsurprised when I did.

What I learnt in the end is that too much anger stays with you if the trauma isn't acknowledged. I think I had been taking out some of my anger on the men I was with, like I could avenge myself against the entire male sex that way. Or maybe I wanted them to make it up to me, and was pissed off and inconsolable when they couldn't. Maybe I just didn't trust them after what had happened to me and perhaps because of the force involved in rape, that complete invasion of your body, the trauma was just coming out in rage.

After nine years, it just wouldn't stay quiet any more. I didn't want to be angry, because it unsettled me, and society had little place for 'angry' women, however justified their anger was. But above everything else, I just didn't want to *feel* it, and have to live like that.

Life doesn't rotate around one event alone and it's possible to experience trauma and live simultaneously with laughter, happiness, achievement, excitement and joy. I've had all those things but I also believe that confronting something a decade later, or two, three, four decades later, is still better than never confronting it at all and making yourself live with the silent weight of it alone.

When I began writing this I was shocked to realise that if I was the reader, I'd want to know what the author looked like. When I tried to understand why, I recognised that it was because I'd hope to see in them a reason that it had happened. A hint of weakness, a vulnerability, anything. A 'reason' that it could happen to *them*, but couldn't happen to *me*. It's way scarier to imagine that rape could happen to any of us, it being rarely about us at all, but about the rapist, and a system that still deters victims seeking help. But I look strong and I'm tall and I wouldn't have been easy to drag anywhere so maybe it was just because I was drinking Prosecco and bubbles are easier to slip a drug that might fizz into without anyone noticing.

Wrongly, our society has always told us that rape is as much, if not more, the fault of the victim than the perpetrator. The person attacked must have done something. Said something. Wore something. Led someone on. Wanted it. But rape is not a *women's issue*, it's a man's issue. Currently the language we use to describe male violence towards women is about *women's safety* and takes men out of the conversation entirely, suggesting they have no agency at all in the violence they inflict on us, but also on other men, sexual or not.

The thing that stayed with me the longest after Madeira were the comments from Ava, the nineteen-year-old who'd told me a man accused of rape must have been given *some* permission. She was just two years younger than I was on that ruinous New Year's Eve and I wanted her to know so much more about the world than she clearly did, and more than I did too at her age. I wanted her to be able to protect herself better than I'd managed to. I wanted her to know that rapists are not just one kind of man in the same way victims are not one type of person and therefore can't blame themselves for being attacked. I wanted her to know that you can't judge someone's morality by what they do for work, or how successful they are, or whether they have bought their mother a house. I wanted to live in a world where teenagers knew that shallow things like popularity and looks didn't make you a good person and that those traits in others shouldn't persuade you to do whatever they want you to do.

I wanted her to know that consent wasn't following someone else's idea of what they deserved and that you weren't 'lucky' to be singled out if you didn't want their attention. I wanted most of all to tell her that there was no such thing as 'some permission', a bit of permission or half permission. That it is impossible to give permission if you aren't conscious and that without concrete, ardent, ecstatic permission, no one else in the world should be going anywhere near her body.

Dear Lucy,

Enjoyed catching up with Holdeniana this morning. What do I think of Ronaldo – better not say. I think you manage to write with a nicely lifted eyebrow. As for the rest, I'm not tempted either to eat Gucci pasta or buy a falcon, and Annabel's sounds like my idea of hell on earth.

Also – gym parties? Really? Let me crawl into my rabbit hole and sleep away my birthday. It is only the necessity of a heart condition and threatening diabetes that gets me to the gym, and it is certainly not pleasure. Whilst there recently I was thinking idly that the changing menu at Pizza Express over the years is an index of the changing tastes of the Brits. Nowadays chili and spicy sausage are to be found on the majority of pizze, the old favourites like 'quatro formaggi' and 'capricciosa', which were not at all spicy, have disappeared, and anchovies hardly make an appearance at all.

Hope you are happy and prospering in all life's departments,

Everleigh

11

THE OLD CURIOSITY SHOP

'Good news,' I told Peter, who sat opposite me at the breakfast table as the credits were cued to roll on another year.

He peered at me over the top of *The Times*.

'Cohabiting intergenerationally is actually good for our *health*,' I read from the screen of my laptop, seeing the studies had changed since I'd last been a boomerang child. 'A study of fifty thousand people by the London School of Economics blah, blah, blah, has reported that those over fifty were less likely to be depressed if grown-up children were living with them. Apparently, I have a greater effect on your mood than any daily activity and influence the tone of your conversation so it's not all about death, sickness and old age but youth, parties and girlfriends. How is computer dating, currently?' I added, given Peter dated more than me since I'd given up men and alcohol entirely since moving in with him three months earlier.

'I'm seeing the violinist for coffee later,' he said.

'*Josephine?*'

'No.'

'*Jane?*'

'No.'

'Jesus.'

'No. Female.'

I gave up. Living with Peter was like being able to live with my parents in London. He was in his mid-sixties but for the last few years I'd been as good a friend with father as with son and so living there felt like being home, in some ways. It was safety and sanity, given Peter didn't throw midweek parties until 3 a.m., scream at computer games, fail to wash up for two weeks, entice bailiffs, boyfriend swap or wake me up by pouring a milk carton of White Russian down my throat.

He was reliable, if a little set in his ways – but hey, no one liked soggy bathmats and I quickly learnt you couldn't put antique silver in a dishwasher. If anything, he just reminded me more of my dad in those moments, which was amusingly comforting. The difference between him and my dad was the fact that Peter and I talked about dating, and from our chats I learnt that relationships weren't much different in your sixties to your twenties. Jealousies, insecurities and concerns were as universal as love itself but when you were older both parties were more likely to own their own home and be able to escape back there after an argument, I realised. Space seemed to help.

After another boozy summer I'd become worried my pursuit of hedonism since I'd been back in London had been edging towards total madness and so I'd made the decision to give up booze in order to quit the other extracurricular activities that trailed in alcohol's sloshy wake. No one had sex in the bathroom with someone they'd just met at a bottomless Bacchanalian brunch, gallivanted Soho until sunrise or called dealers *sober*, I told myself. By October, I was off booze and collected enough to look with lucid steadiness at the boyfriend who'd slapped me but apparently wanted to marry me and wonder why I'd not left already. Also he farted at picnics. Practically on top of the charcuterie.

The previous year I'd already done one stint as Peter's lodger when I'd needed to escape the lighthouse of locals who heckled me from the street every time I tried to go to bed at Polly's, but this was to be more permanent and as the Rastafarian drove me across London to what felt like my second home, I decided to give

up men for a while, as well as booze. By this point I'd had so many
relationships I felt like I was dragging previous conquests behind
me like a Scandinavian trawler, with maybe half of the fish still
talking to me, and so I was content to leave dating to Peter, whose
generation had no problem with sober dates, I quickly found.

'Have you been to Portobello?' I asked, early one morning, when
I heard him letting himself in upstairs. Peter was an antiques dealer,
which was way cooler than any millennial *marketing* enterprise.

'No,' he said.

'The bread shop?'

'No.'

'Why are you being so weird?' I asked.

'I'm not. I just . . . went to Alison's.'

'At eight a.m.?'

'We had coffee and . . . stuff,' he said.

'You did not have a *date* at eight in the morning?' I squealed,
overjoyed not to be partaking in any exhausting revelries
of my own.

Living in that house, where Hugo had grown up, also made
me feel that I lived in a real home so much more than any of the
rentals had allowed, and settled me. It was full of *stuff* gathered
over years in a life that didn't move annually, and I walked around
asking: 'What's this? What's this? What's this?' like a magpie. His
home was an old curiosity shop that reminded me of my parents'
house – my dad once making a foray into antiques at the Tramshed
in Bath but finding his stall emptied by lunchtime when my mum
turned up with sandwiches and spotted half their wedding presents
now price-tagged. From those days we still had the (now slightly
tainted) old fox fur, a dishevelled mink, some ancient leather
boxing gloves and a torturous Chinese chair someone pulled the
short straw to sit on if we had guests. Now Peter was teaching me
how to look for a 'piece' of silver, as though I was his protégée.

The fact he was naturally quiet in the same way my parents were gave me a sense of peace I'd not found elsewhere and emotionally it felt like a parental anchoring more stable than my romantic moorings. Peter also felt the pangs of solitude in an otherwise empty house and liked having someone to come home to, he said, now Hugo had left. Divorced years before and with an on-off girlfriend who lived elsewhere, empty-nest syndrome had been inevitable and we cancelled out each other's loneliness.

'There's certainly never been rosehip oil in the bathroom before,' he said. 'Although what on earth that's used for, I don't know.'

'Nor do I,' I said. 'It smells like dust.'

The way our conversation ran on reminded me of the way Everleigh and I talked to each other; differing perspectives on everything to discuss. As Hugo got on with his Holden Caulfield life in New York, my own bildungsroman was coming together nicely with various pieces of grown-up intel from Peter, who now held jazz tutorials and imparted much information about where to source various ingredients I'd never dare cook (onglet – which is never called *skirt*, he said, and guinea fowl, although I should be careful because he'd once had a break-up over guinea fowl in Borough Market, he added).

Other advice included the fact it was nice to start first dates with coffee at Damien Hirst's gallery ('but don't look at the awful paintings, obviously') then descend upon the Queen's Head in Vauxhall for lunch where I would find 'the most drinkable house wine in London and a quite decent cannelloni served by the most flirtatious waitresses.'

'The most flirtatious waitresses in the *whole* of London?' I asked, in awe of such a survey.

He considered. 'No – just Vauxhall.'

Living there made me feel like I lived on the most civilised street in the world after flea-hopping rental life. Lavender, rather than fly-tipped ironing boards, grew in the front garden and Peter had known most of the neighbours for years. They *spoke* to each other, I saw, and called the *landline* to ask if they could borrow *DVDs*, which showed me neither were extinct. Bill, our brilliant neighbour, came round often, or I dropped round the bread Peter had picked up for him, and sat in his kitchen chatting about Joanna Lumley, who had once lived round the corner, or how his daughter was doing at university. Bill had difficulty walking, but knew the street was looking out for him. It was just sort of – lovely, I realised, and then Arla moved further down the road and joined our Stockwell gang, cooking me dinner at hers and restoring that feeling I'd had in Edinburgh of making a pocket of life in a big city and being allowed to feel less lost.

Peter, I also found, didn't have any of the contagious anxiety my generation lived with, which was calming, and he never mentioned blue-ticking on WhatsApp once. On wintery Sunday nights before I'd given up booze we'd sat in the kitchen struggling under the weight of the weekend's revelries and he told me there'd been rumours of marital strife at a party he'd been at in Oxfordshire. 'Could be an expensive third divorce,' he said, holding his phone out to show me the house.

'Is that a Hogarth?' I said, looking at a picture I vaguely recognised.

He zoomed in. 'Something Victorian,' he said.

I was also teaching him things a daughter might have – if he'd had one. Like how to wrap your hair in a towelling 'beehive', he called it, to dry it, or how to hashtag on Instagram, which he realised was a good way to sell antiques now the markets were struggling in the face of online sale.

'Let's have a look,' I said, finding his Instagram and a new picture of a stirrup cup. Beneath it the caption read: #GeorgeIVsilverfoxheadstirrupcupLondon1829.

I laughed. 'Most people just hashtag, like, *yolo* or *foodbaby* – but fine,' I said.

'That one got sixteen likes, so it must be working,' he said. 'I did #shellcameo, but that's only got four likes.'

I nodded. 'It's dog-eat-dog out there.'

I think the assumption amongst friends my age was that it would be too boring living with someone parental. But the first of my friends were buying flats if heavy family help allowed, and if they were renting, they often had jobs more stable than mine, or at least stable relationships that helped ground them. The consensus was that we'd never be allowed to have stability in every area of our life, but needed it in at least *one*, and now I was single, and self-employed, the idea of sharing a decrepit rental with constantly changing strangers was just too much.

The friends of mine who had constantly moving love and work lives, as well as insecure housing, had the highest anxiety of all and I saw how stressed they were waiting for short-term contracts; forever job hunting; forever advertising rooms online and setting up viewings to fill rooms. On the side, they tried to meet someone, facing the myriad micro-rejections involved in twenty-first-century dating and exhausting themselves looking for love in a sly world where ghosting was now normal behaviour.

Juggling impermanence in every area was too draining, and so I needed the calm of that base at Peter's, and his routine and mine, that developed there. In the mornings we drank coffee and I fired up my laptop while he scanned *The Times*. We just read, often, in the evenings, cooked each other dinner and talked. He'd been worried we'd do a bottle of Malbec a night when I moved in, so my sobriety was beneficial to both of us and I could walk in a straight line to my bedroom by the end of the night.

My friends thought my move to Peter's was '*so weird*' but I knew from my relationship with Everleigh that age-gap relationships between an older man and a younger woman were always treated with suspicion. I saw it as a cultural hangover from books and films like *Lolita* and *American Beauty* that suggested there was something predatory in the interest of the men but I knew I was safe at Peter's, even if he admitted some of his friends had made 'the usual' comments, and one of them – before realising I knew Peter, and who was only slightly younger – had even asked me out. Our society was just sex-obsessed and projected it onto everything, but there was nothing weird to me about my tenancy, even if Peter did change his email sign-off to 'Peter (Rachman)' after I moved in.

That winter Emilia Clarke was filming a scene for a new Hollywood movie called *Last Christmas* on our street, a flyer pushed through the door told us, and I watched from the window as it buzzed with 100 runners, directors and crew. Inside, the warmth barely spread from the tall old house above me to my room by the garden and I slept in a hat, gloves and coat, listening to foxes in the quiet outside and wondering if I was Stockwell's Harry Potter in my almost-cupboard under the stairs.

But living at Peter's was freedom and being single for the first time in almost ten years, which meant I didn't have to answer to anyone was liberating. I felt slightly like I'd conducted a quadrant survey of men in the UK and could write many academic papers on the subject, so I was glad to have stepped out of the game.

'You'd move in with a man you met at a bus stop,' Libby said.

'The only person I've ever met at a bus stop and moved in with was a woman,' I implored.

'Fine,' she huffed. 'But your boyfriends are such weirdos most of the time. The news guy was a prick.'

'Which one?' I asked.

'Exactly. Just have a year off,' she begged, so I agreed, imagining I'd walk through 2019 with a blindfold like Sandra Bullock in *Bird Box* in order to stay single.

Instead of drinking and dating in the evenings, I ran around Clapham Common, where I realised I now had an entirely new problem. In men and booze I'd given up my two main hobbies and now had no idea who I was. Suddenly there was so much time, and apart from *write, read and run* (which I did whether I was flirting with vice or not), I didn't know what to do with it.

What did I used to do with *time*, I wondered, as I ran round and round the common Sam had walked me around once upon a time. The thought had first occurred to me at the end of the summer just after I'd given up drinking and I'd realised how many hours I spent in pubs. My solution then was to join two netball teams and was still playing twice a week in Regent's Park and Paddington. But I used to like lots of things, I thought, sadly, and they'd all vanished. I used to play the piano and (briefly) the saxophone. Even more briefly, the violin. Before I'd grown up and become obsessed with chasing the night, I used to swim every week, and if my mum brought me to London, I'd stand in the Tate Modern drawing the art I liked into a little sketchbook. I used to measure the seasons in sports teams rather than whether you sat outside in the sun or inside by the fire with a drink.

I'd once talked of writing a book, and learning to (properly) cook and all sorts of other inspiring, exciting things before getting persuaded to sit in watching box sets and order Deliveroo with someone I'd half cared about at the time, I thought, lamely realising I had nothing to show for it now. Intimacy was my go-to hangover cure, but now I didn't need one. Even better was that, sober, I wasn't telling myself I missed someone I didn't and ringing them up to cry tears of white wine on the phone. Or rebounding just to bandage over the last emptiness with someone new. But the hideous expression 'my other half' had taken on a secondary, awful meaning because now 'whole', and not 'double', made me feel incomplete. That meant room to fill in the gaps, I encouraged myself, as I ran back to Peter's and sat down at the kitchen table to come up with a personality via a list of things I'd always talked about doing before getting blindsided by someone else's life.

My idea was to write down fifty-two options of what I could love, alone, next and tick off one a week for a year and in the process, work out what I liked, I thought smugly. I don't need a man, I thought smugly, like a 12st Pussycat Doll and wondering – with some interest – who I'd find I was now I wasn't just a chain-smoking, fast-drinking, frantically writing, exhausted socialite defined by my relationships.

'*The new me*,' I said, going into the other room to practise my tumble turns by roly-polying on the floor and almost breaking my back. 'Fuck me, that was awful,' I said. To my horror, I appeared to have aged.

Quickly, the list grew as I remembered all sorts of miniature and more elaborate dreams and aspirations I'd had to go to New York, see the *Goldfinch* painting in real life, swim in Hampstead Ponds and visit the Lake District. I wanted to go life drawing and see what RADA acting classes were like; make soufflé, learn to fish, watch live international rugby, see my friend Serena play for the England netball team, go to the Edinburgh Fringe and try to work out when I was there if I'd ever be brave enough to stand in front of a mic myself. I'd been asked a handful of times in pubs (granted) by strangers (granted) if I was a stand-up comedian, but an actor I'd met on Jools Holland's champagne train had offered to be my manager after I'd drunkenly monologued the tale of Flevo-Natuur. Although you didn't even have to be funny for that story to be funny.

My friends were also pushing me towards comedy and in truth, turning everything into a joke had become a coping mechanism, a way to determinedly lighten the dark I'd seen.

'But everyone's *friends* think they're funny,' I told Madi, an American I'd met on the Regent's Park netball court.

'I'm not funny,' she said.

'That is true,' I agreed.

As for the rest of the list, I'd never even done proper millennial things like go to Barry's Bootcamp, run a half marathon or have a bikini wax, I realised, failing modernity utterly, and phoning a

salon near Peter's to right it. When I arrived at my appointment
a week later I was immediately Eleanor Oliphanted by a woman
who lost her mind on my vagina, and knew I'd never go back. 'I
thought I'd take it all off,' she said when she saw the horror on my
face. 'I can see that,' I replied.

But that was exactly the point of the list, I thought as I waddled
home, to work out what I *didn't* like as well as what I did. Epiphany
number one was the fact I did *not* like vaginal waxologists.

The list also grew fast because suggestions were being flung at
me from all directions by people I realised had wanted to do all
sorts of different things themselves before jobs that felt like relationships and relationships that were a lot of work got in the way.
My mum had spent ten years in London wanting to swim in the
Hampstead Ponds, as I now did, and never had, so came up on the
train to join me in the 3D David Attenborough show that was the
ladies' pond, dragonflies careering close to our faces and ducks at
the end of each stroke.

'I definitely just kicked something,' I told her.

'Probably one of the carp,' she said.

'You what?' I asked.

'I didn't tell you before because I knew you wouldn't get in,'
she said, as I swam as close as I could next to her like a child,
totally horrified. But it was invigorating at the same time, the
cold water, and the wildlife up close, then the sun warming us on
the bank after.

'Nature's quite ... cool actually,' I said, while she just looked
at me as though it was the most obvious thing in the world. 'It's
just a shame it has to be called nature, isn't it? It makes it sound
so ... *wet.*'

Everything on the list provided some small, fascinating epiphany in the end and I saw that we didn't make enough time for new
things any more, then quickly got anxious about the idea of trying
anything in the discomfort zone. But once you started, anxiety

turned to pride or at least amusement, I told myself, as I stood one particularly terrifying evening on a dark street in central London trying to force myself through the door of RADA and wishing I still drank so I might have un-tensed myself at the pub beforehand. During the two-hour acting class that followed I realised, to my surprise, that I just couldn't *let go* very easily. Maybe you're not as relaxed as you thought, I told myself, after we were instructed to morph into animals for twenty minutes and I chose a sloth so I could pretend to be asleep on the floor.

It was invigorating to push myself through so many new things and meet all sorts of interesting people in the process, even if they did make too enthusiastic a chicken, I told Peter, when I got home and lit a cigarette by the back door.

'I'm smoking full-time for Everest,' I told him, knowing he disapproved. 'Bear Grylls said it worked.'

That was the biggest thing on the list: Everest Base Camp. One of the girls I'd met playing netball had signed up to a trekking holiday in April and had suggested I come with her.

'All right,' I said, as though I was agreeing to Friday night drinks, which I don't think she expected.

But April was a long way away, I thought, as I booked flights to Kathmandu with money I'd managed to save while I'd lived with boyfriends and then added to by quitting drinking. I'll worry about it nearer the time, I told myself, which was my philosophy with most things.

'You are going to write your will before you leave though, right?' Madi asked.

But how hard could it be, I thought, now I was a RADA-trained, bikini-waxed, wild carp swimmer?

Dear Everleigh,

Happy New Year! How was it? Riotous lock-in at the church where you danced on the organ? Or too many ales at the local hostelry before you fell asleep on a curb? I saw it in in Bath and was in bed by 10 p.m. for the first NYE I can remember. It was great, although I was shocked awake by fireworks at midnight and bathed in a sort of divine light alongside Alfie, shivering with fear.

I was all set for my first teetotal Christmas until my cousin's wedding two days before, where being both single and teetotal in an infinity pool of happy couples I hadn't asked to holiday next to did NOT feel an option. I had a few glasses to compensate and now appear to accidentally be seeing one of the best men.

He lives in Amsterdam. What is it about Amsterdam and me?

L x

PS Do you think *all* nuns were lascivious drunks before they signed up to convent life, or just some?

12

Oranges Are Not the Only Fruit

On the balcony of a penthouse in Borough Market I stood on one leg like a flamingo watching a middle-aged woman have therapy in a room below me. The decking was sauna hot, which required you to hop from one foot to the other to ease the heat, and I smoked through the voyeurism, every window in the flat open and blaring horns swirling up into the air from the street below. An emergency soundtrack.

Since January, when Peter decided to renovate my room, I'd been living with Madison from the Regent's Park netball team. Madi had been relocated from the States and her company was forking out £4,000 a month for a two-floor pad in Borough.

'Well, *how* the other half live,' I said, when she showed me round on move-in day and I saw that her bedroom was the size of some of the flats I'd lived in.

Because she didn't pay rent, neither did I, but instead gave her my friends and took her for dinner every time I had a plus one; an arrangement we were both very pleased with. Despite being polar opposites – Madi was numbers, I was words; she was shy, I was not; she was CrossFit daily, I'd rather die – we got on immediately and spent almost every minute together after I moved in. She was so easy-going she fit into my motley friendship group effortlessly and the flat turned into a series of parties with an open-door policy, people flitting in and out on their way elsewhere.

After a three-month break from alcohol, I was back drinking and knew that while I'd never be an angel, the devil was less in my mind. Sober abstinence had slowed me down and showed me that I didn't *need* to drink all the time, while my taste buds had recovered enough to recognise that you shouldn't drink wine as fast as water, because actually wine was quite a *lot* stronger.

Living with someone Peter's age did undoubtedly help sobriety because while he drank a couple of glasses of red every night, he never threw the kind of raucous parties where loud music and heady youth made you want to drink and dance all night, like Madi and I quickly did.

But I was also still playing netball, going to the gym, ticking off the things on my list and had lost my alcoholic stamina, so drinking had morphed back into an enjoyment rather than something I thought of as a necessary crutch. That had been a relief and it was reassuring to know I could give it up again if I needed to.

On our balcony beneath the tall, glittering Shard Madi and I slobbed about, me chain-smoking 'for Everest' and her practising handstands. Or we spent the evenings continuing her education in British comedy in the open-plan sitting room with its exposed brick walls until she fell asleep, usually.

Every time I left the flat for the shops I walked past the pub where everything had started with Tom and again hoped today wouldn't be the day I bumped into him.

'I ruined my life at that pub,' I said, pointing it out to Irish Bea and Hannah, the WA and GD from our netball team, who were helping move me from Peter's.

Bea wound the van window down and stuck two fingers up at the pub.

'FUCKKK YOUUUU,' she screamed, making the driver in the stream of traffic below us and several pedestrians jump.

'Jesus,' Hannah said, as we sunk as low as possible in the front seats.

'Sorry, lads,' she said. 'London traffic. Worse than fuckin' Dublin. I can't take it.'

Tom and I *had* bumped into each other a year before on my way through Bermondsey and he'd stopped stock-still like a wild rabbit when he saw me. Somehow I kept walking, but memories of Paris, his head on my lap in the sun by the Seine; Brussels – cold and drunken – and a week drinking rum in Havana made me email him a couple of hours later while I sat alone outside José after lunch.

'That was a shock – but I guess we were going to bump into each other sooner or later,' I wrote. 'I'm around the corner still, if you want to talk.'

Our first date had been where I now sat: expectation and octopus.

'There's nothing to talk about,' he'd replied, which jolted right through me, that familiar wave of rippling dread.

I might have laughed if I hadn't felt so sick.

'Um, how about the fact you lied compulsively about being separated, then wouldn't leave me alone when I broke up with you and tried to win me back with JUSTIN BIEBER lyrics, all while being a superior work colleague. Maybe you want to apologise, I dunno?' I started typing, then deleted it, lit another cigarette and posted some pictures of Iberico ham on Instagram.

'Unfiltered,' I said, aloud, which reduced the cuntishness of it dramatically, I thought.

After moving into Madi's flat with its view of therapy below, I'd started to think of watching therapy as halfway to having it myself after the Ronaldo story had brought things more into my consciousness. I hadn't realised I was looking straight into a therapist's window at first but then the woman in the chair by the window cried and was handed a box of tissues. Above her, a cheap classroom blind was pulled to the ceiling, but she never looked up. Brave to have therapy during your lunch break and go back to the office with eyes puffed from tears, I considered, but that's what we all did, wasn't it? Fit trauma around office hours. Fit everything around work.

I admired her, knowing that I hadn't worked much of my own shit out yet and was still rushing forwards while ignoring the past. Part of it was financial, because therapists in London were like theatre tickets: £60 for the worst seats in the house. But I also knew an hour in therapy would do more for me than any expensive night out and so I was also just putting it off, I guess. I'd had a £80 consultation with a double-barrelled surname in an area I now lived nowhere near and it had been brutally off-putting, how quickly she'd pinned labels on me after listening to ten minutes of my complex, gritty life. 'Daddy issues,' Clarity Buckwheat-Epiphany diagnosed as though naming a colour – which I did not appreciate one bit given she'd known me forty minutes. I was many colours, obviously.

On the balcony, I took a drag and wondered what the woman below was talking about as she gesticulated wildly. The options were endless, and the detail, grim, by the looks of the tears. Then she moved her gaze to the sky and I dropped to my knees in guilt and crept into the flat on all fours, stubbing my cigarette out as I went.

At the fridge I plucked an almost-finished bottle of white wine from the door and held it against my head, then walked back out to the balcony and dialled Madi. 5.15 p.m. Three minutes.

It rang twice.

'Yasss, kween,' came her ever more subtle American accent.

'She's not having a good session.'

'You're going to make that woman leave her therapist, you know that, don't you?'

'She almost certainly hasn't seen me yet. I'll be better. Slyer.'

'Did you write today?'

'Three hundred words on vegan ice lollies, but had a *way* more interesting idea, for a book, right? A young, disaffected journalist

watches her boyfriend having therapy with his wife and then – does
something. Like *The Girl on the Train* but more Girl on a . . . Balcony.'

'And autobiographical.'

'Hardly.'

Madi laughed. 'What else did you do today?'

'Pizza Pilgrims, Pornhub, bottle of white.'

'Again.'

'I know. That dough though.'

'Double pepperoni and honey?'

'Yep. DIY honey – their drizzling is weak *as*. Do you want me
to save you some?'

'Nah, it's all right.'

'Good. I ate it all already.'

'I know.'

'Two things about porn, right?'

'Yep.'

'Firstly: does watching it *always* make you a bad feminist? And
secondly: do you get that thing where you're immediately horrified the second it's all over? Like, who put *this* on?'

'That's normal.'

'Good. It always makes me feel like an actual sex offender.'

'I'm getting in the lift. Two seconds.'

A minute later, Madi's key turned in the door downstairs and
her work shoes clopped up the stairs. It was 5.18 p.m. on the dot.
That was another way we differed: she was timetables, spread-
sheets, normal work hours, order. I was a rush and spontaneous
chaos with a veneer of organised creativity; but mainly anchoring
myself through her more reliable routine.

She swung a clinking backpack onto the kitchen counter and
pulled two bottles of rosé out, putting one in the fridge, then
getting a stemless wine glass and coming out onto the balcony
with the other bottle. She unscrewed it and poured herself a glass,
plonking the bottle down on the table in front of me.

'You're the best,' I said, picking it up and pouring a swollen glass of light-pink wine.

'I know,' she said.

'*Please* don't go to CrossFit,' I begged elaborately, a daily ritual.

'Come with me,' she said. Another ritual.

'I'd *love to* but I've had a bottle of wine for lunch,' I told her.

'Don't pretend you'd come even if you hadn't,' she said knowingly.

'I know. It sounds utterly vile. That video of you climbing up a rope made me feel genuinely ill.'

She laughed.

'*Please* don't go. It's hot and sunny and everyone's out there having the time of their office-clogged minds.'

I'd spent half of the afternoon watching people hovering around the entrance to Borough Market, drinking and smoking outside Brindisa's red awnings as waiters ferried bottles of wine and plates of croquettes. The second it hit 5 p.m., a semicircular huddle of pint drinkers spilled around the Southwark Tavern and crowds of smokers breathed tar into the heat outside Katzenjammers and The Sheaf as bouncers boiled in black.

I pulled a face like *The Scream* at Madi, who just watched me like TV.

'Have you been outside today?'

'No – watched *The L Word* and sunbathed. I wanted to watch *Blue is the Warmest Colour* again but I thought it would be too intimidating. Anyway can't you just do handstands on the balcony while I smoke, then we can do something *fun*?'

'Fine. Let's go drunken art critiquing at the Tate and *try* not to go to see Pop,' she added sternly. There was a barely secret speak-easy next door at the Breakfast Club and having to descend only five floors to a bar was too tempting. We were beyond regular and Pop, the manager, had two negronis on the bar within five minutes of us walking in, despite any length of queue.

You see a completely different side of London when you live somewhere amazing and I knew how lucky I was to land again on my feet at Madi's. I didn't dread coming home and I rarely left the flat unless I had a job or slunk through the market to the gym. For the second time in seven years I felt some financial security purely because I didn't have to pay rent, which was as effective an anxiety pill as anyone who's ever been a freelancer in a big city will understand.

Living with a friend was also an antidote to living with boyfriends and I was avoiding commitment at all costs. For inspiration I ordered *Free Woman* by Lara Feigel but fell asleep reading the academic introduction and then just flash-read the sex scenes like a teenage boy with his dad's Bond collection. Being single was going well, although back then 'being single' never meant not *dating*, it just meant avoiding sliding into another relationship, and I hadn't imagined for a second that I'd have a year of celibacy. If I already knew I'd be a shit angel, I also knew I'd be a fucking *awful* nun.

After the false start at Christmas with my cousin's best man (and an eight-day date that spanned four countries as we flew from Amsterdam to London, then Paris, where we both had jobs, before Budapest) I turned twenty-nine and the real year of *no commitment* was beginning, I told Madi, as we walked into Borough Market for a celebratory pint on day one.

'I just jumped the starting gun too soon, you know? But the race has started now,' I said, adding, 'Do you have athletics in America?'

'Yes. People run in America,' she said, deadpan.

'I was just kidding,' I said as we bowled along through the ghosts of my former existence.

'What you need to know about me, if we're going to live together, is that I'm extremely funny and if you don't find it funny, that's because it's British and you don't get it yet.'

'Got it,' she smiled.

Tom was everywhere in Borough Market. At the wine bar-
rels at the back of Bedales, in plumes of smoke outside The
Wheatsheaf, sitting in the window on the top floor of the Bunch
of Grapes, but I was on a high regardless. Places like this were
why people came to London from all over the world, I thought,
and we *lived* here.

While we waited for the netball girls to drop the hire van back
Madi and I ordered two pints at the Market Porter and she headed
towards the bathroom as I stood at the bar and took a huge gulp.
Next to me a tall, dark-skinned man, also with two pints, was
doing the same.

'We're thirsty,' I said immediately, wondering if a lamer sentence existed in the English language.

'Yeah,' he drawled, with a half laugh. *Goddamnit*, I thought,
American. I was surrounded.

'Hey, would you have some recommendations for things to do
around here?' he asked earnestly, big brown eyes and over-6ft fit.
Ripped, you could tell, under a white T-shirt, jeans, jacket.

'For sure – it's all right here,' I said.

'Dope.'

'If I were you, I'd walk along Southbank to Westminster, have
a drink, look at the books, pop into the Tate.' He didn't look like
an art guy, or a book guy – but fuck it, it sounded good.

'I'd show you myself but it's my moving-in party,' I said. 'But I
could show you around tomorrow,' I added, not consciously pick-
up-artist-ing, just trying to be nice.

'That'd be super dope,' he said, getting his phone to take
my number.

'Lucy,' I said, sticking my hand out to shake his. 'And Madi,' I
said, as she appeared next to us, as did his also very attractive friend.

We all shook hands.

'Impressive,' Madi said, when we left the bar.

'He was just *super* dope.'

'He was so dope,' she agreed.

'Shall we actually call them?'

'Are you literally going to pull on your first night in the flat?' she said.

I considered. 'Maybe second night? The netball team's coming tonight.'

Their reactions, when they saw the flat, were the same as mine and I lost track of the number of times I was called a lucky fuck from then on in.

After that first weekend in Borough I prised my bleary eyes open to read a message on my vibrating phone. Madi. 'Your underwear is on your door handle. Found it hanging off the corner of my laptop screen this morning.'

I winced. 'Oh fuck. Sorry,' I replied.

'Hilarious,' she texted back. Then: 'But also, what have I let myself in for?'

Neither of us knew what we were in for that year when we became close, and Madi's life in particular was about to change dramatically.

She was still typing.

'Also – just so you know – if American dudes say they're semi-professional basketballers, it's total BS trickery. He basically played for his school.'

'I mean – I'd say we got picked up,' I replied. 'If we hadn't picked them up first.'

We'd re-met the Americans in the market on Sunday and Super Dope had left our flat at midnight like a fit Cinderella, leaving me with the impression that if one-night stands were always this charmingly easy, I should have been focusing on them years ago instead of slipping in and out of more complicated arrangements. The fact that he was flying back to New York that morning meant no post-sex dinner date, no texting and no accidental relationship. I'd remained safely single. Win.

Thank you and goodbye, I thought, opening my door to unwind yesterday's pants from the handle and noticing a yellow Post-it note stuck on the wall opposite. Madi had drawn a cartoon of a basketball player before she'd gone to work. SUPER DOPE, she'd written beneath, which I had to agree it very much was.

But a few months in, things had become slightly tangled by the fact Madi and I sometimes woke up to both sets of our underwear scattered all over the flat. The first time this happened I'd emerged hungover from my room and edged upstairs to drink fourteen pints of water when I'd been stopped in my tracks in the same way I imagined burglaries froze you; that feeling that something's wrong with the room before you know exactly what. Those few seconds pre-realisation exist in their own time frame and go on forever. I got out my phone and WhatsApped Madi.

'Did we . . . ?'

'Yeah . . . My memory is also hazy. But – yeah.'

'*Okayyyy*,' I said aloud to myself.

I wasn't as surprised as I could have been because we'd been inseparable for months and the closeness we had as friends who lived together often felt like it was spilling into something else I couldn't define, and didn't feel the need to either. It felt like we gravitated towards each other, equally protective and amused by the opposite nature of our entire lives. Then it just crossed over, I guess.

There would be millions of ways to try to describe 'why' then if I wanted to. I'd always been experimental, I suppose, usually said yes to new things, and I'd been put off men to some degree. But Madi and I just had chemistry that was above gender and therefore made it irrelevant. In 2019 the societal ease around sex, and who you could say you found attractive, changed the idea of a norm that men like women, and women like men. Bisexuality, even if you didn't use the word, which I never did, was common and I saw sexuality as on a scale, thinking I was probably 80:20 or 70:30 (men to women) if I had to try to pin it down. Maybe new ideas about gender identity were just making straight women and men think differently, too.

Sexual fluidity was common amongst my female friends. Many of them had dating apps set to 'both' and would often get with girls on nights out, even if they didn't go home with them. I've been told that annoys the lesbian community, who often don't like to date 'bi' women because of the association with men, or the fact it's sometimes still deemed a bit fash, or a phase, or whatever else. But either way, many straight women were realising that women were softer, safer, nicer, 'more considerate', 'so different', generally warmer and lacking the harshness men often had.

Madi was so much more caring than so many of the men I'd been with: ordering pizza and juice to the flat from the other side of the world if she was away and I was hungover; leaving breakfast in the fridge or coffee outside my room when she left for work, always with a Post-it note stuck on top that referenced one of our new private jokes. She never seemed to expect anything back – she just thought differently to guys, I realised. I loved men, in some ways, but possibly there was something in my subconscious that said women were less damaging. More trustworthy.

Maybe the consideration that we could now be with the same sex also came partly from the fact male porn was so aggressive, which made some girls I knew only watch lesbian porn, and perhaps afterwards see girl-on-girl as less intimidating. Maybe a more general openness towards sex full stop enabled us to think that even if we didn't know what we were doing, we could just say that, and learn, especially now male ego and male–female power dynamics weren't involved.

By the time I got to university, having a threesome was on the personal improvement checklists of most students, but despite the fact I'd gained that kind of 2.1, I'd found the most remark-able thing about it was that my friend Sylvie and I had stripped off to find we were wearing exactly the same underwear set (to the joy of the man, who immediately assumed we'd planned to seduce him).

I'd kissed various female friends when pissed but generally preferred to think of myself as just the blur of the things modernity allowed rather than try to label it. I had a tomboyish side that I only noticed in my late twenties and I guess I'd started to see gender traits as I did sexuality – both being on a scale. Most people were somewhere off 100 per cent on both and half the women I knew had had same-sex dalliances. Some were super romantic: boat, stars, sea. Others were just drunken fallings for and at each other in bars. That year, one of my closest and straightest friends, who hadn't got the blur at all, felt such a strong mutual attraction to a girl in a club that they'd gravitated towards each other and kissed, prompting her to set her Hinge to women, too. 'I've realised I like Mancunian men and Spanish girls,' she said.

'Mate – niche,' I said.

'I know.'

The apps undoubtedly helped the casualness of it because you didn't need to 'out' yourself as anything any more. You didn't even have to skulk nervously into gay bars. You could just privately change your settings and start talking to both sexes. Women I knew who'd done that sometimes found they were actually way more interested in girls than guys and promoted themselves to lesbian dating apps in the hope they were attractive to (what they called) 'proper' gay women.

'There are so many options on lesbian dating apps though,' one friend told me, screen-shotting them so I could try to help her decide what gender she was out of: womxn, genderqueer, questioning, neutrois, gender-non-conforming, two spirit, pan-, poly- and bi-gender. 'If I don't even know my own gender I might have to go back to shitty men,' she said, with a cry-face emoji.

We had the freedom to experiment more than previous generations, I guess, so I didn't freak out when Madi and I started sleeping together although I was still unready for commitment of any kind after ten years plastered in it. With her, it felt more about mood and chemistry than black-and-white sexuality and it was sort of exciting to let it happen. The friendship and the fact we lived together solidified something, and before long we just looked at each other and knew what the other was thinking. The main difference I suppose was that it felt undeniably more supportive than any heterosexual relationship I'd been in, as though gender cemented something even above love.

As April drew closer and the Himalayas loomed, I wished Madi was coming too, knowing she'd keep me safe, but also not wanting to leave our life for the near-death experience I appeared to have signed up for as a holiday.

Jo, the friend I was going with, was following several EBC Instagram accounts, she informed me, where people were saying the temperature fell to -10 overnight.

'What's EBC?' I asked, lighting a cigarette.

'Everest Base Camp,' she said. 'Where we're going. Have you got a sleeping bag yet? On Instagram they're saying . . .'

'YES I KNOW,' I snapped, anxious as hell.

I only had boots, which I'd tried wearing in during a pub crawl in the South Downs and had ripped my feet to shreds. I'd also injured myself training for a half marathon I'd signed up to (another thing on my 52 list) and seen a physiotherapist who had lost most of the colour in her face when I told her Everest was in two months' time. She told me to stop exercising completely if I was going to try to 'make it' and I think I realised then that it wasn't a given that I *would* reach EBC. Strong, or stupid? I wondered, as I went home to emulate an Eric Prydz video of strengthening movements on a yoga mat on the balcony.

'Good day?' Madi asked, when she found me at 5.18 p.m.

'No. Apparently I have *disengaged glutes*,' I mumbled, trying to stop a cigarette falling from my lip while I echoed the physio. 'My disengaged glutes haven't been supporting me through life, the fuckers. I'm sure this is where the vast majority of my issues have been stemming from.'

'Have you got a sleeping bag yet?' she asked.

'NO,' I snapped, collapsing.

'When are you going?' a nice woman called Jenny asked me in the shop the next day as I stared at the 'mummy bags' which promised to save you from hypothermia in −18.

'Tomorrow,' I told her. 'I think.' The airline had gone bust that morning so we needed new £900 flights and I was reluctant to drain the last of my savings to buy death on a mountain.

'You're relaxed for someone that doesn't yet have a sleeping bag,' she said.

'Thank you,' I said. 'I'm very unrelaxed beneath the surface,' I might have added. This is how I dealt with extreme stress and fear – silent, slightly amused horror.

In the walking sticks section she told me to call them 'poles' and picked out a pair, then handed me a headlamp.

'Bit Chilean miner, no?'

'I did Killy,' she said simply.

'You killed who, sorry?' I asked.

'Kilimanjaro,' she said. 'I climbed it. Walked down with a broken foot.'

'Jesus,' I said, gripping the Kendal Mint Cake I'd picked up from the counter like it was a stress ball.

I'd already had three jabs and been prescribed Diamox, the anti-altitude sickness pills, from a pharmacist who said they'd give me 'fantastic nightmares', but the terrors seemed to have started without me taking a single pill. Out of pure fear at the approaching trip I carried on watching *The L Word* to try to work out if I was gay, while half-heartedly scrolling through EBC forums Jo had sent me two dozen links to, in case anyone on there knew how to survive. 'In Tibet they used to wear the same thing for a year, then wash themselves with yak butter and change into a new set of chubas. When in *Rome!*' someone had written, as I scrunched my face in confusion.

'What the hell are *chubas?*' I asked my phone, now wishing, quite seriously, that I was just going to Rome.

Advice on how to remain alive on the mountain was so conflicting, even down to the socks, that I gave up in the end. *What will be, will be*, I thought vaguely, remembering the huge list of medical supplies the tour company said we needed to carry in our packs. If they were correct, I'd have flu, nappy rash, diarrhoea, a bad cough, blisters, blue hands, insect bites, a headache and my period as soon as we arrived on the mountain.

Irish Bea wanted to come round the night before I left to say goodbye (potentially forever – she added) and found me staring at Madi's trekking gear in bewilderment, not yet having packed.

'Take me to a bar for my last supper,' I asked them, wanting four courses of negronis to soothe my journey to hell, and so off we went downstairs to say goodbye to our friends who worked there.

'Guess what Lucy's doing tomorrow?' Madi and Irish Bea asked every single person in the bar after we'd arrived, then shouting 'WALKING TO EVEREST' before anyone had time to reply.

'Not the summit,' I added, as mouths dropped, but by then we were being bought another tray of shots and it was 2 a.m. when I finally went home to pack.

When we got to the airport I realised I hadn't remembered a single pair of pants and had a vague memory of staring at a drawer of entirely inappropriate lingerie half-pissed before I'd gone to sleep. 'What's your excuse?' I asked Jo, who had forgotten her anti-altitude sickness pills but remembered to pack twenty bars of Fry's Peppermint Cream.

After two long flights and a stopover in Hong Kong, we arrived after almost twenty hours of travelling to darkness in Kathmandu and had only three hours' sleep before we were being driven through the night to Ramechhap airport for an internal flight to Lukla, the mountain starting point. Lukla airport is described online as the most dangerous airport in the whole world because its landing strip runs right to the end of a cliff. That and the fact that visibility in the Himalayas is regularly so poor made casualty rates sky high and my fear morphed from a fear of the unknown into something more concrete as we got closer to the riskiest flight I'd ever make in my life. The danger was so much more tangible than it had been in London, which helped to validate my feeling that fear, if not a heel-digging refusal to go any further, was highly reasonable. But it was the speed of disaster as soon as we arrived at Ramechhap that was the most shocking.

At 5 a.m. we were turned out of a minibus rolling with the boiled eggs they'd handed us for breakfast into a ramshackle airport that looked like a refugee camp and found it clogged with people delayed by cancelled flights into Lukla. The previous day a plane had crashed into a helicopter, killing two and landing everyone else in hospital. Pure horror set in then, that we couldn't even trust we'd be landed on the mountain safely. In the airport we stewed in the heat in gear meant for wintery mountain conditions and waited, while I wondered if caring about staying alive meant I should turn around and go straight back to the hotel.

Then thick clouds set in and visibility was declared too precarious for planes. There was a scram for helicopters and Jo and I got on the last one out of there feeling like we were being evacuated from a disaster zone, already. The feeling that I had no idea where I was safest in this nightmare place just sat in me, making me quiet but steeling me against what was coming in a grim resolve that I would make it all the way. It felt like going to war as we flew into Lukla and saw the crashed helicopter and plane nosedived into the earth below like an Imperial War Museum exhibit.

At Ramechhap I'd been so tired I'd fallen asleep sitting up and G, one of the Australians in our group, was already throwing up from altitude sickness pills by the time we reached Lukla. She'd taken a whole one, instead of the half-pill-a-day required, and lay curled in a ball as we were told that, because we'd arrived so late, we now had to walk the first 10 kilometres in complete darkness. The determination in the group to reach that night's teahouse without catastrophe bound us together as we snaked one by one up the mountain with headlamps clamped to our foreheads, hearing only the rush of water somewhere invisible below us. On day two, we lost the first member of our group to the altitude sickness which caused hundreds of people each trekking season to be flown quickly to hospital in Kathmandu, the risk being death if you didn't get the hell out of there. The soundtrack above us was the whir of helicopter blades, and every time one passed overhead you knew someone else was in a critical condition inside.

Who altitude sickness affected, and how, when and why, was almost completely unknown and therefore terrifying. We were told it sometimes felt like flu, or food poisoning – but most people had symptoms of one or the other on the mountain thanks to the teahouse cuisine in the places we stayed and the cold, which dropped to -15 at EBC. Essentially, you had to *guess* whether you had it, which made it feel like you were playing Russian roulette with your life.

Including those in the plane crash on day one, four people had died close to where we were walking within the first three days, one pushed off the mountain by a horse, we were told. Higher up, the queues at the summit were the worst in history, where dozens more dropped in the 'death zone'. There you couldn't breathe without oxygen tanks, which were running out in the queues. Lower down we walked like ants up the tracks, overlapping the same groups and then watching their numbers dwindle. One day you'd see someone hunched over a rock, in tears, with a pool of sick at their feet, then the next day, they'd be gone. Most of the time we never knew what became of the evacuees.

I just put one foot in front of the other like *heel, toe, heel, toe* and hoped I wouldn't fall, still feeling it dramatic to admit the chances of staying alive reduced daily in higher altitudes, but knowing they did. More than anything, it was a lesson in not worrying about tomorrow, but *today* and taking it an hour at a time. Not falling in the moment was all you could control.

The survival aspect of it reduced life to the very basics. We ate breakfast, walked 10k, ate lunch, walked a similar distance, then had egg-fried rice for dinner at a teahouse – the extremely basic hostel-style accommodations run by the Nepalese for mountain tourists – and went to bed. Technology was almost pointless – phone signal invisible and access to Wi-Fi rare – but when I could I texted Madi to show her I was still alive.

Halfway through the week it took us to climb to EBC, we'd arrived in Namche Bazaar and found an Irish bar perched on the side of the mountain, so Jo and I had got joyfully pissed with two Australian lesbians in our group, one of whom seemed to want to have sex in the bathroom. 'I think I'm being considered a REAL LESBIAN,' I messaged Madi that night. 'Great work,' she replied.

Our group held itself together like a regiment as we walked, looking out for each other, sharing food and water or the chlorine tablets that made it drinkable, carrying packs when we each had a turn at being hit by the altitude and felt every step twice as hard. The camaraderie makes me shiver with awe now in memory of how meaningful our dynamic was as we wound our way through a beautiful, ever-changing Nepalese landscape: a different world in a day. We'd started in a humid, tropical green land at 3,200m, which became dusty tracks with basic, dilapidated huts, and finally the crater-like other worlds higher up. Those were barren *Game of Thrones* landscapes where blizzards swirled and only shaggy yaks, after relentless streams of donkeys and horses lower down the trail, could carry life to those that survived on an arctic moonscape at 5,000m.

Most of the paths were so narrow we had to leap up the sides of sheer cliffs like mountain goats to avoid being pushed off the side by the marching bulks of the yaks and every time we got to a new teahouse, I opened a notebook and wrote 'arrived at hospital' before having to cross it out and write 'hostel'.

'Do you think that's a bad omen?' I asked Jo, who tipped her entire backpack upside down on her bed every time we arrived at a teahouse.

'Have you seen my tobacco?'

'No.'

'Swap a Diamox for a chocolate bar?'

'YES.'

The altitude didn't hit me until over 4,000m, but then I woke unable to breathe every night, and had to sit bolt upright in my sleeping bag drinking water until the weight sitting on my chest went away. The panic with it. Higher up, the feeling I'd been run over by something invisible got worse after a blizzard and I had to persuade a teahouse owner to sell me some local rum, swigging in my sleeping bag while the group played cards in my room and feeling then like a frat boy who'd been flattened by a truck. The way altitude sickness came and went with sleep was disconcerting and the day after my attempt to cure myself with a version of Nepalese hot toddy I woke feeling fine, only to climb higher before being rushed back down the steep hill we'd just ascended for altitude training. The sensation as I tried not to fall on the way back down and the guide grabbing my pack off my back, knowing what was happening, was so overwhelming it had brought tears of shock to my eyes. But another night in more oxygenated air cured me before the last leg of the trek.

I was lucky because not everyone was going to make it. The next day I felt so strong it was like I hadn't even struggled for a day, and carried on at the front of the group again knowing we were just two days away from EBC. But then Sarah, a fit 21-year-old Australian, had developed what sounded like a ninety-year-old tobacco merchant's cough and then became so sick the night after I had that she'd had to be evacuated by helicopter a day before we reached EBC. We sang her happy birthday before she got in the helicopter because she'd turned twenty-one that morning. Her birthday present: five days in a Kathmandu hospital with pneumonia amongst other things.

I knew on the final, worst stretch, as we walked over steep, slim paths of jagged, uneven snow-covered rock to base camp, that she'd never have made it – but we'd told her we'd do it for her and I was determined. When we finally arrived I just grinned, realising how strong you had to be to climb even this far up Everest. And I had. Right, I thought then, let's get the fuck out of here.

It was -15 and the energy I had was seeping away fast in the long queues for selfies at the flag-draped cairns. We still had to go back down the mountain in the quickly fading light to the teahouse we'd left that morning, given that only people climbing higher stayed in that deathly place, and amongst the celebration the fact base camp had become just another Instagram opportunity was depressing as hell. I stood alone watching the tents of those trying to reach the summit blow in a savage wind and heard a week later that a dozen of them blew straight off the side of the mountain, thankfully with no one in them, but just confirming how treacherous our end point was, even if it was only a base to go further for others. Some of whom would never leave this place, I thought. If you fell near the summit, bodies were deemed too dangerous to retrieve and so there you stayed in death with the other ghosts in that mountain graveyard. Forever.

When we got back to the teahouse I felt more alive than I think I ever had, knowing we'd *done it*, and feeling sheer relief on top of pride and exhaustion. A beer had never tasted more like champagne than it did then as we raised our bottles to each other that night. It felt almost religious, that drink.

Three more of our group were evacuated the next morning, scared of the descent, but a Canadian called Shay and I practically ran down the mountain with our headphones on, so giddy we'd made it and could now race 20 kilometres a day in air practically bubbling with oxygen.

'The group has decided that you are – on average – the best at going both up and downhill,' an American political aid called Steve told me one day as we walked, and I smiled, knowing it was a mountain compliment equivalent of being called Heidi Klum. 'What's your work-out routine?' he asked.

'Mainly I've been smoking,' I said, adding, 'Marlboro Golds,' in case he was interested in similar tobacco training.

He wasn't.

'I once trained with the SAS, for a job,' I said, then. 'Because they were letting women in finally – in 2019! But *that* was horrible. Press-ups in the mud and then we got "kidnapped" and thrown in this van and had black bags put over our heads and another journalist had a panic attack. Then we were interrogated in stress positions while an Alsatian barked in my face. The mental stuff was harder for sure. Car tyres aren't light, but I'd rather lug fake artillery about and swim through iced water in December than have my wrists tied and listen to white noise with a bag over my head. Do you know what I mean?' I added, looking at him.

He didn't.

We walked in silence for a while. That was one of the best things about trekking with a group you'd shared survival with – we didn't always have to speak. Comfort was just following each other along and intermittently sharing pieces of our normal lives back home in the ten different countries we came from.

In truth, the SAS day had disorientated me totally because it made me wonder if my mental strength was really so much weaker than my physical ability. But Everest was one hell of a psychological challenge every day, and surviving it made me feel more confident about my mind. Fear, the right sort, I realised, was extremely powerful in demonstrating to yourself what you're capable of. Being surrounded by so much danger made me see life differently too: more valuable and not to be wasted, because death happened all the time on the mountain. By the time I got home, 2019 was already being called one of Everest's deadliest seasons: eleven people didn't come back alive.

In London, summer was closing in and I was still determined not to fall in love. Keeping people at arm's length made that easy, but I'd noticed people seemed to gravitate towards you when you were trying to stay unattached, as though some sort of enticing aura glimmered around your edges. Maybe I just had a glint in my eye having survived EBC, which was regularly celebrated at the Breakfast Club's speakeasy. '*Base camp*,' I added, every time someone seemed to suggest I'd climbed to the summit, but nobody cared – they were just overjoyed I'd returned and I did feel vaguely heroic as a negroni on the house was placed in front of me on the bar.

My uncle likened it to the Bosnian war, which he described as, 'No one really knowing how dangerous it was when I was covering it and everyone just asking how the food was when I got home.'

That pretty much summed it up, I thought.

Whilst I'd been away, Madi had made a photographic diary of her time in London without me with pictures on her iPhone and captions about things she missed about us and our life. It was her way of hoping I'd come back, I think, and things with us were still on and off when I did.

Our non-exclusive rule was working fine most of the time, although Madi wasn't dating anyone else and didn't want to see it if I was, she said. She later said our friendship was just more important than anything else, so she was prepared to give me all the benefits of being in a relationship, without the commitment she thought I was scared of. Occasionally I found passive-aggressive Post-it notes stuck on my bedroom door if I hadn't come home, but mostly we were always together in a unique form of couple, and it was great.

I was still enjoying the perks of freelancing and saw so much of the world that year. I accepted jobs that meant I could travel, and went straight to dates from the airport when I landed back home. Life became hectic when you had to take commissions whenever they came in (not knowing when the next work would, and knowing someone else would win favour by saying yes if you didn't) and I was often doing two things at once, but I loved the constant stream of new people involved with each story.

I'd never been to Scandinavia and it was on the 52 list, so when a commission in Norway came up for a food magazine I said yes immediately, then found myself on the back of a fishing vessel deep at sea and trying not to throw up while I filed a piece about audio porn from my phone to *The Times* magazine, who'd commissioned me at the airport. 'I've got a pull,' Jose Pizarro – who was part of the cod story in Norway – shouted, reeling a fish through the water as I screamed that I was coming and someone else suggested the audio porn feature might not have left my mind.

When we arrived back in London, our Norway group fell into hysterics when I told them I was going straight to a date smelling like the shellfish we'd dismantled for lunch. But it was just a *drink*, I said, overly casual from fatigue and deciding to arrive in the black jeans I was wearing, with my overnight bag slung over my back, purely so I didn't have to go home and waste energy getting changed.

But to my great surprise, the guy seemed to like the smell of langoustine, if not the more casual approach in general, and within two hours he had invited me back to his house for cocaine and champagne. As we sat on deckchairs on his roof with glasses in hand and looked at an incredible view of the London Eye, I really did think something was seriously wrong with modern love. It was absurd that someone should be keener the less you appeared to care, I thought, rubbing what looked like cod roe off my calf.

'I'm pretty sure I still smelt like a Norwegian fishing vessel, which is a bit – warped,' I told Irish Bea, who agreed.

I guess it was just a comment on how non-committal my generation had learnt to become and had learnt to find attractive, secretly craving an anchor to steady us but keeping one eye on the lifeboat in case the ship creaked even slightly and we jumped.

None of the people I saw during that year stuck around very long, because I didn't want them to, but a month after that rooftop champagne date I went home to find my mum reading the paper and asking me if I didn't just break up with a guy with that name.

'Yep, why?' I asked, not wanting to go into the fact we hadn't been together long enough to break up.

She held out *The Times*. 'He's just sold his company for £2 million.'

'*Shit*,' I said, grabbing the paper.

'Maybe call him back and say you've changed your mind?' my dad added, quite serious.

'Yeah, maybe,' I said, knowing he'd not wanted a relationship either.

The main problem with constant dating was Sunday, I soon realised, which was usually an empty night after you'd prioritised friends on Friday and Saturday. By Sunday you were hungover and lonely and started looking on your phone for the company which could anchor you for a night. It was brilliantly religiously inappropriate, I thought. But you also had to gear yourself up *hard* for a Sunday date, I found, as Madi and I recovered on the sofa.

She'd just about started talking to me again after I'd turned up late to a friend's thirtieth the night before, after a Friday afternoon drink with someone I'd known for years had ended with Chinese takeaway and sex against the dining-room table. At that point someone he assured me wasn't his girlfriend rang relentlessly, vibrating his phone amongst the chicken chow mein cartons.

'Fuck off, Louise,' he shouted.

'It's Lucy,' I said.

'No, no. My phone,' he said.

I decided to concentrate on an antique candlestick that had been rocking precariously on the table in front of my face for the last five minutes.

'What's that?' Irish Bea asked me when I turned up at the party, pointing to a slick patch of something on the sleeve of a top I'd by then been wearing for forty-eight hours.

'Er. Sweet and sour sauce,' I said, quickly trying to brush it off. I had a horrible feeling it was something else and that it was also in my hair.

Madi went to the bar then, and I smoked awkwardly outside, exhausted, while Irish joined me for a drag.

'When a girl is calling all night, but the guy says he doesn't have a girlfriend . . . he does have a girlfriend, right?' I asked her.

'Yeah, why?'

'Bastard,' I said, exhaling into midnight air.

Madi and I were recovering at home on Sunday evening when The Sexter piped up on my phone. I inwardly groaned. I'd asked a mutual friend for his number after meeting him in a bar in town, to be told after a couple of monosyllabic messages that he didn't like texting, he only liked sexting. But he was fit. Fit fit. So I'd been acquiescing on and off for a fortnight.

Then my phone beeped again and I groaned outwardly this time, and looked at my screen.

'Come round and jump me at your leisure,' he'd written.

'Shit,' I said.

Madi looked at me, genuinely concerned. 'What?'

'I think I might have to go out,' I said.

She snorted. '*Have* to go out?'

Another message vibrated my phone: 'I want to watch you undress.'

Then: 'I want you on your knees.'

'You know every time you get a dirty text you make a face like Fleabag looking at the cameras,' she said, proud of herself for the reference, because one, it was British and two, I introduced her to it.

I feigned outrage, but my phone beeped again and I accidentally looked down. 'I like the idea of telling you what to do,' it said.

'There you go. It's like Andrew Scott is texting you,' she drawled.

We were a bottle of white in, but I knew I'd need at least another half if I was going to attempt to change out of tracksuit bottoms, which was too much even for a liaison this casual, I thought. Staying in to watch TV with Madi felt way more appealing. I yawned and walked to the fridge.

Downstairs, I realised the only thing that wasn't already lying dirtily on my bedroom floor was a black silk dress, slit to the knee (Topshop, but looked better), so I thought fuck it, being half-pissed and too tired to look for anything else.

'Oh no she dinnnttt,' I told my en suite reflection, putting a foot on the edge of the sink so I could drag stockings on in memory of an ex who said I didn't dress up enough for him. While continuing to be shorter, fatter, older and less attractive in the first place.

Upstairs, Madi's eyes widened when I fell back down on the sofa next to her.

'I think I'm immune to white wine,' I told her.

'He's not going to know what hit him,' she said.

'Well, *Fucking Frederick* said I didn't dress up enough,' I said, as an explanation as to why I'd festooned myself in half a lingerie department for someone I didn't really know yet. 'This is a political statement,' I added.

'That is warped,' Madi said, not taking her eyes off the TV.

'What did he fucking do for *me*?' I asked her. 'Apart from fling a dusty whip about like Indiana Jones. I really don't think recycled sex equipment is OK even if, you know, zero waste etc.'

I didn't add that I was also thin because I was single, less settled,

regularly swapped food for booze and didn't have to eat Fucking
Frederick's speciality sausage pasta most nights (pasta, with cut-
up sausages) so didn't bulge out the sides of the suspenders and
therefore liked wearing them.

'Maybe *Fucking Frederick* should have dressed up once in a while
if he wanted the same kind of return,' I told her, not having studied
economics, but thinking this was essentially the gist.

'Why is The Sexter not free until 10 p.m. anyway?' Madi asked.

'He had to watch the derby,' I told her.

She took one eye off the screen to look at me in the pouty
prom queen way she did when she wanted to pretend to be
super American.

'Football, basically,' I translated.

'Eurgh, what a gross *lad*,' she said.

Driving me out the house was actually a desire to stop sexting,
given I didn't have more than about forty-five minutes of sexts up
my sleeve. It was also quickly boring. Identikit lines with slight
plot variation and you knew the ending anyway. La petite mort.

In modern dating, sexting wasn't the only hurdle, I thought, as I
ordered a cab and climbed into it, the last of the Sunday stragglers
heading home as I was heading out, just because I could. Did sex
and Chinese on a first date because you liked sex and Chinese
make you a bad feminist, or a better one, I wondered, thinking
about the evening my date on Friday had turned into? Protecting
my morals, I decided to believe it was the latter, but secretly wasn't
sure. I could feel white wine lucidness leaving me already and only
bone-deep exhaustion beneath. Did people turn cabs around in
real life, I wondered?

When we finally pulled up at The Sexter's flat, I remembered
instructions to let myself in with a pre-texted code and gasped
with fags and fitness not massively enhanced by the Himalayas up
the four flights of stairs to his door.

'Hey,' he purred, standing there in the kind of grey

ankle-scrunchers that are always on offer at Sports Direct and a
T-shirt that was maybe once white, possibly a light blue.

I plastered a smile onto my red lips, realising he clearly operated
a different tracksuit-dating theory to me. But even in tracksuits
he was really quite hot: blondish, stubbled – the kind of guy I'd
have to be drunk (and was) to pick up because I'd gone out with
so many unattractive men I'd assume this one was *way* out of
my league. After guys in their forties, men in their twenties still
amazed me. Youth made youth seem so effortless.

'Shall we have a drink?' I asked, realising one was not going
to be offered, and curling onto one end of the sofa, while he
went to the kitchen and brought me a glass of red wine. Very
cold red wine.

'You know when red wine's, like, so bad you have to serve it
cold?' he said, when he saw my surprise.

No, I thought. *No, I don't.*

I also realised The Sexter didn't have much to say now I'd come
across London to stop him messaging me.

'Shall we play some music or something?' I said, as he settled
on some trance.

God this is hard, I thought, asking if I could have a fag out of the
window while regret seeped through me. How soon was socially
acceptable to fuck off, I wondered, immediately asking myself why
I was worrying about *that* when I was being served shit red by a
boy in a tracksuit while I wore all of the lingerie I owned. I wondered if it was too late to become the kind of girl who announced:
'This isn't working' and walked out five minutes into a date.

'Can I touch you?' he asked then and I remembered my £17
Uber and thought, *Go on then*.

He slid over the sofa and started kissing me with a lot of thin
tongue, pulling things up and down in an attempt to get them off.

'Shall we . . . ' I suggested, gesturing to the bedroom, partly to
reduce the incoming headache caused by both sound and wine

and he nodded, gripping the crotch of his trousers in a Michael Jackson-ish manner while I started wobbling, stockings and suspender belt round my ankles, towards the bedroom as sexily as possible, trying not to trip. The effect, I imagined, must have been like an unfit father in a three-legged race on sports day.

When we got there, he pushed me face down onto the bed.

'Do you want to be spanked?' he asked.

Jesus, no, I thought, and so I said, 'Sure.'

Five minutes after that I was thinking of Holly Golightly jokes. Holly Toolightly would be a very good (or bad) name for a porno. Holly Toolightly was how I would refer to The Sexter from now on, I decided, imagining Madi's second-hand horror when I recounted the evening. *Oh God, Madi*, I thought, *don't think about Madi while being half-spanked, that is so creepy.*

'Harder,' I said, to distract myself, and also because there's no point asking a woman if she wants to be spanked in 2019 and then failing to spank her. *Even this guy is more of a feminist than me*, I thought.

'HARDER,' I screamed, before he savagely jerked backwards.

'Don't move,' he said, walking to the kitchen and I stayed face down thinking, *Oh my God, he's going to fuck me with a whisk.*

But another five minutes later he was standing whisk-less in the doorway, looking very peaky indeed; the glow of Sloane Square's street lights bouncing off the suggestion of abs.

'I just threw up,' he said, hiccupping savagely.

'What?!' I shrieked, swivelling round, stockings and suspender belt still tying my ankles. Up until this point in my life I hadn't considered that I looked that bad from behind. Then a memory of a conversation from a recent flat party flooded my mind when our neighbour Sélim's friend told us she was ready to shag around again after a break-up because she'd just had her 'ass waxed'.

'Is that what we're expected to do now?' I'd asked, choking on a margarita.

I removed her from my mind and managed to ask The Sexter

if he was OK, simultaneously tugging the duvet up to my chin like a Victorian virgin.

'Yeah. Sorry,' he said, unconvincingly. 'I've got a back thing. Like a slipped disc almost, and I just put it out.'

He started doing some very elaborate back stretches against a cupboard.

'You put your back out spanking me?' I asked, genuinely almost impressed. 'Do you need to go to A and E?'

'No, it's fine. It happens sometimes,' he said, wincing. 'It's just so painful I throw up.'

He reached for the tracksuit bottoms with the scrunched ankles.

'Shall I go?' I asked, suddenly realising how disgustingly awful the whole scene was.

Why couldn't I stay at home on Sunday nights like normal people, I berated myself, having a deep epiphany that this is why people cry after sex with strangers.

He agreed it was probably best, because he wouldn't be 'much fun' now, and I felt the beginning of tears in my eyes at the swirl of emotions: plain old exhaustion following acute embarrassment and multiplied by bad white and cold red. I ineptly collected my stuff and hobbled with the stupid tangle of garments still round my ankles to the bathroom to drag it on and get out of there.

Am I a *slut*, I wondered? Or just single and free and lonely? How did you *know*? Nothing slammed you back to reality quicker than a guy slipping a disc trying to spank you.

'Don't go, please,' he said then, because he was actually quite nice, I realised, but also probably because I was now just straight crying in his house in a tangle of Per Una.

'I'm so sorry I upset you,' he said. 'I really didn't mean to. I can see why that made you feel weird, but please stay and watch telly with me. Shall we get a Chinese?' he asked.

When I got home, Madi was half-asleep with her door open.

'That was quick,' she drawled in a tone gravelly with sleep, and

I stood in her doorway like The Sexter standing in his with his ruined back to tell her the story.

'So basically, I'm unfucked and starving,' I concluded.

'What a hero,' she laughed sleepily. 'Also didn't you have sex and Chinese two nights ago?'

'Something about me reminds men of Chinese food.'

'You've got a very pork ball face,' she said.

'Fuck off,' I laughed.

I brushed my teeth and then got into her bed. It smelt comfortingly like laundry and Jo Malone.

'You're not seeing this bro again,' she said.

'Probably,' I said, exhausted.

'What? THIS guy?' she screeched, waking up.

The next day I wondered if my generation was just too sexually liberated for its own good. When everything went, there was so much choice that we barely knew what we were into any more. We just handed over control to whoever wanted it in the bedroom out of pure fatigue, being desired making us feel like we were doing something right, anyway. If we were going to be pressured into masochistic exercise classes each day for the sake of Instagrammable figures it was a waste of time and expenditure all round if we kept the results to ourselves, we thought, setting up dates and throwing our clothes on the floor at the end of it to make it all seem worthwhile. But dating had become so much part of our identities that we were using it to try to work out who we were. I was testing different waters that year in short-term dalliances that reminded me of my first forays into love and relationships at sixteen; the only difference now was that I was confident enough to look like I knew what I was doing. But did I? Not really. I just made it all up as I went along.

Madi's visa ran out in October and the time she'd have to fly away approached ominously as we ran around the city in the searing heat to theatres and restaurants, pedaloing around the pond in Regent's

Park if we were too hungover for anything else, or just walking, late, along the Southbank where the city glittered either side.

There'd been a tough few weeks when we'd gone back to just being friends – she not needing the space I found I did and hating, worrying, that we'd lost the friendship we'd been determined we wouldn't. But we had salvaged it, and I knew I'd not had a friend as close as her since I was seventeen. Being able to trust someone to always be there had changed me. We'd changed each other. Significantly, Madi had realised she was gay and knew she'd be going back home to the States an entirely different person.

By the end of that summer, I'd met someone too – seriously this time. Someone I'd fallen hard in love with after so long not being interested in love at all. In the early days, Jack brought two bunches of flowers when he came over to the flat, one for me and one for Madi, to make it easier for her, and she loved him too because you couldn't not. To start with he was the most charming, funny and interesting person I'd ever met, and so it was bittersweet, knowing I'd found him but was losing her. Madi didn't want to leave London or me, and I didn't want her to go anywhere either.

'I know you're utterly shit at keeping up with people, but you have to be better with me,' she said as we ate a final Pizza Pilgrims in the flat and drank rosé while a moving company packed up her life around us. 'Swear it.'

'I swear it.'

'I love you.'

'I love you, too.'

It was a strange time of opposite emotions then, extreme sadness mixing with heady excitement that Jack and I would live together now instead. My stuff was already waiting in a house in north London we'd rented for a year. We'd known each other just two months but we both needed somewhere to live and we couldn't have been surer about each other.

'You're going to be married by the time I come back, aren't

you?' Madi said, and I laughed. Thinking – *yeah, probably.* I thought I'd found my future in Jack and the meaning of the whole world in the process. I couldn't have known then that I was leaving all safety behind in Madi's flat, and that when I needed her the most, my best friend would be 5,000 miles away.

As I stood on the street watching her taxi drive away, I cried knowing she wouldn't be there every day, then my phone buzzed and she told me there was a letter for me in the bag of stuff she'd left me with; clothes of hers I'd worn all the time. 'In the pocket of the trousers,' the message said, as I rifled for it.

'I've never had the guts to tell you everything about how I felt,' it said on the envelope, telling me it was all inside if I ever wanted to read it and address the emotions she thought I'd tried to evade. 'It might help or it might not,' I read, before opening it immediately. Obviously.

Amongst 100 other things it said she thought I'd tried to push her away because I was scared of being that close to anyone. That I was scared because we were in too deep for there not to be a lot of pain when she left.

Next to the letter was a tiny bottle of the perfume she wore and a ring.

I already had Jack's grandmother's wedding ring on the fourth finger of my left hand in lieu of a real engagement ring, he said, and so I pushed Madi's onto my right hand. Emptiness hit me then as I walked away, but I had no idea that what was coming was much, much worse.

13

Before She Met Me

Feeling the feverish summer heat rising in London, I fished in the folds of sheet masquerading as duvet for my phone, knowing the feeling that held me awake all night was comparable only with Christmas Day when you're a child and want it to be morning more than anything in the world. Love replaces that feeling in adulthood, I guess.

By the side of my bed there was still a yellow Post-it note stuck to the wall, now a month old. 'Your first handwriting sample, you're the fucking best,' it said. I'd told the man who'd written it, a month before, that my mum had my dad's handwriting analysed when they met, and wonder now what Jack's would have said if I'd done the same.

I walked into the bathroom and stood under the waterfall shower, then pulled jeans on and threw a week's worth of life into an old Nike bag. Feeling like I was retracing Jack's steps to the airport I hopped on a Heathrow Express at Paddington, two hours early for the plane, which was delayed, of course, like only desperately expected arrivals can be. I pictured the one he sat on circling London for a free runway and him as restless as me after a long-haul flight coated in such anticipation.

A month before I'd had the best date of my life with Jack in

London. A non-date, we called it, because it couldn't be a date then, but we'd tumbled close to being everything in those two days in a blazing dream that ripped our worlds apart in the end.

It began with him knocking on my door with a newsagent-blue bag of prosecco in one hand and just grinning at me, when I opened it, cool as hell and as unavoidable in that moment as the London heat swimming in the air. Madi was away and we cracked beers on the balcony and knocked them together, knowing he was due to fly back to his life in California in two days, and not knowing when or if we'd ever see each other again.

We'd only met a fortnight before that non-date, at a party on the thirty-sixth floor of a new hotel in the city, London laid out below us like one of those model boards generals use to plan war. The fact he'd almost left before we met, and I'd almost not turned up at all helped it all seem like fate.

'I just knew you were a someone,' he said later on, after we'd talked all night, mixing gin and cola when there was nothing else left amongst the minibar bottles he'd gone back to his room to retrieve; the light coming up on a city viewed through panoramic, floor-to-ceiling glass of this new hotel I'd come to find a story in. The story was Jack, I guess. Not that I realised that at the time, but he spilled his whole life to me that night, telling me how it had been carried away from London, linked to someone else's. Someone he hadn't loved for a while, he confessed. So what are you going to do about it, I asked?

When he left I'd watched him waiting for the lift from the peephole in my door, then gone to bed only for my phone to buzz with his name and never stop. It only ever felt like the most normal thing in the world. He'd come to a party at our flat a week later, and now here we were with two beers, then popping Prosecco, two days before he flew away.

We walked through Borough Market to the Southbank and past the trestle tables of paperbacks to Westminster pier where we waited on a boiling jetty for a water taxi to Greenwich. Agreeing on the boat that it was amazing how far out of London you felt as it chugged past the London Eye and on towards Canary Wharf; water churning out behind us like the white train of a wedding dress.

We didn't even make it up the hill to the Observatory that time, we just sat on the grass and stared at each other, talking and laughing, and I thought he was the funniest, brightest, most charismatic person I'd ever met. We kissed late that evening, when I couldn't wait any longer, and slept next to each other, not touching but feeling electricity buzz between us all night. Then I woke up with him draped over me, and lay in bed with that intoxicating male smell on the pillow while he went back upstairs to the balcony to smoke and just didn't leave.

Thrice-cooked commuters scuttled sweatily below us that day and we watched the trains with their egg-yolk faces on the toast-brown tracks of London Bridge station. I watched the time like I had with Tom, nervously waiting to be cut off for another life, but he didn't go anywhere until he had to, for the plane, his suitcase somewhere else entirely, but barely seeming to care.

'Are you hungry?' I asked, mid-afternoon, digging around in the freezer for something Madi would've bought months ago and forgotten about. 'There's a venison and Merlot pie?'

'Of course you have a venison *and Merlot* pie,' he laughed.

'Fuck off,' I said, trying not to laugh, too. 'This isn't even mine.'

That was what the early days with Jack were like, everything lit up, everything more exciting, and more alive.

Back on the sofa, we put *Love Island* on so we could half-heartedly care about who was dumping who for whom, a mirror of our own world really, and held ice packs to our heads to cool down.

'My dad loves this show,' I told him.

'No way.'

'He says nothing as Machiavellian existed on TV when he was growing up,' I grinned and Jack put his head in my lap and turned his face up to kiss me.

We didn't stop for two hours, like teenagers, and called it *Love Island* kissing after that, joking about the contestants who seemed to pull all day because there was nothing else to do.

'I don't want to leave,' he said, as evening closed in.

'So don't,' I said, and he didn't.

Later he said, 'I'll come back.'

But I'd heard lines like that before, from Tom, so I said nothing.

'Do you believe me?' he said.

'Not really,' I admitted.

He said he'd prove it, and he did.

It took less than a month for him to fly away, pack his life in boxes and buy a return flight back to me and after Tom it felt like someone was finally changing what I could believe in, I thought, seeing how some people did leave relationships that were wrong if they met someone they thought was *right*. I stood at the arrivals gate amongst the chauffeurs, waiting with a notepad scribbled with his name and wondered how you were supposed to greet someone after a beginning like ours? Then there he was, loping towards me and giving me the biggest hug anyone ever had.

'It's so nice to see you,' he said.

We crossed the airport then to board a flight to Edinburgh where I was finally ticking the Fringe off the 52 list. We sat for an hour on the runway, delayed, but neither of us cared in the slightest; we just ate Duty Free biscuits and knew we could fall in love now he was home. His joy at being back in London, where he'd grown up, shone, and when he talked, I understood how he'd become trapped in a move abroad with someone it should have already been over with, because I'd had the same thing with Amsterdam and Sam. *Life*, we said, feeling like we'd been on parallel paths for years, and were always going to have met each other in the end.

Cities always feel like just yours when you're in that bubble of love and he'd never been to Edinburgh, so I pointed at the castle on the hill, then walked him down the city to my old flat, and my old life, as he talked of the city he'd just left for me; said he wanted to show me that one, one day, too.

At a beautiful flat in the New Town we drank French 75s made of purple gin he'd bought in California in another life and put records on and fell into bed. Two days in he asked me to be 'his girl' and it was beyond a whirlwind but there was nothing else to say but *of course*. I broke my *year of no commitment* rule there and then because he was exceptional, and I already wondered whether he would be the reason I stopped dating completely, forever. I couldn't imagine I've ever need or want to meet anyone else, now I'd met him. Then he handed me two books with long, scrawled dedications written on the plane saying he'd not believed in love at first sight until now and I raised my eyebrows at the word love, and so did he, but we smirked instead of mentioning it. After that it was written and I saw how a single metaphor sews an idea you can't take back.

Edinburgh was perfect as we toured about making new memories in my old haunts, deep in affection, arms slung over each other's shoulders as though they always had been. We'd spoken almost all day, every day since he'd left, but now he was back it was different: we had time, and it felt like the whole world had opened up. This, I thought, as we dropped in and out of shows and bars, is what I'd been waiting to find. Other days we laughed about the fact that we'd assumed it was mythical that people stayed in bed all day.

Both being freelance gave us too much time if anything and meant we never left each other, which we worried later was part of our downfall, but in the beginning felt potent and exhilarating. We'd write in the morning, then go to bed for a 'break' and emerge to find it was dark outside, wondering, vaguely, whether anywhere was still serving dinner. Jack even changed *sex* for me so completely it was like that was entirely new, too. We just fell into each other absolutely and how easily we worked each other from the very start was just another piece of evidence, we thought, for how right it was. Just thinking about him shot heat like electricity through my entire body and made me shiver. We totally consumed each other, in an almost primal way, and we didn't even brush our teeth alone any more. We read, wrote, ran, drank and fell back into bed in a way that was so intoxicating and beguiling it made both of us feel we didn't need to see or speak to anyone else at all.

It was addictive, our world, as we walked streets talking in sitcom scenes, making each other laugh relentlessly. I once heard Francis Bacon described as like a piece of electricity pouring into the room, and that was Jack, to me. He was a world in himself and we tested definitions of love everywhere, agreeing in a pub off Oxford Street that love was sharing the same colour hair dye in your seventies, like the mauve-haired couple at the table opposite us, which we'd do one day, we knew. Secretly, it was a relief, and gratitude that it really did exist, this thing that other people said they'd found, just besotted us further. Later it was hideously ironic how liberating it all felt at the start, but in the first moments I was freed.

'I can't wait,' he said, realising he wanted to have kids for the first time in his life and while I was in no rush at twenty-nine, I couldn't wait either. We started flat-hunting in a honeymoon haze and signed the first rental we saw: a beautiful ground-floor flat with a garden and a neighbour's expensive cat we named Olive. Even before we got it, we sat in the local we hoped would become ours drinking Prosecco to celebrate. Then we did get the flat, and everything we'd dreamed of slid away.

The problem with whirlwinds is that you don't give someone enough time to show you who they are in all their moods, I realised later. Maybe not believing there are traits you couldn't live with when you're so blindsided by love, and then becoming trapped later on after you've seen them, but still wanting it all so bad that you try not to admit things even then.

Jack changed fast in ways I hadn't expected. He read my phone for the first time after we'd signed the flat and spiralled into what I learnt later was called coercive control. We were house-sitting for my parents in Bath and had spent the days on country walks to rural pubs with Alfie, persuading landlords to sell us lemons so we could cook fish for dinner back at the house, getting on brilliantly as usual, adoring each other, and what happened next was an 'accident' he said – although no one I ever told believed you could accidentally put someone's password into their phone and read dozens of old messages.

He brought my phone into the garden looking like someone had died and it was frightening, his reaction, as he stood shaking in front of me, not letting me anywhere near him, having seen that I'd slept with someone before he'd come home; before we were together. In the messages I'd told the guy that I'd fallen in love with someone else as a way of saying we'd need to be just friends again now, but Jack chose not to register that bit.

He left and didn't answer his phone for two days and I just had to try not to fall apart, while I waited, wondering if it was already too late to get out of the flat we'd signed. Wondering whether it was all over already. It was just a tiny taste of the drama he was about to force us into; a glimpse into what living with someone who dealt only in extreme emotions would be like.

Accusations followed quickly after the first one, which he described as cheating. I talked too much to someone outside a pub while I smoked; was too friendly to Uber drivers; had also 'cheated' on him with Madi. He said he wanted to know which of my friends I'd slept with, even if it was ten years ago, and I later found out he'd stalked most of my exes online, not having realised he was piecing together identities as he questioned me.

'He's getting a bit Johnny Depp,' one of my old friends said later when it got really bad.

What the fuck? I thought, horrified. That wasn't Jack. We were in *love*.

But after we did move into the flat, telling ourselves and each other it would still be great – and plus, didn't we have to anyway? – he let nothing go and wanted me to apologise almost daily for things that he wouldn't even try to get over. There was nothing new to say and it started driving me mad. What about forgiveness? I asked. What about the bigger things? How can we ever get over something if you make us talk about it every day?

I fought over the small ones. Of course I didn't want to go on holiday with an Algerian cabbie because I'd asked about their cuisine, I said, thinking he'd see how unreasonable he was being. But he never could, and said he was concerned I didn't try to see anything from his perspective, so eventually I apologised for that, knowing it was irrational, but just wanting it to be over.

The hope you can go backwards, to those early days of love, when relationships sour like that is a huge mistake, I know now. When you stay, you validate their jealousies as being something you don't mind living with, and they only escalate. Paddington station became symbolic of our entire relationship, I saw, as I got trains back to Bath to escape him during breaks and a brief December break-up. It was the ecstasy and the ugly that he was, and that the whole relationship was, too.

In Bath, the good memories wouldn't leave me and I saw him sitting on the side of our bed tying the laces of scuffed Doc Marten's in skinny jeans; grinning at me on the balcony in London Bridge; making me laugh all the way through whatever shit telly we watched, and my broken heart swelled.

I thought of the way he looked when he woke up and how radiator hot his body got overnight, how we stuck to each other. How even our toes touched all night. I remembered how, in summer, we'd held an ice pack against the other to cool our skin and in winter how he'd taken off his gloves in New York when it snowed and put them on my violet hands. He'd also ripped my underwear off me then, too, to stop me leaving the Airbnb, and walked in a stony, ranting rage around Central Park because I'd been 'nicer' to a couple next to us in the bar than I was to him, he claimed. But if I could block the bad memories, I could still believe there was a way back. I tapped out messages on my phone telling him I missed his height and his hair and his crinkly green eyes. Then I threw it at the bed, at war with my own mind but knowing what was good for me in the long run wasn't what I wanted *now*. I had an instant gratification personality, saw reflections of Jack everywhere and missed sharing everything I'd read and watched with him. The people I'd seen, the conversations I'd heard. It all felt like a massive mistake, like the world didn't make sense without the other in it any more.

It was delusional, but we believed we could change and always met, inevitably, a few weeks later at a gallery in London or a bar in town where it felt like day one again. Love, absolute, as we ate oysters and fell back into bed. The intimacy was therapy to me after the awful fallout, and I didn't think I could live without it. But he weaponised affection in a game of cat and mouse; awarding it only once I'd apologised for two hours for whatever new or antique wrong I'd committed.

Our desperation for it to work made us pin hope on the problem not being us, but the flat, which was cursed; our landlord was a nightmare, the neighbours had heard too much. Was it London? It was too expensive (for me, at least, he often said), and if I wasn't behind on rent while I waited for small, unreliable pay cheques maybe he wouldn't resent covering me. Did we need to move?

We hatched wild plans to move to Margate and have kids and started naming them. *Margot*, first, then *Olive* and maybe a boy.

'Margot of Margate,' he said. 'She'll be famous in those parts.'

In Margate, things would be different, we told ourselves, genuinely believing it as we looked at houses and dreamed of buying one and being happy and calm elsewhere. Too much had happened to ever go back, but you always believe you can, until the catastrophic end.

Before that I felt like I was staring at a blank TV screen after the credits had rolled, thinking I'd just watched the wrong film entirely. But I couldn't forget what I'd seen.

Normality is so malleable, and his rages were now part of ours. So was me throwing glasses across the room if he pushed and pushed me. I guess staying had implied I could live with his anger but I couldn't and the inhumanity of it snapped me eventually. If he pushed me into the corners of rooms, I pushed my way back out, then I was the 'violent' one. When he confiscated my phone in order to read everything I'd ever sent, and only isolating me further, I flailed at him to get it back and then I was the *abusive girl-friend*. It was darkly funny in the unfunniest way you can imagine. Because in those moments I felt like I saw straight through him to someone he'd tried his whole life not to become. It was tragic, more than anything else.

When an argument stirred, he went to the shop and came back with bottles of wine and rum, lounging on the floor of the sitting room in the middle of the week in the middle of the day, smoking inside and drinking relentlessly until his entire face changed. I'd leave then and hide out in a pub or the library just to get away from him. Sometimes that worked and he begged me to come back. More often he threw me ultimatums until he scared me into returning. Either way, I turned my key in the front door with more trepidation than I'd ever felt about anything, listening for the volume of music I knew was an indication of how out of it he'd be, and how unpredictable.

Because I was quite strong, and as tall as many of the men I knew, I wasn't used to being physically intimidated by a man, so it was an uneasy thing to get my head around. I didn't understand that the anxiety I felt around him was fear, for months. But he was six years older, a lot taller and knew how to fight in a way I'd never learnt to. Plus he was a loose cannon when he drank so while it's a cliché to describe someone as being like Jekyll and Hyde, there was no other way to explain how he split into two people. When he was in a rage, I just looked at him and he was unrecognisable, and I wondered how the attractive, happy person I'd fallen in love with could have disappeared whilst standing right in front of me. The details of what Jack did as part of his emotional abuse of me are too gruesome to recount and, without fail, he blamed it all on me. While he told me what 'I'd' done to him, I felt like I was looking at someone who'd lost it completely – his malleable face hard and menacing and I just froze over in those moments. No emotion seemed safe.

I'd never dealt with someone so manipulative and I didn't know what to do when he got like that, because I could never win. Nothing stopped him raging in those moods and the list of crimes I'd apparently committed were recited over and over. The most frightening thing was that I really think he believed his warped version of events. The violence that emanated from him, in those moments, was uncontrollable and the flat was too small for him, let alone me, as he thrashed about. To give him the space I thought would calm him, I'd walk into another room and just wait, but he followed me around trying to force me to talk, blocked me in rooms and spat in my face, shouting that I was a 'whore', a 'fucking cunt', a 'filthy slut' or a 'grub', which felt like a pretty *Lion King* insult, I thought, darkly, but was just part of some terrible outpouring of language I hadn't known he had.

How I felt at those times is almost too hard to explain. It was as horrendous standing there with him screaming in my face and blocking the door as you can imagine. I felt pure panic at how trapped I was, in the room, in the flat, in the whole relationship, in London with him and after the freeze, I vibrated with shock and fear; took multiple propranolols to stop the physical effects of a panic attack and walked London alone, if I could get out of there, feeling stoned from the pills and like my heart barely beat at all.

Often I waited it out at friends' houses but the only escape in the middle of the night was the bathroom with its lock on the door, so I shut myself in there when his rampages started and tried to sleep on the bath mat while he screamed abuse through the wood, banging, kicking and shouting so much I never slept a wink. It was too cold to sleep anyway, with a towel for a duvet in winter. I only got through it by telling myself I'd leave as soon as it was light, and hoping he'd have passed out by then. I took my laptop in there with me, knowing he'd smash it or trawl through it looking for anything to be angry about if I didn't, and I wrote everything that happened as proof I hadn't made it up the next day when he claimed, without fail, that I had. I don't remember writing it in third person, but it veers into that at points, presumably so I didn't have to feel it was happening to me.

If ever I told a friend about the bathroom tactic, their faces showed me how abnormal my life had become, but normality had arranged itself to the bath mat and when it was happening, I almost didn't think about how harrowing it was; I thought about it only as a necessity. I once took a knife and drew it across my leg while I sat on the floor, wondering if you really *did* get a release from pain that wasn't just in your mind. I only made shallow slices, and the scars are invisible now, but darkness was visible then as red dots of blood popped on the lines I'd drawn.

I've since read about coercive control and know it works by taking everything away, as Jack did to me over the worst months. He poured drinks over food, so I couldn't eat. He tipped anything I tried to drink down the sink. I wasn't allowed to use the butter or salt, or anything else he claimed was his because I owed him money for rent, sometimes, while I waited to be paid. He told me to transfer the entire contents of my bank account to his if I wanted to eat or sleep in the flat. I wasn't allowed to sleep in the bed, which was ours only when we got on, and his when we didn't.

Somehow I could write in any mood, even when I was a shaking wreck of anxiety, which he hated, so he tried to take that away from me too: my job, but also my escapism. I wasn't allowed to sit at the desk we'd found at a Hampstead antique market in our early, wonderful days because it was half his, and he once tipped me off the wooden chair onto the floor while I worked there. The chair hit my head as he tipped, and I sat on the floor stunned from the hard wooden back of it and touched the new, hot pain to see if there was red. Blood.

'Don't exaggerate,' he said then, slamming my laptop shut and spilling a glass of wine over the top of it, and I never stayed sitting again if he came raging into a room.

He removed the Wi-Fi and hid my laptop charger and told me I was insane for thinking he had. He unplugged the TV cord so I couldn't watch anything at the house. There was a list of people he said I couldn't speak to if I wanted to be with him – about six male friends and Madi. I sent inappropriate messages and had cheated on him before, he said.

'You're the cheat,' I said once, hating him. 'You weren't exactly single when you slept with me.'

But that was entirely different, he said, because it was *me* and it was love at first sight. I blocked the names anyway, bar Madi, because I was too scared he'd kick off if they messaged me and I didn't want to hear screamed abuse about someone I liked and who'd done nothing wrong. Internally I took some grim joy in the fact all he was doing was making me like these men who'd meant nothing to me before more than I liked him. You *can't* like someone if they treat you like that – it was just letting go of an idea of love I'd thought was my future that was harder.

Later, in lockdown, as I learnt more about coercive control I

saw Jack ticked almost every box. It was an aspect of domestic violence, I was shocked to read on the Women's Aid website, that was
designed to make you entirely dependent on the person inflicting
it. Women's Aid was a domestic violence charity I hadn't known
existed until now. But why would I have, I thought, when I didn't
even know coercive control was a *thing*?

I still thought it was love.

As the world watched the Amber Heard and Johnny Depp trial,
so much of the detail reminded me so eerily and uncannily of my
situation with Jack, who claimed he couldn't remember any of
the awful things he'd done, in the same way Depp said his actions
weren't his but those of a monster who lived in him. Because Jack
'couldn't remember', he said I must have made them up.

The mind is a powerful dam and I'd managed to seem fine
for six months. But in reality I'd been taking propranolol to stop
the panic attacks and jumped when he came into rooms I was in
which made him sneer and accuse me of faking it. I shook when
he shouted at me, or cried, and he just stood in front of me, doing
impressions with his fists balled up in his eyes and telling me
to grow up.

Everything blurs in those situations until you don't know what
you think any more, and amidst wondering if I was weak for staying, or stronger for putting up with it, I just wanted to sleep. His
mood changed faster and faster, over nothing, and he went from
charm and affection to violently abusive with the speed of a tennis
ball over a net. I walked on eggshells every second of the day, and
felt like I was watching someone lose their mind.

'You're just a shit version of Phoebe Waller-Bridge,' he
screamed once, which was a great insult, but I bit my cheeks
because I thought if I laughed, he'd punch me.

He was always good at not punching me, as though he knew
that he wouldn't be able to deny what was happening if I had
a black eye, so he made sure the worst marks were on himself

instead, telling the people he was closest to that *he* was the victim. That made me hysterical, knowing they'd never know the truth, and knowing they wouldn't believe it anyway, because families and friends have to side with the person they know out of loyalty. I'd seen that on the Ronaldo story. I also knew they wouldn't want to believe he'd become as abusive as the estranged father he'd grown up with. As far as I know they just told him to get away from me, but why would he have done that when he wasn't scared of *me* in the slightest? Ironically, his behaviour was only ever designed to make me never leave him.

When he pushed me across rooms all he said was that he bet I was happy now, now that he'd 'finally' touched me, and I felt nothing but hate, knowing it wasn't the first time at all. He claimed not to be able to see the bruises I often had on my arms in the exact shape of his fingerprints, or the purple marks from his feet when he kicked me out of bed that morphed to green before they finally faded.

He claimed they were nothing, even when I finally called the police and they took photographs, then walked him to a police car while I hid with the neighbour upstairs and watched from the window, hoping he wouldn't turn and see me.

After that I had to go back down to our smashed, beautiful, bloodied flat to give a statement. The flashbacks didn't leave me for months after I'd gone through it in detail with a policeman who had the same name as Jack.

I remember being pushed around, tipped on the floor, I told him. Locking myself in the bathroom. 'I never touched you. You hit me,' being shouted through the door, lies constructed, as I waited until it was early enough to text a friend who lived close by: 'I need help.' Having a shower to try to wake up and get out of there as quickly as possible, and then my friend was already there with her boyfriend in case Jack tried to stop me. Jack screaming at them from the front door like a wild thing, then coming into the bathroom and backhanding me in the side of the head, which made me hysterical, finally, after having held it together so long, and my friend saying pack a bag, quickly, quickly. And he'd hidden my coat. In February. And hidden my laptop charger.

But we left and I was being walked to their car and then dropped in Notting Hill so I could hide at my brother's house, shaking on three trains of commuters I tried not to look at; knowing I looked like a junkie who'd not been to bed.

My brother had gone to work but his girlfriend let me in that morning and cooked me scrambled eggs, as I tried to respond to conversation while feeling underwater and then tried to sleep. But after two hours I'd woken up beyond panic. No one was there. I walked around, lost and disorientated beyond belief, and noticed a dinner reservation on a calendar in his bedroom for a week's time. A restaurant my brother and his girlfriend had wanted to visit for ages.

That was all I needed to see life without Jack as too empty even to contemplate and so I let myself out and practically ran back to the flat, unbelievably. What the fuck was wrong with me, I think now, of course. But something was still dragging me back to him.

I stood shakily smoking in the doorway to our garden while the policeman waited, sitting on the edge of the sofa opposite me. Jack's cigarette ash was everywhere. Smears of cocaine and glasses full of half-drunk booze and fag butts.

'I'm sorry it's such a state,' I said, as he just shook his head. No apology needed.

That was something it took me a while to change. The feeling I needed to apologise constantly for things that weren't my fault.

'Why did you come back?' he asked.

'Love – and a laptop charger,' I said, with a sound that was supposed to be a laugh of disbelief, but he gave me such a knowing look, I knew he'd seen it a hundred times before in a hundred smashed flats. Women going back to violent men because they'd confused love with fear and control.

'What happened then?' he asked, so I carried on.

I tried to go to sleep in the bedroom and he dragged me out of bed and out of the front door, I remembered, easily. I was wearing pyjamas. I had to beg him to let me in so I could get changed and he threw stuff at me, telling me to get dressed outside. Slamming the door. My toothbrush and a phone charger crushed in the frame; the blood from his knife cuts all over our door number.

'I don't have any shoes,' I said through the door, wondering if I could walk to the Tube station to get to Paddington in socks.

'You can come in if you talk. Are you sorry?' he said through the door and I said I was, without knowing what I was apologising for. But it was an interrogation.

'What for?'

'Everything,' I said desperately.

Then I was back inside and he was following me around while I looked for shoes with shaking hands. Then I was being picked up, dragged again, thrown out again.

That's when I called the police. Stay outside, they said, and I waited on the street, freezing. I saw the neighbour in the flat above gesturing at me from his front window and so I tiptoed upstairs and sat with him, empty and exhausted while he handed me his vape and told me he'd be a witness if I needed him. They heard Jack all the time, he said. Then Jack's name rang on my phone again and again, and messages collected on the screen. 'I know you're close, come back and fix things.'

'Can he hear us?' I whispered, eyes wide with fear and thinking I could hear him move around the bedroom directly below us. My neighbour put the TV on, loud, and it was the longest forty-five minutes of my life, waiting for the police. I don't even remember what we were supposed to be watching because it felt like there was a hurricane in my mind and I couldn't concentrate on anything but breathing.

'I'm sorry about the next questions,' the policeman was saying now. 'We have to ask them.'

'OK.'

'Are you pregnant?'

'Has he ever stopped you seeing family and friends?'

'Has he been controlling?'

'Have you ever thought he'd hurt you with a weapon?'

'Do you have fears he'll hurt your family?'

'Is he a suicide risk?'

'Yes. Will he be in a cell?'

'Yes.'

'Oh God.'

'He can be watched . . . Are you scared of your partner now?'

I wondered if these questions were really being asked me of Jack? But I *was* scared of him. I'd never been more scared of anyone. Then the policeman gave me the number of a domestic violence helpline, and I just stared at it, thinking, Is *that* was this is? I couldn't believe it.

I reached for my phone and realised it was our six-month anniversary.

I was hit by overwhelming fatigue after that, when the police left, not having slept or eaten properly in months. I packed everything I could carry and went back to Bath, knowing I was supposed to be performing a stand-up comedy gig to ninety people at a London venue in three days' time. I'd signed up to a five-week comedy course in December and our final show was doubling as my thirtieth birthday party. All my friends had tickets. The idea of standing on a stage and pretending I was fine for even five minutes seemed a joke in itself, I thought on the train as I just tried to focus on getting home. *Heel, toe, heel, toe, heel, toe,* I muttered every time I thought about Jack in a cell.

The next morning I woke to two messages from Cricklewood police station. They appeared to have lost half my statement, they said, and Jack had been released on bail at 6 a.m.

*

Three days later, I made myself get up on stage for my friends, half-drunk and shaking from trauma none of them yet knew the cause of. But I also did it for me, because I'd loved the course and the other amateur comedians I'd spent a month of Saturdays with. I refused to let Jack win. He'd not wanted me to do it, and I wondered if this recent violence was just an attempt to stop me.

He will not win, I told myself as I got the Tube to Angel and then walked to the Bill Murray, where we'd fallen in love in the front row watching Tim Key, a metre from where I had to perform. When people I didn't even know came up to me afterwards to say it was brilliant, I applied the mask I always applied, the one that said life was comedy, not tragedy but knowing I'd cracked entirely beneath the surface.

Then later I told Amy, Frankie and Risha and they stayed with me at the flat all night so I didn't have to be alone, and my cousin Tom came the next day to talk; then Cece came after work, and SJ cooked me dinner. Emily came in the middle of the day and Irish Bea walked me around and around the park.

I didn't know where Jack was during that time, or what story he'd concocted for the people he was presumably still pretending not to have done anything wrong to, but it was a consolation knowing he couldn't turn up without breaking bail conditions. Not that I slept properly in our flat without him there, because I expected him to arrive in a drunken rage and then – I don't know what. I didn't want to think about it. But to my relief, he never came. He stayed away just as long as he had to.

I'd told Madi as soon as it had happened and she'd immediately bought a plane ticket back to London to be with me and so I filled the two days before she arrived with other people, checking the locks I couldn't change because it was only a rental 100 times before I went to bed and hearing the February winds blow branches against the bedroom windows with scratching-finger sounds. When Madi arrived she saw my fear immediately and bought an alarm for the front door that rang on my phone if someone came in when I wasn't there. Then Danny arrived on Saturday. It was my thirtieth birthday, and my oldest and newest closest friends did everything to try to make me smile that day.

I'd been supposed to be on a flight to New York with Jack, who'd not cancelled the tickets, I saw, in the relentless emails that kept telling me to check in, my heart stopping every time they appeared. I wondered if he was going to the airport. Wondered if he expected me to be there. But he was still on bail and I heard nothing from him all day, turning thirty in the only way I could face without him. Oblivion.

Later that week I told the police that I'd drop charges, not wanting to be dragged through the courts on a 'he said, she said' trial, and Jack turned up within days at our flat. Luckily Madi had just left to return to the States because I hated the idea of him turning on any of my friends more than I hated the idea of him turning, again, on me.

I thought he might apologise, which is kind of laughable now but shows how long it took me to give up hope. All he said was that he couldn't believe I'd had him arrested. He cried, telling me how awful it was, with a woman screaming like an animal in a cell near his. Over and over again he said: You had me *arrested.*

'Why don't you ask yourself *why* you were arrested? You were arrested for assaulting me,' I said in disbelief but he never apologised, once, for any of it. He said I should apologise to him, and I almost laughed then. Because of course that's what he was going to say.

I wished I'd never met him, then, and thought about mental illness and whether you could or should blame or excuse things because of that? How do you know when to accept it's too much – and then is it better to stay or go? What's better for them, or for you? Who should you prioritise? I still thought that I could fix him. I expected him to turn back into the person I loved in the beginning and stay like that. But he couldn't and I felt like the person he made me believe he was when we first met didn't actually exist. It had all been a performance. A lie.

When he was on bail and I was alone in our flat, I'd opened two suitcases of his things that had sat in the corner of our sitting room since we'd moved in and found dozens of long, dramatic love letters from a girlfriend he'd told me had cheated on him years ago, filled with apologies for minor things. One of them a sorry for admitting she'd once fancied a woman, because she'd clearly never been allowed to forget about it. Then the realisation that she'd probably *never* cheated on him, that he'd invented his own story entirely like he had with me, hit me like a car crash. This is just how he liked things to play out, I saw with horror, in the language he used and made her use; a language of jealousy and delusion; constant, fatal apology and a love he implied you could never leave.

I phoned the domestic violence charity, and no one answered. So I told the landlady what had happened and said we needed to move out but she wouldn't let us. She was a policewoman who'd managed to get into an argument with Jack herself, during one short visit to the flat when I'd not been there, and she told me she'd known he was an 'abuser' from the off – but we'd signed a contract, she said. I didn't know what was more awful – more laughable – then. Her or the officer for the case, who implied prosecution would get nowhere, and told me that Jack wasn't *like* most of the other people in the cells in a way that suggested I should consider whether he was really that bad. I knew police had a reputation for being stupid, but this man had clearly never heard that psychopaths could be charming.

Knowing I now had to work it out with Jack alone, I suggested we split the time left of the contract we couldn't get out of yet and live there one at a time, but he wouldn't agree to anything that involved not being together at the flat. I tried another route and asked him to get therapy. '*You* need therapy,' he said, of course, telling me I had an obvious, very worrying mental health condition.

In arguments, he often just repeated what I said, like a child, but I'd noticed he often copied what I *did* too, immediately signing up for writing classes after I started the comedy course, as though we were in competition.

So in the weeks I had to be in the flat, which he never left, of course, I decided to try to prompt him to do the same with help and got fast-tracked through to the NHS's talking therapy service, hoping he'd do the same. Online you had to submit a form rating your mood and admit if you were worried you'd harm yourself, which I was and had, so it only took them two days to ring me and say they would see me as soon as possible. But then the pandemic hit and they called again to say they were being diverted to the front line alongside dentists, to help doctors cope. Meanwhile, Jack had one private session, he claimed, and never went back.

LESS THAN FOUR WEEKS LATER
23 MARCH 2020, 8.30 P.M.

We sat apart on the long grey sofa in the sitting room waiting for Boris Johnson to appear on the BBC after rumours there'd be a big coronavirus announcement that night.

'It's going to be lockdown,' Jack said, crossing his legs.

Then it did come – finally, and I felt panic washing through me. Jack reached for my hand.

'The world is crumbling around us, but we don't have to,' he said.

I looked at him, wondering if he really thought my panic was about the virus alone, even if it was already whipping London into a frenzy thanks to quickly rising death tolls. I felt more panic about being trapped further with him. I wanted it to save us, but felt I already knew it would only bring us closer to the edge of the cliff.

Our empty fridge showed how little we'd been taking the pandemic seriously up until now, but we'd been hearing about police on the streets in Paris, keeping people inside, and whispers that the army could be brought into London to enforce a lockdown here. Both sets of our parents were asking if we were going to get trains out of there while we could, but they lived far apart and we didn't know when we'd next be able to see each other if we left.

Our mutual dependence was devastating and because things had been going well for a few days, I latched on to slim hope that we could do it together, while feeling very far from home. The day before we'd walked through Little Venice to Paddington station where boards listing cancelled trains showed exit strategies dwindling.

Ignoring the fear, we bought a pink picnic of pale rosé and pork scratchings in the station and then sat by the canal, drinking, smoking, still in love – I thought – and persuading ourselves things could change if two people wanted them to so badly.

Behind us the sound of Prosecco corks popped in the park and the sense that summer was coming overrode the death, doom and isolation we were beginning to hear about in the news. It didn't seem real yet. Jack was real: tall and gorgeous in skinny jeans and my sunglasses, topping up our plastic cups with wine. I didn't realise then that I felt more in love with him in those moments out of sheer relief that he was in a good mood.

When the lockdown announcement did finally land, it was hardened after a weekend of photos in the papers of packed beaches and queues on Snowdon that defied government guidelines not to leave the house unless you had to, and I remember feeling something close to glee, even, that we were being forced to stay together. A morphing of Stockholm syndrome with a new lockdown syndrome, I guess. Lockhome syndrome.

It was confusing feeling so protected by Jack when he was being nice, *normal*, and I clung to him like a child scared of the dark as we walked, late, to Sainsbury's after the news to buy everything we could carry home from the quickly emptying shelves, reality recasting around us and the new, almost dystopian world changing people's perspective on everything fast.

Professor Chris Whitty's health announcements felt as Orwellian as *Nineteen Eighty-Four* and flashing Lord Kitchener billboards urged us to 'Stay at home. Protect the NHS. Save lives.' The wartime comparison was haunting, and panic changed the atmosphere of London entirely. Before a brigade of volunteers stepped up to help out, it felt like dog-eat-dog, each household against the world in a 2020 version of Cormac McCarthy's *The Road*.

The atmosphere of confusion, with people already furloughed or let go from struggling or shutting companies, had spurred some of my friends to evacuate already. My brother and his girlfriend both had the virus, and she'd called an ambulance when his temperature hit 40C. But hospitals were already crowded and there was nothing medics could do until his condition deteriorated enough for him to need a ventilator to breathe, they'd said, leaving him at home to get through it, which took weeks. In Bath, my dad hadn't left the house since the start of the worry, knowing he was at extra risk by being seventy and having high blood pressure. My mum was isolating with him, aside from doing a weekly food run, which now felt self-sacrificial.

A dark curtain of uncertainty hung in the background and for the first four days, Jack and I were normal again, joyful again, until he turned back. Then I had to start defying the government's instruction to stay at home in order to walk to Hampstead Heath to escape him, sitting alone and watching the same breed of green parrots that sat in the tree in our garden. On the way there I'd walked past a new poster that was getting a lot of attention in the press: 'Abusers always work from home', it said, raising awareness that domestic violence was up 50 per cent in lockdown, but I didn't think of myself as being included in those figures. Neither Jack nor I mentioned it to each other.

The density of people in cities and a lack of space in crowded flat- and house-shares was contributing massively to the general stress of the unknown and the extreme nature of what was going on. Rumours circulated constantly, with nothing clear and no one confident the government knew what they were doing either. The air felt full of angst, as well as the invisible virus, everyone on edge, and a woman chased me down a road in Hampstead shouting that I'd walked too close to an older person, while her husband bitched about the ignorance of young people behind me. *Hypocrites*, I thought, knowing his wife was breaking the two-metre rule to spit at my back. Facing so much conflict at home made me unable to cope with it in the street too, so I just kept walking, pretending to be deaf and thinking, *If you knew, would you care?* Vigilante do-gooders were doing more harm than they realised, but on the Heath there was shouting, people telling each other to fuck off, others coughing elaborately onto those who chastised them; murder in a splutter the new violent threat.

It was horrible feeling London so jumpy and tense and finding loo roll and hand sanitiser costing a tenner in the newsagents. The greedy wanting to fleece those trying to survive. I felt invisible, alone and slipping through the cracks once more as I walked the streets late at night to get away from Jack, with a plastic bag prop that made me feel like Will Self in a Sainsbury's ad. My outing *was* essential in many ways and the streets were so dead then it felt like midnight by 8 p.m. Ironically I'd never felt safer in London than on those empty roads. But through the lit windows of other flats, I saw happy-looking couples having dinner together and I felt pure envy and bottomless loneliness, thinking that shared contentment and care looked unreal and so unreachable. It felt like I was saying goodbye to the city as I walked loops round the car crash my life had become, not wanting to live amongst sirens and police any more. They'd come to the flat again in lockdown, called by my neighbours this time, and I'd stood on the doorstep to run through the questions I knew too well.

We lied and said we were fine. Apologised. They said we seemed like nice people and were so different from the *usual kind* they had to see 'for these sorts of things'. We both had huge cuts all over our hands from smashed glass, Jack claiming privately I was responsible, but to the police we didn't look the 'types' to be in a domestically violent relationship, so no one was very concerned. Maybe we seemed too middle-class, or too well-spoken. Behind us was a beautiful flat on the posh side of the road. If they'd looked closer, they'd have seen blood smeared everywhere, as it often was when there was smashed glass, or when Jack was on a rampage of self-destruction.

Two weeks into lockdown, I finally left. At Paddington station, calling my mum and asking her to please let me come home, the guilt felt absolute, knowing I could bring the virus into the house. But what if staying in London killed *me*?

'Just get here and we'll work out what to do,' she said, as I stood in the empty station, pigeons fluttering in the rooftop making me jump, and her words making me want to cry.

Dear Lucy

Just wondered if you were still in London, or had beaten a
retreat to Bath or elsewhere?

We are now dutifully confined to barracks – and though
this should mean I get down to all sorts of mindful things, I
find I can't concentrate on anything at all. I suppose it's being
branded 'elderly with underlying medical conditions' that
somehow saps the will.

There are certainly advantages to living in a rural place –
lambs jumping in the field opposite our house, and what look
like bovine board meetings, plus plenty of scope for rural
walks without leaving the village and two children living close
by to do the shopping. I do wonder what, if anything, will be
the long-term consequences of the enforced changes we've all
lived through. Will more people work more at home? Will
the NHS be better funded by the Tories? Will the mutual
helpfulness that we've experienced up North continue, or will
we all slip back into the solipsistic preoccupation of the past?

It's interesting, I suppose, how the modern reactions of
selfishness, panic, altruism and the rest have their parallels in
past plagues.

Hope you and your family and friends are avoiding
the virus.

Stay safe.

Everleigh

14

THE PLAGUE

In Bath I lay in a field with headphones on, drunk, and staring at an empty blue sky that reflected nothing of the chaos in the world. My flattened patch of hay, invisible from the road, scratched at my skin as the sun scorched it and I turned tipsily for the hundredth time to check I wasn't going to be ploughed by a tractor. I sat up, lit a cigarette and huffed. Below the fields flashed the seaweed-green of a London train speeding along the tracks and I imagined my former life at the end of it but felt more like it had been tied to the line and careered over at 100 mph. Where did I now stand in the new order of things, I wondered, now I'd left London and Jack, and my friends had scattered all over the UK?

The fears I'd had about coming home and accidentally killing my parents had eased after two weeks quarantined in my teenage bedroom without symptoms, but we were on high alert after my brother's experience with the virus, seeing how it could wipe you out completely, even if you were fit, healthy and twenty-eight. He was still yet to fully recover, and so what it might do to my dad was too worrying to think about. He liked any excuse not to leave the house and had quit friends about thirty years previously, so he only missed Waitrose, but we were being careful. 'Don't read pages twenty-three to twenty-four of the newspaper,' my mum told him after a sneezing fit one morning. 'I just accidentally covered a picture of African tribespeople.'

During my self-isolation, my parents left trays of food outside my door like zookeepers and I realised how much they'd anchored me my entire life.

'My compliments to the chef,' I shouted downstairs after a room-service delivery.

'Don't worry, we're thinking of all sorts of jobs you can do when you're out of there,' he said from somewhere below, so I went back into my room to work on my cough. It was currently too dangerous for me to wash up, which was pleasing.

Alone in my room, hard, jagged loneliness spread through me in the aftermath of Jack, who'd been the heightened extremes of everything. The whole world had gone quiet, every house shutting its doors in order to try to stay alive, and my loss hung thick in the silence. I felt like seaweed tossed around in the waves, but my mum sat in the corridor outside my room, propped up against the bookcase, talking to me as I tried to fasten around the chain of her anchor.

I looked around my room at photos of who I once was and wondered if I'd ever feel again like the girl in the Cornish-blue school uniform or the grinning teenager who hadn't yet been broken by men. I had PTSD – but didn't know it yet, and I was too scared to be alone with my own mind, so I ordered the wine boxes the entire country seemed to have decided was coping mechanism number one in a pandemic. Only when my shoulders dropped after a glass did I realise how tense I was all the time, despite having made it to safety, but by the evenings I was quietly drunk and feeling so lost I wanted to talk to Jack, missing him torturously but knowing he made everything worse. It felt like a piece of me had been cut out and so staying sober when the day stretched out so emptily was too much to handle in the beginning. After self-isolation all I could focus on was getting to a point in the day when it wasn't too despicably early to pour a glass of wine, then sat in the garden amongst the birds, letting the approaching summer heat and the liquid zap me of energy I didn't want, or know what to do with. Jack was begging me to go back to the flat, but not this time, I said. Not now I'd risked my parents' lives by coming back to their house in a pandemic. My head liked that I was being kept away from him, but my heart felt like it was about to stop completely.

Overnight my unconscious dredged the horrors of my previous life, and in Bath I shouted myself awake. I dreamt I was in bed with a horse and being kicked out of bed by hooves in the same way Jack kicked me out of bed in London. In my nightmares I was on dates with tigers and locked myself in a bathroom while they raked at the door, or on motorbikes that don't stop at red lights or trying to apply my make-up in trenches while the world was bombed and woke with the kind of panic I'd had at 5,000m in the Himalayas, not knowing where I was or what had happened to me and then drifted through the days feeling so broken I was barely there.

I blamed myself for everything and wished I'd never made it to the party on the thirty-sixth floor where I met Jack, swapped numbers, invited him round. I regretted 100 other *Sliding Doors* moments that led to the acute pain I was feeling now. Our public life together had been deleted by both of us as our life crashed and having our private existence shut down too enhanced the extreme disorientation of feeling upside down in a world falling apart at the seams.

The dystopia we were now living in heightened my despair and I cried at the news as it listed countries and death tolls; tragic stories about frontline workers getting ill and older people isolated and alone. Ice rinks had become makeshift morgues in Italy and whole houses of elderly dead were found in care homes in Spain. Watching the news now felt like you were watching a constant, highly emotional film and I wondered if this was what real war felt like – crying every day at the news? We got up to death every morning and feeling too shattered to fix myself, let alone help anyone else, made me feel even more heartbroken.

I guess my mum knew, or saw quickly enough, how much of a wreck I was and floated the idea of therapy from the corridor outside my room. But I didn't even know what I'd be going for? Addiction? Abuse? Toxic relationships? She didn't yet know about the New Year's Eve incident, and I dreaded having to tell her about it. Could you tell therapists you needed to talk about *everything*, I wondered, then remembered I'd been given a pack of antidepressants in London after Jack was arrested and held them in my hands, wondering if this was the answer. *What do you need?* I asked myself, and something answered 'Jack' but I knew I needed to listen to something else. In order not to pick up the phone and call him, I imagined the daughter we'd wanted crying every time he screamed at me, and how unsafe she would have been in a house of flying glass.

At night I couldn't get to sleep out of fear Jack was going to turn up at my parents' house. I lay with my eyes open like a traumatised car-crash patient, which in a way I was, and when they finally closed I felt like I was in *The Exorcist* being rid of demons as I slept.

Feeling severed from everyone I knew, I sat in my library of a bedroom and plucked books off the shelves, wanting to be any-where other than with myself in the void. Am I in *The Plague*, I wondered, as I read in Camus' fictional tale of lovers separated and pining for each other, while families were denied the chance to say goodbye to dying relatives, food ran out and an army of volunteers tried to help anyone who wasn't just drunk on despair.

Alcohol had become the first immediate crutch for a lot of people and vice had exploded everywhere behind closed doors in newly private lives. It turned out it wasn't just me having night-mares; the whole world was dreaming nightly of mortality and choosing to disassociate completely. You were in danger of being fined hundreds or thousands of pounds for parties, but people always took risks in war to feel alive. The night before a lockdown was the new New Year's Eve.

I listened with wide-eyed fascination to friends who'd not moved back to family homes and told me *the scene* had just gone underground. Raves too huge for the police to break up surged on hills around Bath; there were lock-ins in Brighton, Danny said, and 'Covid positive' parties on university campuses, another of my netball friends, Beth, informed me, where you were only allowed entry if you had already had the virus.

In London, Alex described bouncer-ed parties in Mayfair apartments rigged with lights, a bar and West End DJs; the owner of the flat selling tables in his own front room like it was a cool new club. When the parties were inevitably shut down, convoys of Ubers carried them elsewhere and Alex was at the next spontaneously offered venue two days later while paraphernalia turned up at the door every five minutes: the usual suspects, plus laughing gas. People always find a way if they want it enough, I thought, wondering if I missed it, but imagining how he felt the next day and realising I didn't.

Another friend was surviving lockdown with a £500 bottle of mushroom oil she assured me wasn't for risotto. Hallucinogenic micro-dosing was used to treat depression and the menopause, she said – despite being thirty and perfectly happy, pre-lockdown at least. Now her wedding had been cancelled, she'd been furloughed and there was nothing to do and nowhere to go.

I guess it was easier to misbehave in private and we'd been psychologically bent in the chaos, so the idea that we were surviving the end of the world raged in private Epicureanism that turned carnivalesque when we were allowed back out onto the streets. With the future invisible, the present had become everything, but having used hedonism as escapism for years, I refused to slide back into the flames.

After my initial isolation I was allowed downstairs to eat dinner in a rocking chair that my dad had rescued from a skip and rocking while you ate really did make you feel like you were in an asylum, I realised, wondering whether that was appropriate for my mental state.

My parents' house had again become a recovery site after London excess but now I was back indefinitely, I saw it in more context and knew it was time to kick bad habits that ruined your mind. I thanked the apocalypse for forcing me to address it, but text messages from London dealers who were working overtime in the pandemic and encouraging bulk-buying still flashed on my phone as though trying to tempt me back to sin city.

'Stay positive and we'll get through this together,' I read, wondering since when dealers got so witty and considerate, then deleting every number I had. Addiction followed you around if you let it, I realised.

'I've been saved,' I told Alfie, like a born-again Christian. Then I got a call from a number I didn't know and it was another dealer asking if I could tell him what existentialism was again?

'You're a good egg,' he said. 'I've been reminded to surround myself with good eggs.'

'Thank you,' I said, glad he was having a lockdown epiphany of his own, but blocking him anyway.

From the rocking chair, I realised that in the middle of the countryside, in a pandemic, all my vices were utterly impossible. The slow lane was mine at last, I thought, rocking manically and wondering if I could also give up smoking so I could avoid having to swap the hoovering for my mum's cigarette runs to the garage.

There would be no more highly unhelpful comedowns for me, I thought, marching back upstairs to my library and opening *Cocaine Nights* by J. G. Ballard where I found half a gram of antique MDMA wrapped in a ripped-out page from *A Room with a View*. Wondering if it was mine, or had been stashed by someone I'd once lived with, I started Googling 'Does MDMA have a sell-by date?' then realised it was a test and flushed it down my parents' loo. I didn't want the view from any room I was in to be altered by chemicals anymore.

It wasn't without fear, however, that I realised all of my usual coping mechanisms were now gone. Aside from the bad habits, I couldn't even escape via the respectable routes of cinema or theatre, or jump on a train or a plane to make the world feel exciting again. The world had shut down completely and, like a lot of people, I realised fast that I wasn't used to spending time on my own. I rarely stopped running around enough to just sit with myself, and I wasn't sure I liked it, or knew how to *do it*, even. The stillness unsettled me totally.

For the first time I realised how much an inability to be alone had pushed me into the wrong relationships, where, once in them, I put up with fights and baggage and insane jealousy because I thought it was better than being single. Only in the silence could I understand how much noise I'd lived with for the past ten years. No wonder I was heading for a breakdown, I thought: it just wasn't a sustainable way to live.

In my previous life no one had ever accused me of going to bed early, but now I was in bed by 10 p.m. I wondered if I could undo some of the extra years I'd aged due to all-nighters. All-nighter years probably worked like dog years I thought, making me bio-logically closer to forty. Then in the morning I woke up to bucolic statements from my mum. 'I dreamt about my asparagus bed last night,' she'd say, as I realised no one dreamt about asparagus beds in London; they had Excel nightmares and choked nocturnally on smog and angst. Meanwhile my dad was working on a painting called *Is Your Journey Strictly Necessary?*, which I realised my meta-phorical version definitely was.

Running helped, I again remembered, and my mum joined me for the first time, which was helpful in stopping me listening to

Anastacia and hating on men as I ran warbling through the lanes. I'd get home from those runs emotionally as well as physically shattered because Anastacia was as sick and tired and outta love as I was.

Starting a day running around country lanes, where my mum and I shared a route with a woman and her horse, felt more enlightened all round, and it was good to feel like I was padding back to health alongside Sprat, who was doing the Couch to 5K, its owner told us.

'Luxury stables, with a couch in it,' my mum said as we jogged away.

'I need to stop smoking,' I said.

'One thing at a time,' she soothed.

In the face of new and extreme financial insecurity, around 80 per cent of my single renting friends had left London in lockdown for their parents' houses and having our freedom snapped away was causing a huge identity crisis, regardless of how brilliantly supportive our parents were.

But that was sociologically interesting because the plague was causing a London brain drain that looked like it might change the landscape of the UK entirely, if those who'd evacuated decided they liked slower life elsewhere or just didn't have anything to go back for. There was a dispiriting sense that the lives we'd tried to carve for ourselves had imploded but from a distance, London had suddenly been revealed as an extortionate merry-go-round and because we'd not been able to afford to buy our own homes there, there was nothing tying us to the capital.

From saner, smaller cities we looked back at city life once so full of promise and saw that the reasons we paid double to live there had vanished. Whether you were into restaurants, bars, theatre, comedy, music, sporting events or the weird and wonderful one-off experiences that happened all over the city every night, they were gone. Shut. Over. London was a ghost town of good times and Friday night, as we knew it, was dead in the water.

Our only escape and our only entertainment was technology, and we needed it desperately, I saw, as a fascinating shift occurred. Over the past five years technology had been treated with more and more suspicion, headlines telling us screen time meant kids played on iPads instead of outside with other children; primary and junior school pupils were sexting because they had smartphones; by secondary school social media was ruining self-esteem and fuelling anxiety; cyberbullying was causing teen suicide. Our physical health was shot alongside our mental health as studies showed too much screen use damaged eyesight, disrupted sleep, destroyed attention spans and caused weight to fluctuate. There was even an iPhone injury called 'smartphone pinky' that suggested we were going to pass on bent fingers to our kids.

But in the pandemic, technology wasn't enhancing isolation and ruining mental health but was alleviating and soothing it instead. It was all we had, especially if you lived alone, and seeing the faces of those we loved on screens helped hugely. My generation stopped texting for the first time, instead picking up the phone to have a proper conversation or a video call.

While friends sat determinedly on Zoom until 5 a.m., reluctant to let the idea of Friday night be buried completely, I stayed off it at first, not wanting to have to run through the sordid detail of my downfall (as I saw it). But as I started to recover, I remembered how much old friends anchored you and during new, virtual socials it didn't matter that everyone was spread around the country or even the world. I could FaceTime Madi in America everyday if I wanted to; call Mat in Colombia on WhatsApp; and my uni friend Jess could bring her new baby boy onto camera to meet our friends from the course. Friday nights edged a little way back to what they were as I arranged Zoom drinks with the Newcastle boys or the netball girls and we 'met' in houses all over the country on screen. We were speaking more than we ever had, as though an understanding of the fragility of life was bringing us closer to those we really cared about, people who'd known us for years and who we wanted to know were coping OK in the crisis.

Chloe's concern was that her vagina was 'closing up' in rural Hertfordshire, I heard, halfway through lockdown one, but she wasn't the only one.

'When are we next going to be able to have *sex*?' Hannah asked, two months in.

'What's sex?' I replied. I'd forgotten.

Those of us who'd moved back home were beginning to wonder whether we should have set up a Hinge date before leaving London, given that touching anyone you didn't live with was currently illegal and the algorithms in the countryside were less than inspiring. My friend Lorna had decreed that all men anywhere near *Bloody Berwick* were farmers, and Beth asked if I'd seen that two pandas in Hong Kong had mated for the first time in ten years. 'Even pandas are getting more than me, and they have no libido whatsoever,' she said with a sad face.

In America, Madi had made the snap decision to have a date move in after a month-long introduction to the gay dating scene. 'She's only a corona girlfriend,' she told me, when I suggested it was fast. 'I'm going to cut her off after lockdown.'

'Brutal,' I said.

'Sex,' she replied. 'Five times a day.'

This is why prisoners marry pen pals in jail, I thought: to alleviate isolation behind bars.

But sex was just another escapism that helped disengage us in the Covoid, and Boris was perhaps destined always to bring virility to Downing Street. By April, the PM had a seventh child (at least) and by Christmas three friends and my cousin were pregnant. Not by Boris.

I guess it shouldn't have been a surprise that a dating-addicted world asked so quickly how and when it would get its next hit. Two weeks in, the world looked so bleak that sheer fear of being alone during global collapse set the apps on fire. The idea that someone else was out there was enough to ease the panic for a lot of my friends, and what a thing it would be to tell the grandkids if you *did* find love in a pandemic, they said.

Yet trying to fall in love had become a health risk and sleeping with someone could kill them, which risked a funeral, if not a wedding.

Even weirder, given married couples were now locked tighter together, was the fact the illicit encounters website Ashley Madison had been adding 17,000 new members a day with a new strapline: 'Life's short. Have an affair.' I guess it was appealing to those who wanted to tick something off their bucket list before potentially kicking the bucket itself. I'd seen in the Himalayas how an atmosphere of death made people want to jump into bed and with Tom how an atmosphere of fear after the terror attacks made us think it was now or never. But affairs were too obvious now you had little or no excuse to leave the house, and the unfaithful were being smoked out everywhere.

Even if you were single, lockdown hook-ups were precarious and I was glad that I was too heartbroken to be interested while other friends were slinking illegally about in order to have one last liaison. Carrying a yoga mat that suggested she was on a legitimate exercise ration, one of my friends drove 20 miles to meet a Tinder date in a park and experienced her first yogic cunnilingus, she texted me, before he asked if they could repeat the move while she held a Webex for thirty people.

Then Alex messaged to tell me he didn't think there'd ever been a better time to date. '*Really?*' I asked.

'This week I find myself in what I can only describe as a nude crab handstand fighting off the extreme pleasures of a perfectly executed lingam massage from my newly found Russian tantric practitioner,' he said.

I had no idea what half of it meant, but decided not to Google it.

I just listened in fascinated alarm to all sorts of lascivious exercise/ dating the government had accidentally prompted nationwide.

Sex really was everywhere, fast, and those lucky enough not to be talking about ventilators were discussing vibrators, or which household objects buzzed enough to do the trick. Virtual orgies had become a thing on Houseparty and Zoom, exes were being re-dialled for phone sex and millennials were rearranging their teenage bedrooms at family homes so they could take naked selfies without a backdrop of trophies showing they were once good at geography. Or the high jump.

For months I couldn't bear the idea of seeing anyone who wasn't Jack, knowing they probably wouldn't have his frightening side, but doubting they'd have his captivating brilliant side either, yet the millennial Neighbourhood Watch scheme I was operating from my bedroom suggested I was getting less action than most of the septuagenarians on my parents' street. West Country Sue appeared to be sleeping with the man that cut her hedge.

'Good for her!' my mum said.

'It's lockdown,' I said.

'Oh yeah,' she said, pulling a face.

Helpfully, the inevitable divide between those taking the new regulations seriously and those continuing to date meant you could quickly gauge if you shared a similar enough mindset to get on in the long run.

Before Alex's dating epiphany he'd had coronavirus, then a corona break-up and then gone straight onto apps where a match quickly became sexting; then a socially distanced walk.

'I bailed the first time, for social responsibility reasons. But then – you know – a few days later ... '

'What did you do?' I chastised in my most Chris Whitty tone.

'Well, she lives near Buckingham Palace. Not in it, can I stress? Near it. So we decided to meet for a walk. But two metres really exacerbates sexual tension,' he whined. 'So we went back to mine. Candles, music, wine. But I couldn't get it up,' he added, dejected.

'The idea of overwhelming the NHS didn't turn you on?' I asked.

He considered. 'I think I'm not over my ex.'

Exes were resurfacing everywhere, suddenly, with virtual versions of Tracey Emin's tent springing up worldwide as we decided to check whether everyone we'd ever slept with was alive. One friend was receiving nude selfies from a French policeman, a dalliance now two years past and presumably re-invigorated while he was walking around Paris trying to enforce Covid distancing. I realised then how globally spread hook-ups had become for a generation who'd travelled the world with such ease. Until now. But the international check-ins were sort of sweet, in a sexty kind of way.

'Everyone's in the same boat and no one's got anything to do – or at least anyone to do,' Alex said. 'That's the real issue here.'

I was pretty sure the real issues were death and the NHS but decided to leave it.

After the immediate, primal question of whether we'd survive the virus if we got it, other existential questions quickly followed. Were we happy? Did we like where we lived? Were we in the right relationship? Were we in the right job? Did we like the personality and the life that we'd carved?

The chance to go backwards is something desired by many but afforded to few. Yet when the pandemic hit it was like the world had failed a level and thrown us back to an earlier one where we could pick a new character and start again.

Who did we want to be now?

As lockdowns stretched on and on, having to stay in and just 'be' held us static in a form of national paralysis and we realised we were being given the chance to rearrange ourselves in a newly recast world. *Milk costs more than crude oil*, we laughed in horror, mixing quarantinis from whatever bottles we disliked enough to have let collect dust in the house, and raising a concoction to the worst year of our lives. The emotional rollercoaster surged and we stood in driveways with gout from too much comfort eating and bashed wooden spoons on saucepans to celebrate the people trying to keep us alive.

My parents' sober routine was helping to settle me. On Mondays, my mum did yoga and so my dad made a northern dinner of egg and chips for himself and, to my horror, Alfie. Tuesday was Catch up with Jeremy (Paxman). Wednesday was Wednesday Wine Night – still alliteratively acceptable. Thursday was a free-for-all and Friday the double whammy of Friday Fizz and 'MONTY', my mum screeched at the telly, before saying without fail, 'Don't you think he looks like dad?' and then 'Monty has seasonal defective disorder,' like this was a luxurious new plant and not winter depression.

The good thing about both *University Challenge* and *Gardener's World* was that they made me feel drunk in a way that was cheaper, healthier and now more reachable than Soho.

'Starter for ten,' Paxman said. 'Najand heeioko keratina walalabad bhey suskun?'

'Great Wall of China,' my parents and Jesus College, Cambridge answered.

'Correct,' Pax said.

'What the fuck? said I.

Gardener's World was more like being on an acid trip in the Eden Project, as Monty popped up mellifluously in a hedge and they cut to all sorts of other people who wanted you to see what they were bunging in soil up and down the country.

'Tulipa Bastia is like a muppet gone crackers,' a millennial Alan Bennett said on screen.

'Who is this absolute lad?' I asked my mum.

She ignored me.

'This tulip looks like something out of Cleopatra's temple,' he continued.

'Seriously, Mum, who is this person?'

'I'm not engaging,' she said.

My mum didn't believe in the word retirement and still worked part-time in a museum, but both my parents were more used to being at home than they once might have been, so the pandemic didn't massively change life for them, they admitted, brave-facing it. Meanwhile, I was still freelancing and commissions about the various complexities of lockdown life trickled in as constant new developments tumbled into the news.

I'd always been determined I didn't have FOMO – not wanting to have any acronym – but now I was out of the fray I saw that the way I'd lived, not planning anything and flitting around, was nothing *but* a fear of missing out. It was a natural consequence of a fast, materialistic life that didn't exist any more. For that reason lockdown was almost a relief for some of us. A pause. A break. For women particularly, who didn't have to worry about what they looked like on top of everything else, and for a show-offy, look-at-me generation who'd been filtering every part of their lives the anti-vanity movement couldn't have come at a better time. My friends were now letting their hair curl into festival tangles and stroking their legs as they watched telly, newly fascinated by a Chewbacca furring that could stand in for both pet therapy and touch which was now illegal. In the midst of world confusion, we'd become more desperate for the *real* and turned our backs on anything that wasn't, vanity the first to go.

Then we started the cull. Now that I couldn't meet them for a drink, some people from my fast life in London slipped away totally and with the distance I realised that most of my PR 'friends' in London were actually more like colleagues. Now I was back home I didn't ring a handful of people I'd spoken to often while I lived there, and they didn't ring me either. Situational friendships were shown to be just that, rather than tight, loyal connection, and I felt honoured to still be able to call so many *real* friends, knowing the kind, intelligent and funny people I knew might have been pushed away if I'd stayed in so poisonous a relationship with Jack.

Sometimes you chose less contact because you know your friends think you should already have left a relationship, and you haven't. Or you can't bear to hear advice you know is true. Again. Maybe you just don't have the energy to pretend you're fine with people you know will see straight through you. But when I'd been alone in that flat in London and learnt to say that I didn't feel strong all the time, tears running down my face and sometimes theirs too, my real friends were all there, and continued to be during lockdown when I didn't feel strong *any* of the time in the beginning.

In London something had been breaking in me for a while and the cracks must have become more visible, because an actor I'd been casually dating before Jack had once asked about the sadness he thought he saw in my eyes. In London Bridge, our neighbour Sélim, who saw how often I stayed up all night alone after the parties were over and the people had left, had taken me aside to ask if I was actually *happy* beneath the Mrs Dalloway act I turned on every evening. Then Irish Bea admitted six months into our friendship and even after we'd been on *holiday* together that I was still an enigma to her, which shocked me but made me think about how much I'd been surfacing over things even with my friends until now, as we coached each other through personal confusion daily. Everyone was worrying about something, whether it was ill, elderly parents or joblessness or relationships that now didn't feel right, and we needed each other more than ever, given the public horror show we lived in. I saw then that I'd never really been alone when I was single, because I had my friends as well as my family. Their duty of care was currently keeping me alive and I wanted to be able to return the favour if and when it was needed.

'Do you like five boys?' my dad asked one morning in lockdown one.

'Do I like *five* boys?' I asked, quite shocked. 'You know I've literally just had a break-up, right?'

'The burger place,' he said.

'Ohhh. Five Guys.' I replied. 'Er – not especially.'

He described several burgers in detail, then added that every one of them was too expensive unless you got *all* the pickles.

I looked at him. 'You look ... nice,' I said. It was 10 a.m. and he was wearing a Ralph Lauren shirt.

'Yeah, I got sick of not dressing up and walking around in pyjamas all day like ... Fleabag,' he said.

As I recovered from my fast, vulnerable life, I realised that my thirties and the following decades would flip vulnerability, at some point, from child to parent and unless I sorted myself out properly this time, I wouldn't be in a position to pick up a Five Boys order, or help with something more serious.

At thirty, I couldn't even offer to do their weekly shop because I couldn't drive, and what if they needed to go to hospital and I had to wait for a taxi? It hit me hard then that I needed to unravel myself enough to be strong when *they* needed *me*, and for that my temporary bandaging technique had to be over. But I knew I couldn't address my whole life alone.

'This is the one I thought would be good,' my mum said, having researched local therapists. She pulled the website up on her laptop, which looked weirdly like Tinder, with the therapists' faces displayed above their name, bio and location.

'*That* one?' I asked.

'Don't you like him?' she said.

'Well, isn't he a bit ... attractive?' I asked, scrunching my face up with uncertainty.

'Everyone falls in love with their first therapist, it's fine,' she said.

For someone who might possibly have a love addiction, this didn't sound ideal.

'Who was *yours*?' I asked.

'A fusty woman I didn't have the guts to leave,' she said. 'But there's loads of unattractive ones near Bath if you keep scrolling,' she added.

'Why do I feel like I'm on a dating app?' I said, completely disconcerted by the similar judgement the website was inspiring in me. It didn't help that they were all registered members of UKCP, which I read as UKIP for the first three pages. 'I'm sure the one you found is fine,' I said, just so I could stop looking.

So *William* it was, I thought, and I'd just not think about the fact he looked like Jamie Dornan. Especially given Jamie Dornan had once played a serial killer therapist.

I wondered how stupid it was to expect another man to change my life for the better.

But at least this one was qualified to try.

Then on the anniversary of VE Day, Jack emailed me a note that was designed to get me running back to him.

It felt like a trap, but what do you do when someone you still love tells you they're about to disappear completely? Even if the person has treated you worse than anyone else ever has, do you ignore them?

Having got this far, I didn't want to phone him so I sent other people to the house to check he was OK. But he was fine. He had answered the door, absolutely fine. Then a week later he wasn't and there were pictures this time.

I still doubted him completely and felt like I was losing the ability to gauge what was real in the tangled fabrications of his deceit. Was I crazy for talking to him on the phone, or just empathetic? I didn't know how to work out what was happening, or how I felt about any of it, but I sat for hours on Zoom to try to breathe some life back into him, just in case.

That was also why I agreed to meet him once more after that, at Paddington when the first lockdown was over. I wore a yellow dress, like the girl in *A Gentleman in Moscow*, which we'd bought together in a charity shop near the sea. Despite everything and despite being forced apart for the longest time we ever had, I stood in that station and watched him coming towards me and we just grinned. It was the airport all over again.

We sat in a hot park and smoked in the heat, wrapped around each other like comfort blankets, and it was magical being back together, eating pizza in bed and running my hands through his hair as he lay quiet and calm. He was *alive*, so alive, and it was two days of blazing June heat and constant affection until he was drunk and rambling and talking of the men I'd *fucked* and then I was in self-inflicted pain again. I watched him walk away from me in Regent's Park, not moving, but knowing that this, *finally*, would be the last time I ever saw him. I'd realised, as we'd sat there that day and I sensed he was losing it, that I'd unconsciously checked for witnesses. I understood then that the fear I still felt around him would never go away.

It takes a while to believe something you don't want to believe – but if you're right the other person can't help but show you. You only have to keep your eyes open. I also knew that nothing would change if I didn't make it. I wondered for a while whether he'd always be a part of me. His touch, his different looks, the way he woke, babbling with energy.

Untangling myself from Jack and London was the hardest thing I've ever done but during the months I'd been away from him I'd realised that what I'd left behind was like the reflections of the boats on the canals in Little Venice we'd sat by the night before lockdown was announced. They looked so solid on the surface they might have been real, but then the wind blew and they shivered and disappeared and then you realised reflections were really nothing at all.

*

As the summer rolled on, I listened to friends embarking on social-distance dating and realised romance had taken a massive, old-fashioned step backwards. Not knowing when I'd be back in the game, I listened to the world asking itself whether it was possible to fall in love two metres apart, and what exactly a date *looked* like, now that pubs, bars and restaurants were closed. The options seemed to be a picnic or a turn around a park. *Welcome to 2020*, I thought, wondering if I should get calling cards printed so I could have one delivered to a potential suitor's drawing room and extend the feeling I was in an eighteenth-century novel when I next started dated again.

Comparisons with war romance were rife, but the main difference between the Blitz, say, and corona was that the battlefield was not a faraway place, but much closer to home, and the person you saw as a moment of comfort and safety might be the enemy. Was this what AIDS felt like to a previous generation, we wondered? Dating had become a personal risk assessment that pivoted on your age and whether you were a single parent, self-employed or looking after elderly parents. Some people just couldn't afford to get ill, while anyone who wanted to risk it found themselves in a love triangle with a prospective shag and the NHS.

When we might be able to safely have sex again was yet to be addressed by Chris Whitty, but a news story that sex workers in Switzerland had gone back to their unique offices (in only doggy-style and reverse cowgirl) had gone viral.

As I always had, I wondered if meeting new people could fill the void I felt in the wake of Jack and so knowing I was safely covered by both enforced distance and not being in Switzerland, I downloaded Hinge halfway through the summer. There was something about the apps that made you feel less alone, at first, but the West Country options were quickly more depressing than the idea I'd never fall in love again. In the country, handfuls of men said they were just looking for a girl to water their courgettes while they were away.

'Away *where*?' I asked my phone. 'Sainsbury's?'

'You know I'll like you if . . . on Sunday morning I poach you an egg and smash your avocado,' someone else said, as I winced and scrolled on to the next man, who said the most surprising thing about him was that he was 'actually' quite intelligent. *Jesus*, I thought, swiping yes to no one. Mainly I just carried my phone to my mum, to say: '*Look* at this one. He says the most spontaneous thing he's ever done is eat an After Eight mint at 7.30pm.'

'No,' she said simply.

'Do you think I'm a badass with a nice ass?' I asked her, seeing that's what another man was looking for.

Worrying I was being too fussy in a way only women do, I 'liked' a tobacconist thinking I'd at least get cheaper cigs, then realised I'd misread it, and he was actually a tobogganist. *Goddamnit*, I thought. When I asked if he was joking, he said he was Team GB.

Geography undeniably changed dating pools, I realised, and after the massively diverse and metropolitan dating options in London, smaller city romance was hugely uninspiring. Bath was full of students, tech types and cheesemongers while Bristol was inundated with vegan stoners with nose rings. Despite promising to do the opposite, Hinge quickly only exacerbated how alone I felt because scrolling through reams of bleak profiles made me feel like I'd never meet anyone enticing ever again.

Suddenly the most persuasive thing about the whole enterprise was that anyone I met would have to remain two metres away from me at all times. For a generation so quick to jump into bed the idea that you couldn't have sex on a first date felt antiquated, but hugely less pressurising, I realised. While the men I knew argued there was too much sexual chemistry at two metres, the women argued there was too *little* without the usual ingredients of direct contact, music and bar surroundings acting as relaxants. More of a concern was corona goggles: 'the new beer goggles' that made everyone look more attractive because we were desperate not to die alone.

Letting go of the idea that dating could help excite me about a world I felt severed from when I moved home was a slow process because I was desperate to believe in life after love, as Cher had before me.

I lasted two months on Hinge before I deleted it completely, but for the first time in my life dating just wasn't a welcome distraction any more and the micro-rejections from people you had no interest in anyway were destroying the mood I was managing to lift better without them. To be happy I didn't need to meet highly anxious Hinge girls who messaged me about loo roll or boys who laughed at none of my jokes because their previous girlfriends had been 'slow', mock-punched me in the face when I told them about my horrible last relationship or haggled for gone-off lamb sausages they said they could cook me for breakfast if I stayed over.

There was a big sea change, I realised, because whilst it had been exciting to feel everything new again when dating was back on the cards, actually the pandemic was changing my generation profoundly. The vacuous nature of sleeping around was more obvious and sexually liberal millennials who'd previously been enamoured with the ease of hook-up culture now realised we had nothing to show for it. The bars had shut, one-night-stands were illegal and I'd realised sex and intimacy were not the same thing at all. Intimacy was rewarded only on the way to love and not in the beds of strangers who didn't really know or care about anything outside of the moment. On the other side we knew we'd be looking for something realer.

In consistently on-and-off lockdowns, no *stable* connection tied you to new acquaintances either and they disappeared fast, we were able to realise, now our lives were emptier. Instead it was our friends and the people we'd known for years who'd get us through the crisis.

By the end of the summer, I'd starting talking to the boyfriend I'd had at sixteen, who'd since become a personal trainer and said that while the days of carrying me up the hills of Bath were over, he could get me fit if I didn't moan during the sessions. 'Well, I will,' I said. 'I know,' he laughed. All sorts of memories, like the mini-fireworks display he'd surprised me with one November 5th, came back to me then and I laughed in memory of a tree burning with a Catherine wheel jammed in too tight as he desperately tried to put it out.

Sid, the chef I'd gone all round Europe with, was still here too and had left the restaurant trade in the pandemic after seventeen gruelling years to retrain as a plumber. He'd settled down and bought a house with someone he thought he'd marry, before it had gone wrong, so we met in a pub garden by the river to talk about our similar heartbreaks and laughed about all the places we'd been.

'I always thank you for that Europe trip,' he said. 'I still never would have gone to half the places without you.'

'Remember that row we had in the Colosseum in the rain,' I laughed. 'Such an epic setting for an argument.' But he didn't; he only remembered the great bits and let go of the rest, reminding me that some people just did.

From Brighton, Liam sent me a book he thought I'd like with a little note saying I was amazing and needed to remember it in the face of the storm. I remembered him sitting on the balcony in London Bridge and telling me he'd always wondered whether our future would be together. How ironic if it had been him all along, I thought, then.

Sam came back, too, his girlfriend having had a pregnancy scare before they had a traumatic break-up of their own. 'It's reassuring to hear your voice,' he said, as we started talking on the phone again about everything and nothing, like we always used to.

I saw the communications with my romantic past as threads tying me to the good people I'd been close to; a collective anchoring that helped remind me how far I'd come. '*Look at you,*' Sid said. '*You did it.*'

Until then, I didn't realise how much I'd lost the idea of what I'd achieved since I'd left home and gone to London where there was always someone doing better than you were, it felt like. I saw then that it was only people who really knew you that could help you remember who you were, and how far you'd already come, and in trying to forget my past completely, I saw who I'd left behind.

I did have friends, I remembered, in Bath, not only in Sid but in Serena, who I'd known since I was sixteen and who told me it didn't matter what state I was in when I came to see her. 'Just come,' she said. After that we started cycling to the pub, trying not to run over her sausage dog Bobby en route, but ticking off exercise before a pint. She was the captain of the England netball team so I don't think she thought of a meandering ten-minute bike ride as exercise, but it was better than nothing.

'How's living back home?' she asked when we sat down.

'It's good,' I said, having a sip of Amstel. 'Just feel like I'm drinking too much. I need something that doesn't involve booze, you know? I wish I liked yoga but it's just so . . . *smug.*'

'Yoga's shit,' she agreed. 'But have you tried meditation? I know what you're thinking,' she said, when she saw my face. 'But I've got this great app called Buddhify. It's like quick, mini-meditations rather than long, intimidating ones that make you think you've got to sit there forever, failing to empty your mind. It really helped when I wanted to get to the next level in netball and was stuck in a rut.'

If it helped calm a professional athlete, I thought, surely it could calm me. Her *job* was speed and I knew from our teenage gallivanting in Bath that we had similarly short attention spans. Before I stopped going into school, we'd often snuck off at lunchtime to joyride town on her moped and in the evenings pre-drank to Justin Timberlake's *Future Sex/Love Sounds* in my room, trying not to fall down the stairs on the way to the pub (where one of us inevitably fell immediately down the stairs).

'Christ we were so *young*,' I remembered. 'I still drank Malibu then.'

Then there was Em, the school friend who'd invited me to my first party, straightened my hair and handed we a blue WKD. We laughed so long in the pub the first time we saw each other again, we had to cycle home in the dark.

'I almost swallowed a bat,' I told her. 'Felt like Ozzy Osbourne.'

'The canal was *frightening*,' she replied.

I just didn't need dating any more, I saw, realising how little time I'd given myself between commitments during ten years of serial monogamy. I knew when I finished a book that I could never start a new one immediately, characters from the last still sitting too real in my mind. But with relationships, I'd been starting new ones to get over the disappointing epilogue of the last. You couldn't get over anything or anyone when you did that, I saw, realising that ironically time revealed that you didn't *need* anyone at all.

And if I didn't need anyone, the chances of getting it right when I next considered a relationship were raised a thousand per cent, I thought, a feeling of mature epiphany settling into me with the prospect of staying alone. I was quite sure this is what Isaac Newton must have felt like when he discovered gravity.

In the meantime, vibrators were a grown-up way to deal with libido, I thought (like thousands of women in the pandemic before me), ordering one and accidentally opening it in front of my mum.

'That is *not* the book I was expecting,' I said, slamming the box shut.

Dear Lucy,

I've just caught up with a couple of your pieces including the record of determination to live quietly in the country. I wonder if it will persist?

I'm also sure you'll be horrified to know that you figured in a dream last night – married and pregnant! I've been having long, surreal narrative dreams; this one was something about debt, and I was trying to find you – though I'd forgotten your name – to write a piece on the subject (amongst a tangle of other things). Some people have claimed that dreams prompted successful artworks but I don't think I'm suddenly going to emerge a novelist.

I'm heartily fed up of not being able to get into the Brotherton library, but am actually in the middle of a bit of health scare. The main feeling as another problem lands (this has not been a good year) is just of weariness as another bit of the aging body falls into the sere, the yellow leaf. I actually think that Shakespeare is obsessionally good at writing about old age – the sonnets, *Macbeth* (from which, I don't need to tell you, that phrase comes), *Lear*, *Tempest*, etc. His is definitely a country for and of old men.

Very best hopes for 2021,

Everleigh

Dear Everleigh,

Please don't go anywhere yet.

    I always wanted you to play the organ if I ever walked down an aisle (outside of a supermarket) and there may well be a new menu at Pizza Express for your idle consideration once this is over. How will the taste of Brits change after a virus has wiped out tastebuds full stop? There may well be anchovy on EVERYTHING.

L x

15

ANY HUMAN HEART

As we entered another lockdown and then another, it was hard to know who to feel most sympathy for in a new, still entirely uprooted world. Those at school missed months of education and were sometimes stuck with parents who wouldn't or couldn't help them; university and college students were denied the normal, social, carefree experience. Those who'd slogged to secure good, bottom-rung jobs now found there weren't any vacancies and further down the line, younger employees were less likely to have kids, so there was less guilt from employers about furloughing or firing them. Those with kids *needed* their jobs, but were now also their full-time carers and teachers, too. Suddenly offices we'd never liked looked like paradise lands you'd pay to visit. Generation rent were huddling around one kitchen table with flat-mates they often didn't even like, fighting to talk over three other Zoom meetings and eventually locking themselves in bedrooms they now had to spend twenty-four hours a day in.

Two things became very important for my generation then: compatibility with those we lived with and outside space. Those that didn't have a garden, or even a balcony (because who could afford to prioritise *that* in London?), boiled inside small flats in the heatwave and tried to drink cabin fever away. Mental health issues surged.

New mothers, including some of my old school friends, didn't have the support of their parents in early difficult days and grandparents didn't know if they'd meet the next generation of their families before it was too late.

One of the most dystopian moments I had was driving past a care home in Bath and seeing a singer with a 1950s fringe and a polka-dot dress singing into a microphone for a window of wheelchairs above the car park. It made me want to cry, that effort to cheer them, knowing they probably hadn't been outside for months and seeing how inhumanly trapped they looked. The very vulnerable – which included my godmother Kate, who'd had a heart transplant over ten years ago and lived alone – were experiencing the most isolating isolations going. Shut doors separated families to try to keep the vulnerable alive but caged them in the process and as hospitals filled, families worried, medical staff died and war comparisons prevailed.

Single women in their late thirties and early forties wondered whether they'd meet any one in time to have kids and rushed to freeze their eggs. The risk of dating raised with age and the older you were, the more you worried about when physical affection would next be safe. 'Don't kill Granny,' *The Times* front page said in September, directly quoting the health secretary as another wave of the virus swept the UK, but by then some of my friends' grandparents were saying a hug was worth more than, what might be, their last Christmas alone.

Above all, I felt most sorry for the homeless, knowing the terrifying fear of being kicked out of a house with a few possessions, but knowing – too – that I had a home to go back to which was not an option for all children, grown up or otherwise. Parents who couldn't cope like mine, as well as illegal evictions and violent home lives were putting tens of thousands of people on the pavement ahead of a winter in which an invisible virus raged. A national identity crisis had also become a new human rights crisis and while the homeless were rushed to be housed in the lockdowns, what was going to happen afterwards?

With its soaring infection rate and huge rents for cramped flats, London had started to look even more frightening from a distance and having been thrown off my escalator life to stumble on slower ground, I was wondering, by early autumn, when I'd want to go back, if ever. Back to a city where millennials were rushed through ruinously late shifts, late nights and even later love, then turned around to realise they were fifty-five but looked seventy. I'd already had free Botox once for gonzo journalism purposes, but I didn't want to have to pay £400-a-syringe to delete the stress lines that lay in wait if I rushed back, I thought.

By the end of the summer, I had decided to have another complete break from drinking, and only after that could I suddenly stand the idea of time and felt it flow more easily. Forever, I'd thought it was the other way round: that alcohol helped time run faster until you reached idyll. But giving it up when I moved to Peter's showed me I could and I now saw *not* drinking was a coping mechanism.

The time to slow down after such a frenetic decade was invaluable and once I'd righted myself enough to see that, I didn't want to waste it. When would we ever be given a chance to stop everything? After the initial flocking to vice, it was like the whole of the UK was sitting amongst empty Virgin wine boxes, with a hangover, and deciding it needed a healthier way than degeneracy to colour in the gaps of an emptier existence.

I saw my breakdown as just one star in a huge constellation, knowing major or mini crises of self were being experienced by everyone. My friend Janey had spent three months living in a tent in her parents' garden having been kicked out of Australia by a government who didn't want foreign nationals stuck there in a pandemic. She'd just started a new life as a teacher and being thrown home made her feel like such a failure she couldn't bring herself to walk through the front door of her parents' house yet.

It was a relief to feel I was starting to fix myself enough to help those who were breaking for their own reasons and soon I'd joined an army of NHS volunteers and a '*Mission Possible*' theme was ringing constantly on my phone, which meant someone was struggling in isolation elsewhere, sometimes not having heard another voice in days.

Through another phone-volunteering service I met my immediate favourite, an incredibly spritely 94-year-old widower called Arthur who'd been shielding since March. 'I was talking to myself at first, and then I started talking to the wall,' he said. 'But I'm assured I should only be worried if the wall starts talking back.'

'Shirley Valentine talked to her wall, and then a Greek rock,' I told him.

'You're very easy to talk to compared to the wall,' he said, as he told me what it was like to watch the start of the Battle of Britain from a field just outside London when he was a boy. 'No one's really asked me about the war before,' he said, which was shocking to me but showed, I guess, how silence had once upon a time been the norm.

Living somewhere with a sense of community that was rarely reached in London suburbs meant we were all looking out for each other and when a neighbour turned seventy-six, I snuck to her house to tie balloons to her gate, knowing she wouldn't be able to have dinner with her son for the first time in years and she emailed to tell me what a lift they had given her when she saw them blowing in the wind. 'Everyone keeps thinking I'm partying in here now!' she said, but luckily no one called the police.

The world outside of the home had largely vanished and public selves had died everywhere. All we had were newly personal worlds and an identity crisis that confirmed a 'work–life balance' had been mythical. We'd made time for nothing *but* work, and now barely knew what to do with ourselves.

In Fulham, my brother bought an electric piano and started Zoom lessons, as I started drawing and my mum bought an origami book and worked on her Japanese accent. Realising now was the time to become who you wanted to be, my neighbour bought a convertible and took up knitting, while my dad upgraded to posh kitchen scissors.

To my combined surprise and glee, I'd realised *nature* was also something that made you feel more like a real person and less like Pete Doherty. In Bath, roe deer leapt about the fields at the end of our garden, which looked straight onto a vineyard of happily undrinkable wine, and I lay in the garden with goldfinches flying metres above my face. Everything was different: the sound, the colours, the pace, the mood.

I'd begun to like life far from the maddening crowd and now spent the weekends at National Trust properties with my parents, and looking back on the all-nighters like I looked back on exes who I'd fancied at the time but now retched at the thought of. Not to say I'd never have another too-late-a-night ever again, but I was realising how blindly you lived when you skipped from one thing to the next with a drink in your hand. Balance made me trust I was saner than the benders often led me to believe.

Was I regressing, I wondered, through family trips to the seaside and early bedtimes, or *progressing* because I now agreed to days out without needing to be assured there was a bar when we got there? City life was so bottomless that women got hammered during blow-dries in 2019, and time floated less surreally when you weren't drunk at the art gallery or cinema or the fucking *squash court* just because all-you-can-drink Prosecco was available, I realised. It was an economical push, but greed had turned us into a drunken city who wanted no glass half empty.

It was only the insistence outside of big-city life that pouring alcohol over everything didn't make it better that was starting to shake my deeply ingrained patterns of requiring booze to relax. Maybe I just couldn't say no to the opportunity, which arose constantly in London. But the countryside and the sea, as we drove to Studland Bay and walked along the beach trying not to look at the naturists (now I was a prude again), made alcoholic calmers so unnecessary, I realised. As my mum and I swam out from the beach the cold hit my skin like a panic attack before it became, ten seconds later, drug-like in exhilaration.

'This is why people take cocaine in London!' I gargled at her with a mouthful of sea water.

'Are you drowning?' she shouted back, unable to hear me through a cormorant-ridden wind.

'I'm not sure,' I choked. My heart felt like it was growing again and I wondered if I'd become the Grinch in London, or whether this was just the heightened clarity you had before a heart attack.

When my godmother emailed to tell me life was a marathon not a sprint, and if I slowed down, I could enjoy the scenery, I realised that this is exactly what I wasn't doing when I raced through life, only thinking of the next best thing. The collectively hectic rush in London combined with Peter Pan syndrome meant that by thirty we were ready to retire like injured footballers. The difference was that we were still expected to run another forty years on the pitch, because we weren't Son Heung-min. I knew I wasn't the only one who felt like they'd been thrown off one of those fast-moving walkways in airports when lockdown hit. Normal pace felt like we were loping in slow-motion on the moon before we got used to it and realised it was just that – normal.

In therapy, which was able to take place in person by the end of the summer rather than on the phone, William was teaching me that the point was to just 'be', and I was bent on learning how to do it in my new slow-worm life. Unbeknownst to me, the being was actually the doing, apparently, rather than what I'd been doing for the past ten years: the complete opposite.

'But what do people do when they just do . . . being?' I'd asked when we'd started our weekly sessions.

'Anything you like,' he said. Then presumably remembering my past life: 'Anything relaxing.'

'Like ... watching *Match of the Day*?' I asked.

Footballers were now playing with a sanitised ball to empty stands, elbow-bumping hellos to sound effects from a fake, cheering crowd.

'If you find that relaxing, then yes.'

This told me that he did *not* find *Match of the Day* relaxing but I was getting more used to not asking questions: another complete overhaul of all I'd been doing for a decade.

Initially, I'd found the idea of phoning someone to talk about myself for an hour – which was against both everything I knew as a journalist, and everything I knew about curiosity and manners – immensely difficult. I was also wary, having had one boyfriend who'd been turned so inward by psychotherapy that he couldn't level his sight back to anyone else. I was scared that would happen to me if I became used to rambling on a virtual chaise longue, but I had to start unravelling somewhere given I'd ceased to believe in my own personality. I hadn't told William that yet, thinking it was too twatty to paraphrase T. S. Eliot less than six months in.

But my identity actually seemed to be one of the main problems. A frantic social and chaotic work life during my twenties meant I could barely remember who I was before I'd been run over in the fast lane. I'd sensed that a couple of years ago when I'd written the 52, but I now saw how my list had centred around experiences and life had narrowed so completely that ticking off similar self-improvement would have been impossible. I fished an old reporter's pad out of a box by my bed and wrote 'Who am I?' on the page, then stared cluelessly at the words.

William was also keeping a list in our sessions but was unfortunately having no problem adding things. It was a list of the words I was banning in order to try not to get put off entirely.

So far it included: mindfulness, wellness, journey, nature, personal *growth*, survivor, victim, be kind to/love yourself, the inner *you* and yoga.

'What is it about those words that you don't like?' he asked.

'Don't they just make you want to throw up?' I said.

'No.'

'Eurghhhh. I just really don't want to have to spend seven minutes eating a raisin to practise mindfulness,' I drawled elaborately.

'Nor do I,' he agreed.

I found myself allergic to the hippy-dippy, pseudo-intellectual, semi-homeopathic-sounding enterprises of people who'd had city breakdowns and then left to start a hot yoga pod in Burton upon Trent. They were the people I should have trusted the most, I guess, given they'd had rat-race epiphanies before me, but the cultish expressions of serenity on their faces when they told you they'd 'got out' unnerved me.

In my black-and-white thinking I knew I'd considered London was 'it', life, and everywhere else was 'not it'. But believing I only needed to be tougher to survive was changing in lockdown when I saw most of William's banned list just included things which involved being outside or conscious, or just empathetic towards yourself and your emotions. Which was fine. I just didn't like the mushy avocado buzzwords.

To trial my discovery of the natural world, and see if it could fix me, I went wild swimming in rivers around my parents' house and rented a canoe so I could propel myself around and pretend I was Kya in *Where the Crawdads Sing* – who was pretty much the queen of isolation anyway. Nature did help, I realised, glad to be back on a level with water, having grown up in the sea.

Now I'd come out the other side, I didn't blame myself for falling back into bad habits at the start of lockdown when the world had felt too difficult to exist in sober, and single, but with time I realised that the world wasn't empty, it was just quieter, and I liked the new volume after believing the drama and noise of my previous life was not only normal, but preferred.

'I can't wait until I'm old enough to get into gardening,' I told William that week.

'Can I frame that quote?'

'I don't believe in framed quotes.'

He added framed quotes to the list.

Like antidepressants, which people said made you feel worse before better, therapy had started brutally with fears of phoning; often tipsy or full of resentment when I did; once flat-out drunk and having a panic attack William had to talk me down from on the phone. I felt overwhelmed and drowning, often, in the beginning, having blocked so much for so long. The retraumatised reactions were horrendous and, in the darkness, I tried to tell myself that I only had to put one foot in front of the other, like *heel, toe, heel, toe*. It had worked in the Himalayas. But now I was static I found every minute felt like an hour while I was getting used to myself again. I was as impatient as I always had been without anywhere to go.

In the mornings I wanted to stay in my dreams, happier unconscious, but that fuelled insomnia that made me prowl my room like a trapped animal at night feeling reality too awful, the silence absolute. I wanted to die then, when that feeling didn't leave me, and I looked outside to see the world upside down on top of me, death everywhere. I felt like I didn't know where I was or how I got here, and wondered if I'd ever be able to undo the ruin.

William had informally diagnosed PTSD from both the situation I'd escaped from in London and historic trauma involving the night on New Year's Eve that I'd been trying to forget since 2011, which was helpful in making me feel less unhinged but at one point, early in the summer, I'd really not wanted to be in the world any more. I wasn't used to thinking about suicide and I didn't like it at all that my mind had gone there in the first instance and now did so more easily.

I wondered also if I was locked into a genetic battle that would take me to the darkest places there were. My grandmother's past sat heavily on me, and knowing virtually nothing about her, I wondered if her fate was mine too.

There was also Adele. My mum had been talking to her regularly on the phone, or via email if Adele was going through a bad patch, ever since I'd found her again from Edinburgh. Adele had a quiet, hugely solitary life in extremely remote surroundings, her life a crevasse that she pulled herself out of. She had a partner, but besides him knew and talked to no one but her doctor. She had found some happiness in small things: puzzles and the birds in her garden, and made my mum CDs of her favourite songs that arrived in the post and we listened to in the car, thinking with a shiver of emotion that all the time we'd not been in touch, we'd been listening to half of the same tracks. She was also still on heavy medication that sometimes didn't feel enough, so my mum had been waiting for Adele to ask to see her, not wanting to scare her off with the idea that a family she'd not spoken to for twenty-five years would suddenly descend on her doorstep. Then the call came. Adele was alone, her partner working away and she was losing it. She needed someone to be there fast if something really bad wasn't going to happen. My mum drove four hours to be that person and stayed four days, during which Adele talked about her own trauma for the first time in decades and emailed my mum afterwards to say so much had lifted from her, finally, just by saying the words. From then on my mum understood better why she'd disappeared, and for me there was the realisation that unaddressed trauma had the power to destroy you. I wondered whether Adele's earlier life would have been easier for her if the therapy available to me had been an option back then, when it was only stigmatised and uncommon.

William had helped me to see that the weight of my family's

history with mental health issues sat heavily in me, making me fear any low mood, and so chasing the highs. I guess it was then that I decided to ask my mum to tell me what had happened with my grandmother Celia, wondering if knowledge could ease the unknown I felt shackled by. I hadn't wanted to ask for fear of upsetting my mum, but she said she'd assumed neither Charlie or I were that interested, and that just showed me how misunderstandings can blight life, if you let them.

What she told me was a story of small and large proportion. A raging wind Celia hated in the fields around the house; medication not strong enough to bear life alone after her youngest child had left home; and her husband moving to Ibiza with a woman closer to my mum's age than hers. A desperate, hoarded overdose. Booze. A chain of phone calls starting with neighbours that finally reached my mum's desk at the London publishing firm she worked at in her twenties. Trauma closed off a lot of the detail for her, too, after that.

'I think I must have left work,' she said, trying to fill in memories of her own. 'What the mind does in those situations is ... who knows? I remember going out to buy a black coat for the funeral – silly,' she said. She was told it was better not to see the body after the post-mortem. 'But the thing about never seeing their body is that you always expect them to come walking back through the door,' she said, eyes filling with tears. She'd been younger than I was now.

I imagined Celia, then, sleeping badly, having nightmares about moving house *again*, because money issues made them have to pack up and downsize constantly. Her husband, my grandfather Alan, expected her to write a great novel, like he had, but she was also expected to look after three children and make dinner. My mum was convinced Celia's life would have been different if she'd married someone else, seeing the ultimate difference in a father domineering and sociable, and a mother squashed by his world. I wished so much that I'd been alive when she was. That I'd been allowed to meet her. That she'd been able to go on.

'Things were different then,' my mum said. 'We have to remember that. There wasn't the help we can find now.' I saw then that I was breaking the cycle just by *talking* about it in therapy, and that I'd broken the cycle by not marrying Jack and by not being squashed by him. I felt the chains loosen slightly, just knowing things were and could be different. Destiny felt less doomed; my own choice in things more powerful.

I saw Celia, Adele, and me all standing together in a line – three generations of women who'd all struggled with their moods and minds. But I saw the outcomes were changing with every one of us. The idea, for Celia's generation, that you didn't ask for help had ended with her suicide, but Adele had survived with medication and by talking to my mum, even after twenty-five years of silence. I was still here too, and so far I hadn't needed antidepressants and hospitals to keep me standing. Therapy had been enough to ease the fear and I saw that you learnt so many valuable things about the people who'd existed before you if you didn't ignore the past, in turn improving things. Hopefully it would mean any daughter I might have one day would be even better equipped than me to deal with the same issues, if they affected her.

A month after that my mum brought Adele to meet me on Zoom and I just loved her immediately. She was funny and cool and vaped sweet clouds of blueberry smoke nonstop. She was naturally questioning and had a girly side my mum didn't, but I did and there were other tiny traits that I knew were mine too, and could only have come from her. I never would have known, I thought.

Horrendously, I noticed that suicide was in the air in coronavirus; mental health shot at dawn and the trappings of cabin fever too much for troubled minds everywhere. Someone I knew bought a rope before being prescribed antidepressants and someone else was having his first suicidal thoughts since walking into traffic ten years ago, and had quickly restarted therapy. Another asked me if I ever thought it would just be easier to jump out a window and end it all, like he did.

It scared me more than anything else that all of these people took cocaine. Was the drug, that ruined sleep, and crashed you hard the next day, pushing suicidal thought? Or did the people who took it like it because a propensity to depression pushed them towards the high that provided a few hours' relief?

Either way, I'd begun to see how dangerous it was and that my very late nights and the drink and drugs and the dating had all been a precarious way of trying to escape consciousness entirely. I fuelled myself to run faster and faster away from the truth, which was that I wasn't OK, and instead looked for the truth in overheard conversations, in the faces of older people in pubs and the stories of strangers. In my life everyday as a journalist. I never looked for my own truth because I didn't know how to begin, and didn't sit still long enough to give myself the time to feel anything at all.

'Trauma can often make you feel frozen, as can abject terror. But we need to feel pain in order to get over it,' William said. 'You have, essentially, a logjam.'

'Great,' I said. That sounded fun.

By Christmas, he'd admitted that when I'd first started talking to him, I'd reported everything in a way so detached it was like I was telling him details of someone else's life entirely, holding myself away from it to avoid having to think that some of what had happened, had actually happened to *me*.

It wasn't exactly as though rape was my favourite subject, so I probably *was* avoiding talking about it with any emotion at first. On my own I'd learnt to say the words but not *feel* them, yet slowly William and I started discussing it in a way that made it as bearable as it was going to ever be. In an hour, we might talk about it for ten minutes, then veer into other things, which reduced the panic that surfaces when you have to go over something like that. At first

I'd wondered whether it wouldn't be better to go through it with a woman, in an absurd thought process that maybe a man wouldn't think it was so bad, but being backed by William helped massively. I think what he validated most valuably was my anger by explaining that I *should* be angry, and that it made *him* angry, and that *anyone* would feel angry if it happened to them. Up until that moment I think I expected myself to just get over it, partly because I didn't want to think about it, because I didn't want it to have happened. I felt like I was giving the awful man who'd done it power by admitting he still sometimes followed me around in my thoughts.

I don't think I'd known how to be vulnerable or cope with feelings of despair after the breakdown I'd had at school, and so therapy had to become a wrecking ball at the wall I'd built tall, before we even got to the experiences I'd hidden behind it. But there was strength in breaking it down and working out how things had affected you, William taught me, because you could better control your reactions to them. They were less likely to sweep you off your feet with grief.

As time passed in weekly sessions, I did unfreeze, gradually, and could reflect on a rock bottom I didn't know could be so low. For months I'd slept with a wall of pillows next to me in bed like a widow, feeling my bed too empty without Jack. Love, when it ended, was a form of death, too, because is anyone ever granted the chance to do everything they wanted to do with someone before life, a shared version, is taken away? All I thought about at first was everything Jack and I had never done, and would never do now.

But the longer I spent away from him, and the more I talked to William about the relationship, the more clearly I saw how everything in that eggshell life was influenced by his moods. I saw that it wasn't my fault at all, but film-star levels of narcissism and gaslighting so violent I hadn't known it could exist. I learnt to see what 'normal' actually looked like, and realised it had never been my life with Jack.

When William and I talked about Tom, I understood that my relationship with him had made me feel dead for a while; hardened me and made me cynical about commitment and loyalty and then distrusting of relationships in general, doubting they were ever as happy as they were portrayed to be. Doubting there wasn't something going on behind closed doors, which might be partly why I stayed with some of the men who came after him as long as I did.

I saw everything as connected then and in my room I looked back at the ringletted girl in Cornish-blue school uniform, barely having learnt how to smile for photos, and I felt so angry that anyone had treated her like they had. I felt protective of *her*, more than I'd ever felt protective of who I was in the moment. But as the walls came down, my different selves were becoming more aligned.

I guess one of the worst things about rape is that it destroys simultaneously your self-worth and any idea of boundaries or rules because the ultimate physical boundary of your body has been violated. With perspective it became possible to see that anger and numbness had pushed me towards 'drug rush men' as William described them; men who swept me up so quickly that I felt more alive with them and their drama than I did beneath the surface, in the hurt and the pain.

'Then the comedown,' I said.

'There's always a comedown,' he said.

I knew that people living in conflict zones got used to hearing bombs drop and I saw how my normal had twisted into a relentless, threatening drama that wasn't dissimilar from the hard news that had triggered me to drink in the past. It was only now that I realised why abuse trials and missing women made me reach for a bottle of wine. I guess I was looking at something so big I couldn't even see it, or maybe the picture was too close up for me to be able to note the detail. William's distance from it meant he *could* see it, and could help me recognise and name what I'd failed to.

When Christmas arrived and my brother was stuck in a new Tier 4, unable to come home as thousands evacuated London, I had flashbacks to my own escape in the spring and felt the panic and the torment and anguish afresh as I watched the news, so grateful to have got away. Then Boris' third lockdown announcement in January included a line about domestic abuse victims being free to leave the house if they needed to, and I thought about all those people who hadn't yet been able to escape, relief washing over me that *I* had, but so much sympathy and fear for those who hadn't.

The difference with the emotion I could feel again after the wrecking ball had started to swing was that I now had the ability to observe the *why* and *how* and could breathe through it until it went away, rather than rushing off on a whirlwind bender with a pocket full of artificial ego boost. My constant, fight-or-flight life had swerved into the slow lane and a basic CBT phrase – 'choose again' – had the power to turn damning thoughts around before they stuck.

The future worried me as much as it worried all of us during that time, having been taken out of our control entirely; life suspended. I had a dream about stamping on two dozen eggs and when I told William he said, 'You know what that means, don't you?'

'YES,' I said. 'Fertility, and that I think I'll live with my parents forever and never have sex again, or children, which I thought I'd have with Jack but now obviously won't and worry that I won't meet someone great and ambitious enough outside of the city which destroyed me and I'll probably have to freeze my eggs and do it alone in between hoovering for cigarette runs.'

'Is that what you think?' he said.

'A bit.'

I knew, as he said it, that I just had to bring my racing mind back again and six months in, the shift from chaos to calm was easier. My world felt lighter as the pain of the past began to lift. I started to see that I'd been acting for a long time and projecting something untouchable while I cracked under the pressure of the performance.

'It's like you've come off a stage with make-up on and an audience cheering, but now they've gone,' William said.

'So I'm now an out-of-work actor?' I asked.

'I think they're called resting actors.'

'Well, rest is *mindful*,' I said.

'Exactly,' he smiled.

In changing a pattern of silencing my emotions, I saw that I'd lived my entire life disliking the idea of the past, chasing the future and wishing I liked the present more. But now I had to like the moment – we all had to – because chasing the future was impossible when you couldn't see a week ahead. That was one of the biggest shifts in the national consciousness, I think: that we had to learn to sit in the grey waiting room of the unknown. But in the waiting room sat balance, and we saw it as something we'd never really had.

I realised, only in therapy, that I'd felt safer if I was always moving not only from years of constant change and uncertainty in my personal and professional lives in London, but because my main memory of the night of the New Year's Eve party was from the morning after when I knew all I had to do was just move, try and move, away from the danger, and that stayed with me subconsciously, I think. Staying still always seemed too frightening but I'd never understood why until William helped me see that I'd been desperate to move away from the scene of the crime that day because if I didn't, I could be attacked again.

In Bath I walked the countryside with my mum who plucked wild raspberries from the hedgerows and held them out to me in the rehabilitating tranquility. I felt my perspective change almost physically in the fields with the horizon stretching away from us, in a way that felt like my eyes saw further and opened wider. I sat by the canal sometimes, alone, and watched two mallards chase a female duck like *Jules et Jim*. A mother cycled along with her little girl sleeping in a baby seat behind her, and I realised that I was smiling; that the world had started to gleam once more and that I felt like myself again, finally. The sun helped these cop-out epiphanies, I knew, but I felt so fucking relieved to be back.

When distance and time allowed me to see how I'd chased temporary happiness in hedonistic distractions, I knew I wanted a more concrete, stable version that I could rely on not to leave me at 4 a.m. I'd thought I was lucid when I was glazed with white wine or felt the first chemical rush of blood to the head, but I realised now that I hadn't even been close.

I also saw how angry I'd been. For years. Masking over it but having it scrunched tight inside me all the time. Never admitting it in a way that let it dissipate, as it was said to, but only running hard and fast on treadmills and drinking non-stop at night to try to exhaust it.

But I was fucking angry.

About the way kids were being forced to break under the pressure at school; about boys who didn't know the meaning of consent. About Tom and about Jack, maybe Jack most of all and how he dared to tell me he loved me and continued to talk about a baby he hoped would look just like me when she was born, while he pushed me around behind closed doors like a coward who couldn't show who he was in public realms.

I saw that feeling angry about some of what had happened wasn't only right and normal but self-protective, and saw that rage could be a driving force in justice, change and in good. After bottling it all up for so long, the lightness was more than bearable: it was a fucking dream, I grinned.

My generation is as flawed as every other but our strength is honesty, I think, and our refusal to be as complicit as women felt they had to be in the past. When I spoke to a woman a generation above about some of the sexism and harassment she experienced in a job like mine in the '70s and '80s the first thing she asked about this book was whether I'd regret writing it?

I understood that she'd lived in more of a gritted-teeth world and that saying anything for her, then, could have lost her her job. But I refused to be silent and let it continue for another generation, now things could change. I knew when I wrote this that if only one reader in the whole world believed afterwards that they could get over anything similar, or start to talk about it, like I did, then I would never regret it.

What I regret is not saying some of this years ago, but I don't think I had the language or maybe the strength or the ambition, even, once upon a time. The self has the ability to change profoundly over the years and I'd have liked someone to tell me that I wouldn't feel lost forever. That the future would be bearable – even if it was uncertain. That I didn't need to worry so much that I wouldn't survive. I'd like to have known how normal it is to feel a complicated mix of anxious, lost, excited, resilient and vulnerable; to be completely sure of yourself one minute, then doubt you ever knew what you were doing the next.

Maybe my thirties wouldn't have looked dissimilar from my wild twenties if the brakes hadn't screeched hard in March, but when they did I became determined life would be different. Now I wanted noise, but a very different kind of noise to the shallow, nocturnal soundtrack I'd run on before. I wanted real, confessional, freeing, screaming noise about what can happen to a woman when violence by men is tolerated, unaddressed and unpunished. Silence just isn't good enough anymore – from any of us.

As for the rest of me, the part that liked the thrilling race of life is still here, but it's calmed and rebalanced. I've learnt to see balance as like tectonic plates, never set, just constantly shifting in relation to their parts. I discovered I could be a bit of grey, rather than black-and-white everything, and I let the grey shiver like the ones now visible in my hair in the right light.

I saw I'd been squashing an introverted side for a life in the front seat, but in lockdown both sides of my personality stood tall and got on fine.

The truth was that London encouraged late-night recklessness because it ran 24/7 and could be a fraught, unkind place to live. Those of us who'd moved away from it now recognised that, in a way that wasn't dissimilar to leaving an abusive relationship and only seeing once you'd left how badly you were treated. My abusive relationship with London was the longest relationship I'd ever had. But knowing how many brilliant people gravitated towards the capital made it hard. It was still where I expected to one day meet someone, I told William, who told me there'd be a key difference if I did go back: me.

I *had* changed and was continuing to and I knew things would be on my own terms now. I'd build my own home finally, and not have myself painted over by anyone else. The catalyst was the end of a relationship which was simultaneously the best and the worst I'd ever had and leaving it felt like the biggest decision of my life so far. The fact the timing of the pandemic forced me to go back home and address ten years of mayhem in a city so busy bus drivers brushed their teeth at red lights is almost too neat. The fact that this book will be read almost ten years after the night of the New Year's Eve party is even neater. But still accidental. It was just time, and it takes time to live, Camus says. Like any work of art, life needs to be thought about.

Then, almost nine months after I'd sent him a Facebook message saying I wanted to talk about that awful New Year's Eve, the boy who'd put me on the path of self-destruction replied.

I stared at his name, wondering who he was, until pure shock cut through the confusion, stopping my breath. I stood motionless in my room with my phone in my hand, thinking. Then sat down, wondering if the pieces I'd started to arrange for myself across the board of the past might now be moving into checkmate.

I'd sent the message in February on Dutch courage, alone in the flat, with Jack on bail and wondering how I'd become this person so bruised and scared she jumped at every tiny sound. I knew then that he had something undeniably to do with it, I guess. Had known for a long time and was perhaps readying myself, unconsciously, to go back to the start.

He'd not seen my message, he said, because we weren't Facebook friends and it had gone into that weird other folder people forget to check. Not caring whether that was true or not, I asked for his email address. Then he said it sounded serious. In my room I stared at his words, completely sober, knowing in my former life I'd have wanted to drink two glasses of wine before typing. But I didn't drink a drop. I hadn't for two months.

I looked again at my screen and pushed all the air out of my lungs in one deep breath, wondering if he really didn't know what this could be about? I wondered if he'd ever admitted it to himself, and knew there was a chance he'd already sought legal advice if he had. I also knew this was the one chance I had for closure and a grain of personal justice in a situation where I would be afforded no legal justice.

I felt the shiver of anxiety, and the heat of tears that always came when I had to run through those memories. It was an acid test, because William had Covid and was too sick to talk. I felt, again, completely alone in facing the trauma. But deeper than that, I felt profoundly different about having to, as though being alone wasn't the end of the world any more. The dread and the fear of it was diminished and the fight-or-flight response was more manageable.

In the early days of therapy I'd told William about the message I'd sent, and I remembered what he'd said. That I needed to ask myself what I wanted to get out of it. I knew I needed to be prepared that I wouldn't get what I needed: acceptance. I waited while I thought, and phoned two friends – both women, both lawyers, both with personal experience of rape – and each of them told me to expect to be attacked for a second time. This time with accusations I was lying. That I'd fabricated the whole thing.

But I hadn't, and I needed him to know that I knew, and would never forget what he'd done. I started typing into a word document, re-read it three times, then copied it into an email and pressed send.

Hi,

Yes, it is serious. The word 'rape' might come as a shock to you and I'm sure this email is going to make you very uncomfortable, but I have had a long time to get used to the word and it's always shocking.

I wanted you to know that that is how I think about what happened that night. I'd blocked it out for a huge time, but as is the habit of people who've experienced 'historic' sexual abuse, you find it comes bubbling out of you eventually because things can't be blocked forever and so I've been trying to get my head around it as best as mentally possible in the last year.

Given it was 2011, your memory might be hazy but mine isn't because trauma sometimes makes you remember everything, unfortunately. So I remember having no idea who I was lying next to when I woke up that day; then trying to get away from that bed as quickly as possible; then you telling me I 'was more fun last night' and trying to work out where the hell in the house I was and get downstairs and just get out of there, basically. But we had to travel back together, which was beyond horrendous. You might remember throwing up on the way home? You might not remember the look of absolute guilt you gave me after that. I saw it as guilt anyway. You might remember me barely speaking the entire way and not wanting to look at you when I got off in Bath.

I had doubts for a while, as everyone who this happens to does, because it would have been much easier to think of it as consensual rather than always having to know I was raped, and think about how and who did it. But it always comes down to the same thing: no one can give consent when they're blind drunk, or unconscious, or drugged. I remember regaining some consciousness halfway through and not having any idea who was on top of me and your face moves like horror in my memory still. I remember my eyes rolling to the back of my head in the way a drug like ecstasy makes them (I'd taken it once before that, with a boyfriend) and I remember you boasting downstairs in the kitchen earlier in the night about having pills on you.

I did not fancy you, and I did not want anything to happen. I was seeing someone at the time, although I broke up with them quickly after that because it felt like my world had turned upside down. The photos from that night still make me feel ill — you've got your hand on me in one of them, or you're right next to me or staring after me when I'm walking away. It makes it look premeditated. Never before or after that night have I again woken up and known I was lying next to a man, but not had any idea who they are.

I told our mutual 'friend' what had happened quickly after, and his response was to tell me you'd always been 'weird' with girls, but that he'd thought you'd go quite far in life. At the time he had some mad scheme to build a Warhol-style factory of creatives, and I think he thought both of us would be helpful to it. It was a hugely damaging reaction as you might expect, but says everything about how power works in these situations. I told Anna a couple of years later when we lived together and she just cried. That's what people who love me do when I tell them what you did, they just cry. It's quite awful, as I'm sure you can imagine.

I've never been to the police, as you will know, and I don't want to now. This isn't about that and besides, it would be largely pointless. If you're wondering what I want, then I don't want very much. I wanted the chance to tell you how I view that night. How I know you took huge advantage of me and for you to see how unacceptable it was and is. I don't know if you'll ever be able to admit that to yourself, I know it would take massive strength of character to do that and you might think it's too much of a risk, but I will always know, and I will always have to live with it, so I want you to share that burden after all this time. It's a hell of a lot to carry around and I resent you for putting it on me when I was just 21. It's caused a huge amount of pain and it ruined my view of men and how I thought I couldn't trust men for years. I would love a sorry – but I don't expect you to be able to give me a proper one without admitting it to yourself first.

Not everyone who has been through something like this gets the chance to lay out how they feel to the person responsible and I hoped doing it would allow something to lift from me after all this time.

Lucy

I felt the pressure rise in my chest in a way I knew meant I was going to cry, and felt beyond relieved that my emotions weren't any more heightened by wine. This emotion was all real. Came easily. I didn't need anything else to make me feel.

I knew that there was slim chance he'd admit it. Especially over email that could be used as concrete evidence in a court, if I ever took it to one. But forcing him to read it slightly reduced the guilt I'd felt for years in never going to the police, knowing he might be treating another girl the same way and ruining her faith in herself, and in everyone else she met, too.

Knowing I'd done what I could, I now just had to wait, I thought. In journalism we called it offering someone *a right to reply.*

Four days later, it came.

Dear Lucy,

Your message came as a terrible shock. I am appalled that you have had to suffer this pain, and to hear about the profound effect that it has had. Thank you for allowing me some time to come to terms with what you have said.

Clearly my behaviour was abhorrent. I cannot put into words the shock and shame of reading your email, and of then having to share it with my brother. This is nothing next to what you have been through and it is a waking nightmare.

I must be clear that I remember events differently, but that does not change the pain you have had to carry. I do not doubt the suffering you have been through and I am truly, truly sorry to have played any part in an experience which has caused such terrible distress.

For what little it is worth, thank you for telling me. You are not looking for my opinion but your email clearly took courage, and although I cannot agree with everything in the email I fully accept that I am responsible for doing whatever I can to try to share this burden.

I am not sure what to suggest and understand that this may be impossible, but if meeting might help in any way (ideally with someone you feel comfortable with and my brother present) then of course I would be glad to do that. If you do not want to speak to me you might prefer to speak to my brother, who is the only person I have shared this with.

Sincerely,

[XXXXX]

I read it, and read no apology, and read it again and noticed a detached one. But in his wriggling words I saw the distance he'd created, knowing it would be dangerous, perhaps, to say more. But I felt something close to relief, I noticed, too. In a situation in which nothing would change what had happened, and nothing would be enough – this felt like somewhere *almost* close enough to an apology. Knowing he knew and knowing that he now had to live with it too helped ease the weight I'd carried alone.

Unfortunately, I don't believe anyone ever actually achieves 'closure' after rape. Closure is an unhelpful word because it suggests you can get over something, move on, and never be troubled again by what you needed closure for in the first place. I don't think you ever can draw a line completely under the kind of grief related to sexual assault, or death, but that doesn't mean you can't learn not to let it ruin your life.

Afterwards four people close to me read those messages and every one of them said how powerful they thought they were; 'incredible', even, and they told me they were so proud of me. The most shocking thing, maybe, was how surprised I was by that. I realised then that I'd felt, the whole time, like I'd done something wrong, and their reactions validated that I hadn't. I realised that it was *shame* I'd felt for ten years, although I had no reason to – and certainly felt even less of now.

This was never designed to be a book about trauma. Some bad things have happened to me over the years, but bad things happen to everyone as life goes on. Some of you will have seen worse darkness than me, or similar, or maybe nothing as extreme. But life is never just one thing, and amongst the sadness, loneliness and fear in mine, there was a hell of a lot of laughter, excitement, joy and contentment too, however temporary I let it be in my twenties before blowing it up.

Now I was unfreezing, I knew it would be easier to find happiness less precarious, and I knew I was recalibrating and recasting alongside everyone else, while my anchors held the boat. We all need anchoring if we're not to be thrown about in the waves.

I knew that after very difficult, lonely times, in life and in relationships, finding someone who adds to your life, rather than takes from it, only makes things more sweet. I thought I'd be able to appreciate real affection all the more now, after all the wrong I'd seen so far. Rather than futile, I thought love was even more worth looking for. Older and more aware, I knew I'd be able to value it properly, for however long I would be given in life to keep it.

There's no baby at the end of this story. No ring. No super-neat ending. Life isn't always like that. As readers we seek a bow-tied finale because we want to assure ourselves there will be one for us, too. Like there's a formula for happiness you only need to find and follow. I looked for happiness in other people for a long time, but I guess I finally realised that no one ever holds your perfect hand of cards. It's better to choose your own from the deck. That was where happiness really was, I thought. In liberation.

I'd thought letting my mind run backwards for the first time would help rid me of ghosts, but then I realised that the people you've loved and shared your life with are always with you in a way. Part of me was still on a train to Bath with my hand out the window as Jonnie ran along the platform beside me, turning us into a black-and-white film. Part of me was still in Brighton playing at being a grown-up with Liam on Sunday mornings, drinking coffee and making puffed French toast. I saw Sam dancing around our bedroom and Tom running across a square in Brussels in the rain. I saw Jack in a good mood rattling a spoon around a glass of Nesquik in the kitchen and telling me to come flirt with him while he smoked. I knew Madi would always be with me; that we'd never leave each other now.

I saw life as one big love affair. But I knew in my thirties to be more objective now, knowing myself and where I came from better, and knowing that I had the power to break patterns in family history as well as learnt patterns of my own and redirect the future for another generation ahead of me. I knew I was stronger and could stand alone if I needed to.

In allowing the past and talking about it, I let so many people keep me going. Keep me alive. When you hit rock bottom, your mind goads you. Asks you if you couldn't just disappear without anyone really caring, but as soon as I could talk about it, the names of friends I'd gathered in Bath, Leeds, Newcastle, Edinburgh, Amsterdam and Berlin and from random cricket matches and pubs and jobs and netball matches over the years in London buzzed constantly on my phone. They sent me books and tiny thoughtful gifts and got trains to Bath to sit and listen and pour me a drink or pass me a paddle for the canoe. They all told me to promise not to go anywhere, not to duck out now. They often cried too and gripped onto me as tears ran down my cheeks and I felt the surge of the panic that Charlie and Madi talked me down from on the phone when the panic never left me, in the beginning. I thought I'd feel like that forever – but you never do.

I saw there were anchors spread on the seabed all around me and the feeling of being completely uprooted and unknown had waned. This is a love letter to all those anchors really, and to a life in a slower lane that lets you breathe, think, consider and stay conscious.

I rifled around my room for the list I was writing to try to remember who I was, after that, and I wrote *Anchors*, and then so many other things spilled out.

Walks when I'm on them. The countryside more than I always remember. Fresh air and cigarette smoke; first pints in pubs and how the noise rises each hour; white crab in orange shells; my dad's cooking; my mum pulling into the driveway; how my brother makes me laugh. The smell of oil paint that makes me feel at home. Waking up next to a friend and laughing about the night. Waking up next to Madi and ordering pizza in bed. The important air of central London but being able to arrive somewhere else. The London Bridge tracks that carried us all in and out. Pressing into someone in the night but also sleeping alone, in a starfish. That first electric kiss. The stage in relationships when you shower with the door open so you can carry on talking. Clicking through London in heeled boots or bowling about in Doc Martens. Seeing roe deer kick about the fields like horses. Scoring in a match. Seeing my name in print. The strange luxuriousness of going to bed early. Water, anywhere. The first crispness of winter and how you can feel the cold in the air. The first languidness of summer heat. Being on the back of a boat as it speeds away and your hair flies around your face. Dangling my legs over the side of a pier. Loud music when you're getting ready to go out. Fast cars on country lanes. Rooms that look like libraries but aren't. Texts that make you laugh out loud. Alfie stretching like a cat in the morning. Champagne, and what it means. Holding a lighter to a cigarette and concentrating only on the first flamed puff. That look someone gives you when they first open their eyes. The warmth of other people's skin. The way touch can make you shiver.

It ran on and on and on and my tears fell as I wrote because I remembered how deeply, deeply lost I'd felt when I'd left London. How I hadn't been able to see beauty or value in anything. How I'd been so worried about who I was and how I'd survive. But I'd realised I was 1,000 different things and that we all were, and I knew I'd left unconsciousness behind.

On New Year's Eve 2020, I sat in Serena's garden and we raised two coupes to each other and the least forgettable year of our lives. A fire raged and the fields around us were blanketed in frost, peaceful and quiet. We were both about to turn thirty-one and the next decade of our lives stretched out in front of us, unknown and exciting.

This is exactly where I should be before a new year breaks, I thought, after so long feeling them cursed. I should be with one of my oldest friends talking about our lives so far, and everything they were still to become, and drinking to who we'd be next.

Hope is what I felt then, and what I felt all the way home as I walked back up the hill in the street-lit dusk and smiled, knowing how much happier I'd allowed myself to become since I'd come back here.

To a home I'd forgotten I had.

In a world I now wanted to stay in.

ACKNOWLEDGEMENTS

First and obvious thanks to my brilliant agent Jon Wood at RCW for helping me hone a life into a book (and for making me laugh when it all felt too much) and to Fritha Saunders at Simon and Schuster for commissioning a book that had to be written partly in real-time and for the support and guidance with the prologue especially.

Journalism is a fantastic career, even if it is changing fast and I'd like to thank Nicola Jeal for getting me started; John Witherow for taking a chance on a writer with no training and a weird CV; Grace Bradberry and Vanessa Jolly for putting up with me in the early days when I was writing features like academic essays; and without Celia Duncan I wouldn't have been nominated for a Press Award, and thank you for the support ever since.

The continued support of Jay Rayner and Caitlin Moran has been truly invaluable so I will be forever grateful to them (and have promised to pass it on to the next generation, who always need a hand). I also want to thank everyone who agreed to be interviewed by an unknown student journalist during that time.

The biggest thanks to all of the friends who enhanced life during the decade in this book, and picked me up, took me out and pep-talked me through the bleakest times: Meg, Danny, Frankie, Barlow and Lawson, Harry and Lauren; the Newcastle crew; Leeds lot; netball girls; Emily and Amy, Cece, Katie, Rosie, Jenny, Nick and Sam. To the exes that let me write what I needed to write, and to the others for the content, even if it was hideous at the time. To Hugo and Peter for my second home and to Serena and Bob in Bath for adopting me when I came back to the real one.

To Charlie for the constant hilarity and the phone calls in the rough times and to Kate for trying to make London life easier for both of us. Robin for the book talks this last year. I also *highly* recommend anyone trying to write anything this autobiographical to get a therapist – William, I owe you a lot. Thank you.

My dad's already asked me if he could please support me without reading this so I'd like to thank my mum a million times, because she won't be able to not read it, and without her, our family would be crumbling all over the place.

Lastly, what I never wanted to have to write, but now have to, is that this book is dedicated in memory of Everleigh: my brilliant friend. On a steely grey day in September, I hopped on a train to Leeds and walked through the city I'd only been back to once since leaving university, to get a pint in Whitelock's and raise it to Everleigh on the day of his funeral. I'd received a reply from him that broke my heart in April, just after *Lucid* had been formally announced and I'd emailed him the news. 'Dear Lucy. Great news about the appearance of the book. Unfortunately it seems probable I may not be here to read it' and I cried then as I cried in Whitelock's at the table we used to sit at together. His last words in that email said there was always hope, 'so keep hoping' and I knew I'd always remember that. Everleigh, thank you for everything; this is for you.